Praise for *The Art of*

"Dr. Clare Johnson has firmly establishe
ity, rigor, and a caring heart, she illuminates the darkness of nightmares and will radically transform your relationship to unsettling dreams. Vast in its vision and practical in its approach, *The Art of Transforming Nightmares* is a brilliant book that will show you there is no darkness within—only light unseen."

—Andrew Holecek, author of *Dreams of Light* and *Preparing to Die*

"Dr. Clare Johnson is a 'how-to' guru when it comes to enhancing dream lucidity and the use of dreams for healing. In *The Art of Transforming Nightmares*, she teaches us that bad dreams are not to be feared as much as they are to be considered doorways revealing surprising gifts: lessons in healing, creativity, and more! You'll learn all you need for real growth and transformation."

—Dr. Kimberly Mascaro, author of *Extraordinary Dreams*

"*The Art of Transforming Nightmares* is a personalized and practical guidebook that can help us transform terror to transcendence and confusion to creativity. Offering a comprehensive menu of effective and prescriptive practices, this book is essential medicine for the terrified soul."

—Dr. Rubin Naiman, clinical assistant professor of medicine
and author of *Healing Night*

"Dr. Clare Johnson gives us a wealth of practical guidance on how to use 'bad' dreams and nightmares as portals to healing and transformation. *The Art of Transforming Nightmares* helps you to recognize and work with your personal sleep cycle and style of dreaming....This book issues a vibrant call to us to choose our actions and attitudes in dreams of the night and the dream of waking life."

—Robert Moss, bestselling author of *Conscious Dreaming* and *Growing Big Dreams*

"This is a golden masterpiece on nightmares! Filled with illuminating techniques for better understanding nightmares, *The Art of Transforming Nightmares* is a magnificent resource for anyone interested in emotional healing and spiritual transformation. Take the Nightmare Quiz and discover what type of dreamer you are, develop a sacred dream practice that helps you grow, learn to confidently engage with dream characters by becoming lucid in your dream, and ultimately see how nightmares really are very precious gifts."

—Anna-Karin Björklund, author of *The Dream Alchemist*

"There are few reliable guides for nightmares, so Dr. Johnson's book is more than helpful: it is essential reading. I hope this book goes far—I particularly love how she splits the different kinds of nightmare types up and provides recipes for each. Very practical."

—Ryan Hurd, author of *Sleep Paralysis*

"From traumatic dreams to sleep paralysis attacks to suicide-related nightmares to insomnia, Dr. Clare Johnson has synthesized decades of dreamwork experience into a rich self-help toolbox that nightmare-prone individuals can draw on to build a personalized treatment program for healing and transcending their fearful nighttime episodes."
—Professor Tore Nielsen, director of the Dream and
Nightmare Laboratory, Université de Montréal

"Groundbreaking! Carefully researched and based on the studies of numerous experts along with her own experiences, *The Art of Transforming Nightmares* not only discusses why nightmares happen to many dreamers, but also gives useful and concrete examples for using nightmares as tools for growth and a way to transform the lives of the dreamers. Highly recommended!"
—Jean Campbell, coeditor of *Sleep Monsters and Superheroes*

"A delightful and authoritative book on understanding and dealing with nightmares. Dr. Clare Johnson introduces an encouraging view of the more common forms of nightmares and bad dreams and the self-healing function that they can provide, then offers a wealth of exercises and tools to empower the dreamer to work with them in a healing manner."
—Robert Hoss, director of the DreamScience Foundation

"This revolutionary book empowers the reader with the little-known secret that nightmares can be transformative, healing gifts. For those wanting to reduce nightmare frequency, manage sleep paralysis, or transcend fear using creative, lucid, or psychospiritual methods, this book offers a treasure trove of well-informed tools and solutions. Knowledge about nightmares and the art of transforming them is indeed empowering."
—Angel Morgan, PhD, president and CEO of the International
Association for the Study of Dreams

"Every dreamer should know that a nightmare, like a crying baby, requires special consideration and care. Dr. Clare Johnson treats nightmares as the great gift that they are: with love, tenderness, and curiosity. *The Art of Transforming Nightmares* is a reminder for any nightmare sufferer of the golden opportunity that every unpleasant dream offers."
—Jordi Borràs García, psychologist and founder
of www.mondesomnis.com

"From monsters to zombies, trauma, anxiety, and depression, from PTSD to night terrors to sleep paralysis, Dr. Clare Johnson shows us how all dreams can be a source of healing and transformation. A readable and easy-to-reference manual for all kinds of sleepers and dreamers."
—Laurel Clark, author of *Intuitive Dreaming*

THE ART OF
Transforming
NIGHTMARES

© R. C. Wilkerson

About the Author

Clare R. Johnson, PhD, is past president and CEO of the International Association for the Study of Dreams (IASD). A lifelong, frequent lucid dreamer, Clare has over forty years of personal lucid dream experience. In 2007 she became the first person in the world to do a PhD on lucid dreaming as a creative writing tool (University of Leeds, UK). She has researched lucid dreaming for over twenty-five years, and for the past sixteen years she has taught practical courses on how to access the deep creative and healing potential of the unconscious.

Clare is the author of the acclaimed book *Llewellyn's Complete Book of Lucid Dreaming: A Comprehensive Guide to Promote Creativity, Overcome Sleep Disturbances & Enhance Health and Wellness* (2017). Clare's work on lucid dreaming has been featured in documentaries, magazines, anthologies, radio shows, podcasts, and television. She speaks at international venues on topics as diverse as lucid dreams for the dying, sleep disturbances, transformative lucidity techniques, and nightmare solutions. Her most recent book was *The Art of Lucid Dreaming* (2020).

A novelist, prize-winning short story writer, and poet, Clare is the author of two lucid dream–inspired novels (as Clare Jay). *Breathing in Colour* looks at how lucid dreaming can heal trauma, and *Dreamrunner* explores lucidity as a potential cure for violent moving nightmares. A passionate advocate of dreamwork as a way to empower children, Clare coedited a book on children's dreams and nightmares, *Sleep Monsters and Superheroes: Empowering Children through Creative Dreamplay.* Her book *Dream Therapy* (US title is *Mindful Dreaming*) explores the transformative effect that dreamwork can have on our lives.

You may feel inspired to join Clare on her lucid dreaming retreats. These usually have a beautiful ocean setting, and the creative, healing, wild, and spiritual aspects of dreams are explored in a small group. For more information, check her website or contact her at deepluciddreaming@gmail.com. Clare also leads online Transformative Lucidity workshops and Yoga Nidra for Lucid Dreaming courses. She offers one-to-one mentoring sessions via video chat and has created a new series of video courses on lucid dreaming, nightmares, and yoga nidra for blissful sleep. She is the creator of www .DeepLucidDreaming.com, where she can be contacted for advice on lucid dreams and nightmares.

THE ART OF
Transforming
NIGHTMARES

CLARE R. JOHNSON PhD

Harness the Creative and Healing Power of
Bad Dreams, Sleep Paralysis,
and Recurring Nightmares

Llewellyn Publications
Woodbury, Minnesota

FIRST EDITION
First Printing, 2021

Cover design by Shannon McKuhen

Llewellyn Publications is a registered trademark of Llewellyn Worldwide Ltd.

Library of Congress Cataloging-in-Publication Data

Names: Johnson, Clare R., author.
Title: The art of transforming nightmares : harness the creative and
   healing power of bad dreams, sleep paralysis, and recurring nightmares /
   by Clare R. Johnson.
Description: First edition. | Woodbury, Minnesota : Llewellyn Worldwide,
   [2021] | Includes bibliographical references and index. | Summary: "This
   book is all about transformation: turning the darkness and fear
   associated with nightmares into healing and illuminating gifts. It shows
   you how to befriend your dreams and nightmares and, as a result,
   transcend fear in all areas of your life"— Provided by publisher.
Identifiers: LCCN 2020038056 (print) | LCCN 2020038057 (ebook) | ISBN
   9780738762906 (paperback) | ISBN 9780738763019 (ebook)
Subjects: LCSH: Nightmares. | Dreams.
Classification: LCC BF1099.N53 J64 2021 (print) | LCC BF1099.N53 (ebook)
   | DDC 154.6/32—dc23
LC record available at https://lccn.loc.gov/2020038056
LC ebook record available at https://lccn.loc.gov/2020038057

Llewellyn Worldwide Ltd. does not participate in, endorse, or have any authority or responsibility concerning private business transactions between our authors and the public.

All mail addressed to the author is forwarded but the publisher cannot, unless specifically instructed by the author, give out an address or phone number.

Any internet references contained in this work are current at publication time, but the publisher cannot guarantee that a specific location will continue to be maintained. Please refer to the publisher's website for links to authors' websites and other sources.

Llewellyn Publications
A Division of Llewellyn Worldwide Ltd.
2143 Wooddale Drive
Woodbury, MN 55125-2989
www.llewellyn.com

Printed in the United States of America

Other Books by Clare R. Johnson, PhD

The Art of Lucid Dreaming:
Over 60 Powerful Practices to Help You
Wake Up in Your Dreams
(2020)

Llewellyn's Complete Book of Lucid Dreaming:
A Comprehensive Guide to Promote Creativity,
Overcome Sleep Disturbances & Enhance Health and Wellness
(2017)

Dream Therapy:
Dream Your Way to Health and Happiness
(US title: *Mindful Dreaming*)
(2017)

Sleep Monsters and Superheroes:
Empowering Children through Creative Dreamplay
(Coedited with Jean M. Campbell, 2016)

Dreamrunner
(Pen name: Clare Jay, 2010)

Breathing in Colour
(Pen name: Clare Jay, 2009)

*This book is dedicated to all nightmare sufferers
and all healers of mind, body, and soul*

Contents

Practices

Disclaimer

This book offers techniques for working with disturbing dreams, nightmares, and other potentially fear-inducing states of consciousness arising from sleep. It is not a substitute for psychological counselling or medical advice. If you have any physical or mental health concerns, you must consult your doctor or other medical practitioner. The author assumes no responsibility or liability for the actions of the reader.

Acknowledgments

This book would be a shadow of itself without the compelling and astonishing nightmares so generously shared with me by warmhearted people from around the globe. My heartfelt thanks go out to all of you who shared your brave stories and revelations. It has been an honour for me to channel your dreams through the book and watch them illuminate the manuscript.

I was delighted to work on *The Art of Transforming Nightmares* with my talented editors, Angela Wix and Andrea Neff, and I'm thankful for the care and attention the multitalented team at Llewellyn Worldwide give to every aspect of my books.

I'm grateful to the little dream tiger who let me pick him up at a time when the floor of my writing room was strewn with nightmare accounts and I was trying to get a grip on the masses of material that went into this book. My thanks also go to the vibrant baby girl with alchemical symbols for fire and water tattooed on her kneecaps who appeared to me in a dream to let me know the book was in good shape. Writing this book felt like pure alchemy due to the powerful, transformative nature of nightmares, and I'm thankful to Yazzie and Markus for their love and support throughout the rollercoaster creative process.

As always, I feel honoured whenever I get to meet soulful dreamers and hear their fascinating stories in my online workshops and on lucid dreaming ocean retreats. It's a joy to accompany you on your journey into the thrilling world of sleep, dreams … and nightmares!

The wound is the place where the Light enters you.

– RUMI –

introduction

Imagine you are in your bedroom when you hear a creak. You look over, and your window is opening very slowly. Your heart begins to pound and you watch, frozen with horror, as a spiky metal arm enters through the window, followed by another, and yet another … With a shock, you realise that these monstrous limbs are not arms, but the legs of a giant robotic spider! You see the evil glint of its eyes as it scrabbles over the window ledge and moves towards you …

With a jolt, you wake up in darkness with a bursting heart. You fumble for the light and switch it on. Squinting fearfully, you check that there is no robotic spider in your bedroom, no scrabbling metallic limbs. You are safe in your bed.

Safe, but terrified.

It was so real; you can still see those grasping, tentacle-like legs and the deadly intent in the spider's eyes. Why on earth would you dream something that hideous? To calm yourself down, you have a drink of water and lie back down warily with the light still on, waiting for the feeling of menace to pass.

This is a classic example of a nightmare: a dream that is so frightening or upsetting that it wakes us up. Yet there are many different types of nightmares. For example, have you ever experienced the "dead leg" nightmare, where you try to run but it's like moving through quicksand, or a sleep paralysis nightmare, where your entire body feels stuck and you may feel suffocated or as if you're being attacked by nasty creatures? Have you ever had recurring nightmares that seem to strike whenever you're under pressure, or those heart-breaking dreams where you cry unstoppably? Or nightmares that seem to echo past physical, emotional, or sexual trauma? How about mythical nightmares, where you face fire-breathing dragons or are kept prisoner by unearthly creatures?

Maybe your worst nightmares are apocalyptic, involving tsunamis or devastating earthquakes and nuclear explosions. Or perhaps they are quiet, lonely dreams where you feel yourself to be the only person alive. Do you suffer from unpleasant dreams whenever you're ill or in pain? You may have had those stressful "missing a train" nightmares, or the ones where you have to sit an exam that you feel completely unprepared for, or a humiliating version of the "naked in public" dreams that people so commonly experience. One way or another, we all have had distressing or disturbing dreams at some point in our lives, even if we quickly forget them, and many of us have full-blown terrifying nightmares.

One sunny afternoon, after a talk I gave on the transformative power of lucidity for nightmare resolution, the university students in the audience were not ready to leave. They swarmed around me for about thirty minutes to get advice on their dreams and nightmares. Two guys suffered from severe sleep paralysis; one girl had trauma-induced nightmares that she wanted to cure; a devout Christian was having "fire and brimstone"–type dreams that he wanted guidance with; several young women approached me to ask about disturbing dreams they had never understood; another was scared to go to sleep because she always fell straight into the same unpleasant dream; and I had to refer one lad to a psychotherapist friend of mine who lived in his area, as his recurring nightmares were so traumatic that he was having panic attacks during the day. And this was just an average sample of students!

In fact, in sleep studies, 85 percent of the adult population reported having at least one nightmare in the past year, and 29 percent reported at least one a month.[1] Negative emotions in dreams are associated with depression and sleep disturbances, and large-scale dream surveys reveal that most people regularly report dreams with negative emotional content such as anxiety, fear, or sorrow. Sounds like pretty bad news, doesn't it? But the little-known secret is that nightmares can be transformative, healing gifts.

All dreams come to help and heal us, and nightmares are dreams that cry out for our attention. They yell: "Healing is needed!" or they call in despair:

---

1. Ohayon et al., "Prevalence of Nightmares"; Belicki and Belicki, "Nightmares in a University Population."

"Things can't go on like this any longer!" or they forcibly remind us: "You're still not over what happened when you were eight years old!" Nightmares flag up areas in our lives where healing change is needed. When we open up to their wisdom, we can learn to harness their creative and healing power. We just need to know how. After that university lecture, I realised it was high time to write an empowering practical book of nightmare solutions that anybody could put to immediate use to release their fears and create a happier dream life.

Fear

Mental healthcare professionals tell me that people ask for medication to stop their nightmares. People want to take a pill to make their nightmares disappear. I understand how bad the fear can get, but my hope is that this book will illuminate the enormous benefits of working with nightmares rather than suppressing them. By doing this tough but amazingly beneficial work, we can heal ourselves and move through life from a place of greater awareness, compassion, and understanding.

Why is it so important to learn how to work with nightmares in empowering ways? Every nightmare researcher I've spoken to about this book of practical nightmare solutions and transformative dreamwork has expressed how welcome, empowering, and needed such a book is. Psychologist Dr. Michelle Carr has conducted research at the Dream and Nightmare Laboratory in Montreal and is a researcher at the University of Rochester Sleep and Neurophysiology Laboratory. Michelle and I have both worked on the executive committee of the International Association for the Study of Dreams (IASD). When I told her about this book, she remarked:

> A major problem in sleep medicine right now is the lack of awareness about nightmare treatment. Relatively few sleep clinicians know how to treat nightmares and may turn nightmare sufferers away, telling them to seek other psychological help.
>
> If individuals feel their nightmares are completely beyond their control, they are afraid to go back to sleep, afraid to dream, or even afraid to think about their nightmares. This adds on to the general vulnerability we can feel around sleep, the threshold we cross alone each night. This is why learning to work with and overcome nightmares can be so powerful. It gives a feeling of power back to the nightmare sufferer.

This book provides empowering support for all of the nocturnal horrors and anxieties you or your loved ones have ever faced. But it is not aimed only at nightmare sufferers.

Have you ever experienced fear? Fear of change, fear of a particular situation, fear of making a leap of faith, or fear of looking deep within yourself? Fear can be an enormous obstacle not only for psychological growth but for spiritual development as well. Fear blocks us, freezes us up, and prevents us from living a full and joyous life. Yes, a certain sort of fear can be healthy, such as the fear that stops us from putting our hand in a fire or walking too close to a cliff edge. Fear as a survival instinct makes sense. But the fear we explore in this book is the type that seeps insidiously into all aspects of life, blocking our freedom and creativity, hampering our relationships, and feeding our anxieties. *The Art of Transforming Nightmares* is aimed at anyone who has ever experienced fear.

In many ways, this book is all about fear.

It's about how to face our deepest fears and transcend them in very practical ways. Through the dark but magical lens of nightmares and other frightening sleep experiences, we'll explore how to release crippling fears and anxieties so that we can step forward into a bright and fearless life.

The Art of Transforming Nightmares is not only useful for those struggling with fear, anxiety, or depression. It will also be helpful for anyone who is fascinated by the potential of dreams for creativity, personal growth, and spiritual transformation. Anyone interested in trance states will find plenty of exciting and transformative practices. People who have dreams that they simply don't understand will also benefit from the book, as we'll look at how to unwrap the meaning of dreams, and we'll see how the symbolic and mythical language of dreams creates powerful stories to wake us up to how we are really feeling and what we really want from life.

How *The Art of Transforming Nightmares* Began

The true origins of this book are rooted in what happened when I was three years old. My earliest memory is of a nightmare in which I was terrified because I knew I was about to die.

The dream started well—I was in a sparkling turquoise swimming pool, splashing around in all the beauty. Then somehow I was underwater and sinking fast. I was kicking frantically and trying to get back up to the surface, but sinking deeper and deeper. At that point, in a state of pure panic, I experienced a moment of clarity. I realised that I had a choice: either I could stay in this dream and drown or I could wake myself up. I chose to wake up. I did this by rolling over powerfully in the water, and this dream movement was so strong that my physical body rolled right out of bed! The turquoise water was gone; I was in my dark bedroom, tangled up in the sheets.

Alerted by the thump, my mother came running in. She disentangled me and listened to my story. In her efforts to reassure me, she told me something that altered my perception of reality.

She said, "It wasn't real, Clare."

I was stunned. I knew for a fact that only moments before, I had been drowning in a turquoise swimming pool! How could that experience *not be real*? It felt way more real than the dimly lit bedroom reality with my mum whispering so as not to wake up my sister. Parents are gods, right? They know everything about everything. I was a three-year-old child—what did I know? But something jarred me. I understood that there are two worlds: the solid, consensus-reality world where parents know everything; and the quick-to-vanish dreamworld, which feels amazingly real, but which parents know little about and dismiss.

That sense of there being two distinct worlds, one labelled "real" and the other labelled "not real," persisted throughout my childhood. I grew up with fearsome nightmares, as many children do. I was a sleepwalker, a vivid dreamer, and I suffered from recurring lucid nightmares (when you know you're dreaming but feel unable to act or wake yourself up). Sometimes I had dynamic out-of-body experiences that involved overwhelming buzzing and shaking sensations before I shot up out of my body and zoomed right through the roof of my house. I also experienced years of sleep paralysis, which is when you fall asleep but your brain remains aware, so you feel trapped in your body and might experience horrendous images and sensations. Although I grew up in a loving home, there was nobody to help me make sense of any of my bewildering sleep experiences. "Last night there was a noise like a steam train and then I flew right up over the house!" would be met with, "Please just calm down and eat your breakfast, Clare." In the face of these mystifying sleep events, I had to become very resourceful. Although I had many wonderful, joyful dreams, I also had terrifying experiences. I experimented with my responses to different nightmare environments and transitional sleep states.

For the first twenty years of my life, through trial and error, and with no outside help, I worked through my fear. I learned a lot about the glorious potential of these states of consciousness. I love dreams and sleep, and have made it my life's work to investigate this huge but often overlooked aspect of the human experience. But it often strikes me that not enough is written about the scary side of sleep experiences, and even less has been written about *what to do* when these experiences happen! People are left to work it all out for themselves, just as I had to as a kid: how to release fear, how to feel safe in unfamiliar spaces when terrifying things happen, and how to use the power of your own mind to turn this into an adventurous exploration of consciousness. Having created my own path to a deep understanding of these states, I feel happiest when I can help others work with them for transformation, healing, and empowerment and to release creative and spiritual gifts.

Nightmares frequently ping into my inbox as people from all around the globe write via my website to share their most horrendous dreams, horrifying sleep paralysis experiences, and trauma-induced nightmares. Some tell me they are cursed by dreams of future tragedies—dreams that come true in waking life. Others plead with me for help with their nonstop lucid nightmares. They write things like "I'm desperate—why is this happening to me?" or "I think I'm losing my mind." They make frantic appeals: "I'm terrified to fall asleep. Please help me get my life back." I have a full life, taking care of my family, writing dream books, creating lucid video courses, and leading online groups and lucid dreaming ocean retreats, as well as devoting time to the International Association for the Study of Dreams as past president and CEO. But I take the time to write back to every single person, because these people speak right to my heart.

The good news is that there is a world filled with astonishing marvels to discover, and it lies tantalisingly close to fearful nighttime experiences. In fact, it's a mere thought away. My aim for this book is to share practical solutions for all manner of fearful sleep events, to help nightmare sufferers fling open the doors of their own wonderful inner world.

My fascination for the world of sleep, dreams, and nightmares led me to teach myself to lucid dream at will. As an undergraduate at Lancaster University in 1995, I carried out my first academic exploration of lucid dreaming. This eventually led to me becoming the first person in the world to do a PhD on lucid dreaming as a creative writing tool, at Leeds University in the UK.

My role over the years as a board director of the IASD has enabled me to stay up-to-date with cutting-edge nightmare studies worldwide (some of which are funded by the IASD). In my twenty-six years of dream research and over forty years of personal practice, I've developed many original practical techniques to help people resolve and overcome nightmares and sleep paralysis.

Since 2009 I've had six dream books published, including *Llewellyn's Complete Book of Lucid Dreaming* (my *magnum opus*, which in part explores how to resolve nightmares), *The Art of Lucid Dreaming* (a super-practical book to discover your individual sleeper-dreamer type to fast-track your lucid dreaming), and *Dream Therapy*, on the healing potential of dreams and soul dreams. I also coedited *Sleep Monsters and Superheroes,* a book on how to empower children with their nightmares, and wrote *Breathing in Colour* and *Dreamrunner* (as Clare Jay), two lucid dream–inspired novels that explore themes of lucid dreaming and violent sleep disorders. I have given interviews, presentations, and workshops on sleep disturbances, how to transform nightmares, and how to release fear and embrace calm during frightening experiences arising from sleep. We'll explore these topics as we go along.

What's in This Book?

This is a friendly introductory guide to nightmares, with a highly practical focus. Its goal is to give people the knowledge and practical tools they need to reduce their nightmare frequency, manage sleep paralysis and other sleep disturbances, resolve bad dreams, and tap into the creative and healing gifts that nightmares and sleep paralysis visions offer. *The Art of Transforming Nightmares* is different from each of my previous books due to its focus on disturbing dreams, weird sleep events, and nightmares. It revolutionises nightmares as a creative and healing force and suggests that lucid dreaming may be the world's most innovative insomnia solution.

There are very few books on nightmares on the market that offer practical solutions. Most tend to be directed at therapists or have an academic, paranormal, or historical approach. As opposed to other nightmare books, this book is all about transformation: turning the darkness and fear associated with nightmares into healing and illuminating gifts. It shows you how to befriend your dreams and nightmares and, as a result, transcend fear in all areas of your life. This book does what other nightmare books don't— it gets you focused on yourself as a highly individual sleeper and dreamer and enables you to leapfrog to the transformational techniques that are most likely to be effective for you personally.

The Art of Transforming Nightmares serves as a practical handbook to help you understand, step-by-step, why you are having nightmares or sleep paralysis and how you can work with these experiences to understand their message and harness their creative energy and healing power. The book goes step-by-step through the most powerful practical techniques to help people manage sleep paralysis, integrate their shadow aspect, and gain wisdom, healing, and creative inspiration from all nightmares. The aim is to empower dreamers by giving them practical tools to resolve nightmares and other disturbing sleep experiences in healing ways.

Chapter 1 focuses on what nightmares are, what happens when we ignore them, and how they can help us. Chapter 2 unpacks the rich symbolic language of nightmare images and how to understand them, and provides a quick guide to common nightmare themes. Chapter 3 looks at the role of the dark shadow archetype in nightmares—the term *shadow* is used to describe the parts of ourselves that we are either unconscious of or reluctant to acknowledge. Chapter 4 explores how we can heal our inner child through working with animal-rich, mythical, and common childhood nightmares. This dreamwork enables us to reconnect with our creative, playful, and magical child mind.

The in-depth Nightmare Quiz in chapter 5 is a cornerstone of the book. A key concept of *The Art of Transforming Nightmares* is that we are all unique individuals: our relationship with sleep and dreams is unique; we respond to fear in unique ways; and we each have a unique personal history. The Nightmare Quiz encourages you to identify the kind of sleeper and dreamer you are, and when linked with the best techniques for your personal situation, these will make up the backbone of your Unique Nightmare Solution Programme. I've created fifteen different programmes for a range of different types of sleeper, from traumatised dreamers to insomniacs. These programmes are for you to combine and customise to create your own Unique Nightmare Solution Programme to fast-track you to a joyful and enriching dream life.

Chapter 6 offers healing techniques for recurring and traumatic nightmares, including those caused by post-traumatic stress disorder, which can require specialised therapeutic techniques and a higher level of support. This chapter dives into the power of storytelling as a tool for nightmare transformation. Chapter 7 explores sleep paralysis, a transitional state where we are consciously aware but feel trapped and unable to move due to the natural muscle paralysis we all experience every night. This chapter provides techniques for releasing fear in scary sleep states and using them as a springboard into a beautiful lucid dream. I also share my insomnia freedom technique here. Chapter 8 lifts the lid on nightmares that transcend space, time, and death, diving into telepathic and precognitive nightmares, out-of-body experiences, and disturbing near-death experiences, as well as suicide dreams and nightmares that may appear to be warnings from deceased loved ones.

In the final chapter, the luminous shadow archetype is explored—this encompasses positive qualities such as our higher potential that we deny or suppress. We'll explore the lucid void (a dream space devoid of imagery) and the transformative power of fire in nightmares, as well as the nature of light and the vast spiritual potential of dreams and nightmares. Throughout the book, common questions and dilemmas about nightmares and fearful sleep-related experiences are answered as you are taken step-by-step through the most powerful practices for resolving nightmares, anxiety dreams, sleep paralysis, and other nocturnal terrors. Through exploring the creative and transformative darkness of your dreams, you'll gain a profound and beautiful relationship with them.

In *The Art of Transforming Nightmares,* I synthesise all of the best-known nightmare techniques with lucidity. This can be waking lucidity (when we engage with nightmares while awake), lucid dreaming (when we wake up inside a dream or nightmare and can engage with it with full conscious awareness), or the relaxed lucid awareness of trance states. The transformative potential of lucid trances is one of my main areas of research, and I have been teaching my original Lucid Dreamplay techniques for over fifteen years.

Within this book, you'll find techniques that use creative writing, meditation, visualisation, bodywork, transitional sleep states, and spiritual practice, and you'll discover how to do transformative healing work *while in the nightmare itself,* through lucid dreaming. The synthesis of these healing, creative, and transformative methods will help you get the most out of the rich and powerful energy of your nightmares. Above all, you'll discover ways of transcending fear in all areas of your life, freeing you to live a life of happiness and wonder.

Let's dive in!

PART ONE

understanding nightmares

CHAPTER 1

what Are Nightmares And How can they Help us?

Sleeping and dreaming are incredibly interlinked and overlapping states. Even waking and dreaming are not two separate things! In fact, there is no state of consciousness that is ever completely separate from any other state. How could there be? If we are having a hard time in our nighttime world, it's likely that our daytime world is adversely impacted, too. Our physical, mental, and emotional selves are instantly affected by just one sleepless night. When we suffer from recurring nightmares or are attacked by faceless monsters in sleep paralysis, or when we don't get enough deep, restful sleep because we're scared to fall asleep, you can bet that our cognitive abilities, short-term memory, emotional resilience, empathy, and overall happiness levels plummet. The good news is that there are many simple, practical ways of working with unpleasant sleep experiences that can help us transform our dream life and regain the bliss of serene, nourishing sleep.

What Are Nightmares?

The Art of Transforming Nightmares employs a broad definition of the term *nightmare*. In this book, a nightmare is *any upsetting, fearful, or distressing experience that occurs during sleep*, which means that we are going to focus on much more than those terrifying nightmares that cause us to wake up screaming. As far as this book is concerned, the term *nightmare* also encompasses harrowing sleep paralysis visions and sensations, scary out-of-body experiences, grotesque pre-sleep imagery, fearful episodes of floating lost in the black void, sleep disturbances, uncontrollable lucid nightmares, or any dream that troubles us or leaves us feeling anxious or depressed. While unpleasant nightmares and anxiety dreams are fairly common and can usually be worked on with relative ease, chapter 6 of this book also attends to more severe nightmares caused by post-traumatic stress disorder (PTSD). The severity of PTSD and trauma-related nightmares can overwhelm and impede our natural self-healing process, so they can require a specialised therapeutic approach and greater support.

Dreams and nightmares are honest mirrors, showing us how we really feel about life, relationships, and ourselves. This book shares how to engage with nightmares in transformative and lucid ways, how to dissolve fear, how to receive precious messages and spiritual gifts from our unconscious mind, and how to use our new awareness to guide us into a fearless and wonderful life.

One important maxim I'd like to share is that *even the worst nightmares carry healing, creative, and spiritual gifts*. I'd even go so far as to say that *especially* the worst nightmares can bring us these precious gifts, because they have so much energy! Dreams and nightmares speak to us in the language of the soul. The greater the need of the soul to communicate with us, the greater the potential for healing transformation. Our goal, then, is to find the gifts within our nightmares and distressing sleep experiences, and to understand how these gifts can empower and heal us in our waking life.

Why Do We Have Nightmares?

Fight-or-flight reactions occur in an ancient part of our brain, the *amygdala*, also known as our "emotional accelerator." In the past, if we were walking through a forest and met up with an angry bear, the amygdala would help us survive by creating a sense of extreme fear and urgency, so that we would either fight the bear or run away to save our lives. These days, our stressors are very different: we miss the train we needed to catch to get to an important meeting, or we have to sit an exam we don't feel prepared for. Although not life-threatening, such situations can trigger the same existential fear in the brain because the amygdala makes no distinction between a death threat and other stressors. Then there are also unresolved traumatic experiences we had in the past that have left a memory of fear embedded deep in our brain. During dreaming, this fearful raw material can become magnified into scary imagery.

Because of the zany, creative nature of the dreaming mind, the scary dream may contain comic or ludicrous elements (the train we miss turns into a golden hedgehog that chases our boss), or there may be resolution within the dream story (to our amazement, the dreaded exam question only asks us to draw a rainbow, and we happily get out our colouring pencils and do so). This is great because it means that we are processing our fears and making sense of the situations we have lived through in a healthy way. We release excess fear and resolve our life issues by dealing with them in our dreams. But sometimes the fear gets out of control and becomes amplified into a terrifying nightmare.

In the case of such a nightmare, our overflowing fears and emotions are usually *not* resolved within the dream story; instead, we wake up flooded with dread, our heart pumping. When this happens, we have received a loud and clear message from our unconscious that here is an issue we need to resolve. Nightmares are red flags that point to the areas within our psyche that need healing. Distressing dreams are an invitation to heal from the past, create positive action in the present, and brave up for the future. When we work with distressing dreams, we can complete the process of resolution, insight, and healing.

Imagine your dreaming mind as a kind mermaid who swims up from the depths of your unconscious and approaches you with love, holding something in her two hands. When she reaches you, the mermaid says, "This needs healing." Her eyes are compassionate—she knows how hard this is going to be for you, but she needs to bring your attention to what she's holding. You look down … and in her hands you see the most repellent, ugly, wriggling nightmare. Instantly, you are engulfed with awful emotions: guilt, dread, and a deep distaste. Your instinct is to walk away—who wants to get involved with something so repulsive? You force yourself awake and try to shrug off the images you just saw. But the next night, the kind mermaid returns and she's still carrying the damn nightmare, which is bigger and stronger than it was before, thrashing around hideously in her arms. With a rush of clarity, you realise that you need to face this monstrosity before it gets even bigger.

This is what our dreaming mind does when it produces nightmares: it brings our attention to what needs healing within us.

How Does a Dream Turn into a Nightmare?

Imagine a young parrot who flies into a hall of mirrors. Since she has no idea about the nature of mirrors and the visual effects of bulging reflective surfaces, she is terrified to find herself face-to-face with grotesque parrots with massive heads and distorted beaks, and freakishly long-necked parrots with rolling eyeballs. As her fear skyrockets, the creatures become mythical: here is a griffin, swooping with outstretched claws; there is a wild-eyed harpy, a warped and deformed phoenix... The more the parrot opens her beak and shrieks in horror, the wider these ugly beings open their massive jaws! As she flees the hall in panic, a pterodactyl keeps perfect pace with her...

Outside in the cool air, the parrot feels powerfully relieved when none of the monstrous birds follow her. The pterodactyl who seemed to be flying out too has vanished—how come? Now comes her moment of lucidity: she realises that those birds were silent and she never felt the flap of their wings. She realises that despite their weirdness, they looked uncannily like her and even sported the same smart cap of green feathers! Feeling calm and brave and curious, she flutters back into the hall of mirrors, and as she approaches the first mirror, she understands that these birds are reflections of herself! Now she is able to look into the mirror with full awareness and laugh at the funny images and enjoy this shapeshifting game.

Dreams are mirrors.

Through our dreams, we get to see ourselves as if gazing through a distorted but honest mirror. Dreams reflect back to us our hidden hopes, our shortcomings, our inner beauty, our obsessions, our worst fears, and our strengths.

Crucially, dreams are *thought-responsive environments*.

This means that our thoughts and feelings, as well as our intentions and expectations, are conveyed seamlessly to our dreaming mind in a beautiful telepathic communication. And dreaming is a conversation, so the dream responds. If we are alone in an old house in our dream and we think, "This might be a haunted house!" the dream may well rattle up some ghostly chains in response, or we may see a translucent figure gliding by ... And, of course, if we then panic in our dream and allow fear to rise within us, well, things could get truly nasty—the ghostly figure rushes towards us, shrieking like a banshee with glowing evil eyes ... yikes! We wake up bathed in sweat. Our out-of-control fear turned what could have been a relaxing dream about exploring an old house (and maybe finding hidden treasures) into a full-blown nightmare.

In the dream state, we have to be super mindful about our fear. We need to bring our awareness to the fear, panic, distress, or horror, and remind ourselves that we are safe and will wake up safely in our bed after this experience. We can take measures to calm down and protect ourselves, as in Practice 1: How to Release Fear and Become Calm and Practice 36: Invoke Protective Powers: Ball of Light.

In dreams, as in waking life, when it comes to emotions, there is a tipping point. Up until a certain moment, the dream is not a nightmare. There may be low levels of anxiety present, but things are okay. However, if we get too caught up in the feeling of anxiety (or fear, or dread), then we quickly reach the tipping point where the thought-responsive dream environment creates upsetting imagery in response to our emotional input, and the dream turns into a nightmare. One father dreamed he was exploring a wildlife park with his young daughter. There were animals roaming free and it was fine until he noticed that night was starting to fall. The dreamer's anxiety rose: darkness was coming and wild animals were all around. Because of this increase in anxiety, the dream responded with something far worse: the dreamer noticed his daughter had disappeared! Now frantic, he ran around looking for her while his fear further amplified the dream story and soon his worst fears were realised: a man told him two people had kidnapped his daughter. Assailed by an overwhelming feeling of despair, he awoke.

The tipping point in this dream—the moment it morphed into a nightmare—was when night began to fall, causing fear to rise in the dreamer. Fuelled by this fear, the dream story then escalated into a harrowing nightmare. It's really helpful for nightmare sufferers to practise calming techniques during the day so that it becomes automatic to breathe and calm down whenever we feel stressed, both in waking life and in dreams. This simple technique is easy to get the hang of.

practice 1

HOW TO RELEASE FEAR AND BECOME CALM

Releasing fear is essential for us to deepen our connection with life. When we go through life with fear in our hearts, we obscure our own magnificence and distance ourselves from joy. We feel unsafe in the world. But you have a right to feel safe, in your body and in your life. Remember that you are a powerful spiritual being and the entire universe supports you. You belong here. You have the right to be alive; you have your place in the universe just as the stars and the oceans do. This is your earth to walk on. This is your air and you have the right to breathe it.

Your breath is your lifeline and your path to feeling safe. Whether awake or asleep, you can always influence the depth and regularity of the breaths you take. There is nothing to fear in any state of consciousness because ultimately, everything is one. When you cultivate a feeling of safety, you gift yourself with a huge amount of tranquil power. This breathing exercise can be practised by day and used whenever needed to bring your fear and anxiety levels down and induce calmness:

- Take a few moments each day to practise this relaxing breathing rhythm: Close your eyes and inhale for four seconds. Hold your breath without effort for four seconds, then exhale for six seconds. Keep your focus on this 4-4-6 rhythm until it feels easy and natural. Adjust it if you need to.

- Now keep the rhythm going without actively counting the seconds. Each time you breathe in, think, "I am calm" or "I am safe." As you retain your breath, feel that sense of calm and safety infuse your mind and body. When you breathe out, think, "I release fear." Keep this mantra going as you continue to breathe in a relaxed and rhythmic way.

- Really feel the sensation of calm spread throughout your entire body, through all your cells and muscles, as if light is infusing you. Feel this calmness fill your mind and body from head to toe.

- If you have any difficulty in cultivating calmness, it can be helpful to summon a memory of a moment when you experienced deep peace and total safety, and focus on reexperiencing this moment with all of your senses.

- Once you feel completely calm, remind yourself that you can use your breath to reach this peaceful state whenever you need to, both in waking life and in dreams and nightmares. This calmness is always present within you. When you're ready, open your eyes and smile!

During a nightmare (or in a dream reentry exercise), you can use this breathing technique to remind you that you are safe and that after this experience you will wake up safely in your bed.

Four Steps in Transformative Nightmare Work

Working with nightmares can be very simple—we recall the events and imagery, figure out the symbolism, release fear, and then act on the wisdom of the nightmare to create positive change in our lives. There are four major steps in healing, transformative nightmare work:

1. **Remember our dreams.** The first major step is simply remembering our dreams. Most nightmare sufferers don't have a problem recalling what happened during the night, but if you'd like to improve your dream recall, try Practice 2: Keep a Nightmare Journal (later in this chapter). When we recall our dreams and nightmares, we shine the light of awareness onto them and let them know that we value them and are listening to what they have to say.

2. **Uncover the message.** The second step is uncovering the message of the nightmare—what it's about and what it wants to tell us. In chapter 2, we'll look at the language of dreams and nightmares and how to decipher the symbolism.

3. **Release fear and other unhelpful emotions.** The third step is to work with the nightmare to release fear and other difficult emotions that may be holding us back in life and to integrate whatever we need for healing resolution. There are many practices in this book that help you work with nightmares in transformative ways.

4. **Take positive action.** The final step is to take positive action in our lives based on what our dream is saying to us. Dreams and nightmares show us how we really feel about a situation. They show us probable outcomes and worst-case scenarios, and they offer solutions.

What Happens When We Ignore Nightmares?

When we ignore nightmares, they return in a different form or they repeat in every detail, slapping us with their message until we react. Unfortunately, many people react by becoming frightened to sleep lest the nightmare return. This is a terrible pity, as it blows their much-needed recuperation time out of the water. When people have been in this state of terror and suffering a lack of solid sleep for a while, they find themselves unable to regain their strength, and they may become exhausted, depressed, physically ill, or even suicidal. Severe nightmare sufferers write to me saying, "I think I'm going crazy," "I feel like I won't survive this," or "Please help me get my life back."

If you find yourself feeling this desperate about your nightmares, as a first step, please get professional help immediately. Some nightmares should not be worked on alone! Talk to your doctor or see a therapist who works with dreams, trauma, and nightmares. Some people spend a night being monitored in a sleep lab and discover that their nightmares are caused by a mild sleep disturbance and can be easily treated. Others may discover that there is a past trauma at the root of their nightmares, and can work on this at their own pace with a therapist. Still others may be advised by their doctor to take antidepressants, which may have the side effect of suppressing dream recall. Medication may well be a useful sticking plaster for desperate times, but in the long term, often the only way to reach a lasting, satisfying, and healthy solution is to create a safe space within which to face the nightmare and unwrap it to reveal its gifts.

Our dreams are part of us—we are the dream and it is us. But this also means that we are the nightmare and it is us! Nightmares can be thought of as a part of ourselves that hasn't yet healed properly. They are a red flag that shouts, "Healing is needed!" Nightmares are healing gifts. They may come in ugly wrapping paper, but when we calm our fears and open them up with full lucid awareness, we are gifted with wisdom, transformation, and healing. We are not as helpless as we might think. We are much more powerful than we know. We can change our lives for the better. Every one of us has the inner resources to be able to heal ourselves. It's true. We just need to know how to access this healing so that we can transform our lives—and the lives of others—for the better.

practice 2

KEEP A NIGHTMARE JOURNAL

Keeping a nightmare journal is the number-one practice for empowering ourselves when engaging with nightmares, as it helps us identify common themes and emotions, and we begin to understand the message behind our worst dreams. It also makes the powerful move of showing our dreaming mind that we are listening to it and are open to its wisdom. Since nightmares are pure creative energy, writing them down also enables us to connect with their creative power, and we can work with this in exciting ways to harness that wild, raw energy (as shown in Practice 19: Artistic Nightmare Options for Adults and Kids and Practice 43: Turn Mythological Beasts into Protective Allies).

Nightmares often come in sequences, like the next instalment in a soap opera (or a horror series). As our emotions and situation shift over time, we receive new nightmares that show our progression. One woman who lost all her worldly possessions had recurring nightmares about endless hardship, poverty, and suffering. But the nightmares depicted a gradual shift as her attitude of helplessness changed into one of inner strength. In the final nightmare of the series, she was struggling up a mountain in bad weather with other refugees when suddenly the ground levelled off and the sun came out, giving them all a feeling of hope.

Nightmares that change from difficult to easy, or from dark to light, reflect positive shifts within our psyche, such as a change in our attitude or a new feeling of empowerment and resilience. When we change on the inside, our outer, waking life changes accordingly and things improve, often with surprising speed. Keeping a nightmare journal with spaces for sketches and life context can give you clarity because it helps you spot patterns in your nightmares and see where you are, psychologically and emotionally, at this moment in your life.

- Find an unlined notebook so you can add sketches, or use your phone to record your dreams vocally if you prefer.
- Try to wake up without an alarm clock or wake up slowly to music. This allows you to stay in your sleep position with closed eyes and think back over your night of sleep and dreams. Your overall dream recall will

improve. (It's nice to remember not only nightmares but the beautiful or fun dreams as well!)

- Whenever you wake up in the night, ask yourself these questions: "What was I just dreaming about?" "Who was I with?" "How was I feeling?" The better your dream recall is, the broader your picture of your dreaming mind will become.

- Keep your nightmare journal right by your bed and write in it even if all you recall is a feeling of unease or dread, with no imagery. If you awaken from a nightmare in the night and don't want to disturb your bed partner, either leave the bedroom to write or whisper your nightmare into a recording device. If the nightmare was very upsetting, do take a moment to unwind from it with a few deep breaths and reassure yourself that you are safe. Remind yourself that, horrendous though it may be, this nightmare has come to help and heal you!

- Use the present tense when writing your nightmares: "A black swan lunges at my throat…" "The spaceship fires laser beams at our house…" This tense helps to retain the immediacy and emotional impact of the nightmare.

- Give your nightmare a title. This sums up the main action and makes it easier to identify different dreams when you glance back through your journal.

- Draw or sketch the main images from your nightmares to capture their energy. This makes it easier to do dream reentry practices, such as Practice 8: Reenter the Nightmare and Practice 16: Become the Monster.

- Note any associations or memories the nightmare brings up for you.

- Which emotions are present? Jot these down in the order in which they appear, such as "sadness, followed by disgust and fear." When did you last experience these emotions in waking life?

- What is the context of the nightmare: is there any connection with events in your waking life?

- Be a nightmare detective: Once you have recorded a few nightmares, look back over your journal and ask yourself, "Which stories do my nightmares tell?" Jot down recurring themes or images.

- What is the timing for these nightmares? Do they occur when you are stressed or after you've been out partying? Do you often have a nightmare after seeing a particular person? Try to find links to waking-life events and emotions.

Keeping a nightmare journal (and jotting down pleasant, nonscary dreams as well) gives us a fascinating glimpse into our state of mind. It's easier to do transformative work with a range of different nightmares when we have them readily available to us as written accounts with sketches, associations, and context, so that we can chart their progression and add new insights to them as we go along.

....

Emotional Detachment from Nightmare Imagery

A nightmare is often defined by the strength of the emotions it triggers. One person described a recurring dream of floating in a large cube. "How peaceful!" we might think. But no, for him this was a terrifying space. Sometimes the most horrific dream stories that cause others to flinch when they hear them are not perceived as being a nightmare by the dreamer. This is usually because there is not a strong emotion such as fear, disgust, or guilt present in the dream. Occasionally someone will share a dream with me that contains shocking or disturbing imagery, such as having their limbs torn off by soldiers and watching as their body parts are strewn around the street. Yet the dreamer will say this was not really a nightmare since although they now feel baffled and slightly concerned by the imagery, it didn't upset them *while they were in the dream*.

There may be various reasons for this kind of emotional detachment from shocking dream imagery. Sometimes there is a past trauma that the person has unconsciously dissociated from, and this crops up in the form of disturbing dream imagery, but the emotional element has been frozen out of it to protect the dreamer from its impact. Other times it could be one of those "this is how you *really* feel!" dreams related to a current situation that we think we're handling just fine, but when we unwrap the meaning of our dream, we realise it is telling us symbolically that on a deep, unconscious level, the situation we're in is in fact making us feel "torn apart."

Another possibility is that the dreamer watched a war movie the night before and this imagery seeped into their dreams. The emotional impact would be minimal, as the imagery doesn't pertain to the dreamer's life but rather to an artistic creation—the movie. Emotions (or a lack of them) are important to consider when it comes to any nighttime experience, from sleep paralysis to dreams. It's also very valuable to work with the imagery to illuminate its meaning. There are many wonderful ways of illuminating nightmares, from the simplest method of asking "what was going on in your life at the time this nightmare occurred?" to deeper practices such as reentering the dream imaginatively with powerful allies and magical tools at hand, so that we feel equipped to meet our monsters, befriend angry dream bears, and dance with our demons.

When Are Nightmares *Not* about Personal Issues?

- **When nightmares tap into a wider social dimension and reflect the state of the world or the collective human psyche.** Apocalyptic nightmares sometimes—but not always—fall into this "social dreaming" category. Working with the dream allows us to figure out if this is a social dream or a personal one.

- **When nightmares are triggered by medication, psychedelics, or other recreational drugs.** If you suffer from nightmares, it's wise to investigate any prescription drugs or plant/herbal remedies you're taking, but only change your intake after consulting with your doctor.

- **When nightmares are warnings of real-life events that are about to happen.** Dreams are not bound by time in the way that our waking lives are, and sometimes people report precognitive nightmares, where a shocking or upsetting event occurs in the dream (such as a loved one dying in an accident) and then this actually happens in waking life. Chapter 8 explores such dreams. Please note that the majority of nightmares do *not* come true in this way, and death in dreams is usually symbolic of major change.

- **When nightmares are caused by physical pain.** We'll take a look in chapter 2 at how pain and discomfort can infiltrate our dreams to cause unpleasant streams of imagery.

- **When we cause digestive mayhem by eating spicy foods, cheese, or gluten before bedtime.** This is highly individual and may not be a problem for you at all, but it's worth looking at what you ate before your last nightmare, to see if there's any connection between uneasy dreams and an uneasy gut. Also check your coffee intake.
- **When nightmares are caused by sleep paralysis.** Chapter 7 explores sleep paralysis, which is when we feel trapped in our body, unable to move, and we often experience disturbing imagery and sensations.
- **When nightmares are our response to a horror movie or psychological thriller we watched before bed.** The dreaming mind is a skilled movie-maker: it pulls together daytime impressions, deep psychology, and pure creative imagery to create fabulous living stories. If we've just watched a horror movie, we may find elements from it infiltrate our dreams. Of course, looking at exactly which movie elements our dreaming mind focused on and why can reveal psychological insights, but there may be no particular message for us other than that we shouldn't watch such films if we want sweet dreams!

Who Are You When You Dream?

This is a fascinating question to reflect upon, and one which can help you to shine a light on your dreaming self. Think back on your recent dreams and nightmares, or leaf through your dream journal as you consider this question. You are so much more than your waking self! Who is your dreaming self? The following practice helps you to get clarity on who "dream you" is.

practice 3
WHO ARE YOU WHEN YOU DREAM?

As you reflect on the kinds of dreams and nightmares you generally have, consider the following questions:

1. Who is your dreaming self? How do you act, react, and reflect in the dream state? Do you feel you are an empowered dreamer—do you act to protect yourself and others in dreams, and are you able to state your needs, boundaries, and feelings? Or do you feel vulnerable and unsafe

in your dreams, perhaps often being chased or attacked, or hiding from enemies? Do bad things happen to you, like falling off cliffs or being trapped in burning buildings? Perhaps your dreaming self is sometimes your child self, or perhaps you shapeshift into animals, birds, aliens, or objects in your dreams—in which case, how would you describe the energy of these dreams? Jot down your observations about your dreaming self in your nightmare journal as if you're making a character study. List the traits and personality type of your dreaming self.

2. How do you think in your dreams? Consider your thought process in the dream state. Perhaps you are highly aware in your dreams and have meaningful encounters and conversations, or perhaps you feel you are flung willy-nilly into crazy situations with low awareness of what's going on. Are you able to think fairly logically? Without judgment, consider the way you reflect in dreams, including the thoughts you hide from other dream figures. Pay attention to times when your dreaming train of thought escalates into anxiety, and notice how this causes the dream scene to change in response.

3. What kinds of situations do you often find yourself in? Identify themes and recurring emotions.

4. How do you react to fear? Whenever you feel fearful in a dream or nightmare, what happens? Does your fear get the better of you and escalate, or can you calm it down? When confronted by danger, do you tend to flee, fight, freeze, wake up screaming, or become lucidly aware within that dream? Write down your habitual response to fearful dreams, and also note your ideal response. For example, instead of running away, you could decide to turn and calmly face what's chasing you. We'll look at how to do this in Practice 14: Creative Nightmare Responses.

5. The crucial thing to know is that whoever you may be when you dream, you can change the way you respond and react to your dreams. You can empower your dreaming self. When you engage lucidly with a nightmare while awake (through dreamwork after the nightmare) or while asleep (during a lucid dream), you can change your nightmare response in simple, practical ways. In doing so, you empower your

dreaming self and supply it with the resources, serenity, and flexibility it needs to face the dreamworld. This empowers both your dreaming self and your waking self, because the two are intrinsically linked.

It's helpful to return to these questions as you get into the process of empowering your dreaming self and making changes to your nightmares by using the techniques in this book. You'll find your dreaming self will grow more confident and powerful, more able to respond creatively to situations, and more aware. The Nightmare Quiz in chapter 5 will help you pinpoint your sleeper/dreamer type even more precisely, but it's great to already begin to consider the key question of who you are when you dream.

Three Common Questions about Nightmares

The most common question I get about nightmares is this: *How do I stop them?* My hope is that as you progress through this book, you'll find that the idea of "stopping" nightmares loses importance as the larger picture is revealed. Instead, it will seem far healthier, more exciting, and more relevant to work constructively with nightmares so that their frequency diminishes naturally due to the integrative work you have done. Nightmares are powerful gifts of the psyche that help us chart our path through life. Still, let's address this question, along with two others that people ask me all the time.

"How do I stop my nightmares?"

The best way of reducing nightmare frequency and intensity is to work with them in healing and transformative ways to understand their message and release their powerful gifts. Once we have done this, their job is done, so they don't need to return. Nightmares come with a message, and they often show us the solutions to our life issues. When we suppress them, we don't solve the problem! We continue to live in fear, and that's an unfortunate way to live, don't you think? Sometimes people use sleeping pills or anxiety medication to block out their nightmares. For some, this may work for a short period, but then they report the nightmares returning full force. Nightmares are dreams that shout at us to get us to listen because there is something within us that needs healing. When we befriend our nightmares and work with them in gentle and healing ways, we can spark major psycho-spiritual transformation, freeing up lots of energy with which to create a happier life for ourselves and those around us. It's a win-win situation!

"Are the evil beings in my dreams real?"

When we bring lucid awareness to our nightmares, either during the dream or afterwards through waking dreamwork, we can discover for ourselves the nature of our dream figures. A common psychological approach is that every element of any dream is a part of ourselves. This means that we are the dream (or the nightmare!) and it is us. When we have forcibly repressed an unwanted shadow side of ourselves, this may surge up in the form of a highly conscious aggressive dream figure. Through working with the nightmare, we can discover why this figure has chosen this moment to present itself to us.

Remember what we said earlier about the dream being a thought-responsive environment? Well, it also reflects our beliefs, so it can be helpful to examine and question your beliefs about supernatural powers, the existence of "evil," and the reality (or non-reality) of devils, goblins, sorcerers, or malign presences. Much depends on your beliefs, expectations, and fear levels within the nightmare. When we experiment with calming our fears in frightening nightmares, what we very often find is that the dream responds by growing calm, and the nasty entities vanish into black dust or transform into benign, friendly dream figures. When we conquer fear, we may find that the "evil beings" no longer appear in our nightmares, and that tells us a lot about their illusory nature.

Dream figures (this includes animals and non-human figures, as well as magical objects) do appear to have differing levels of awareness. I describe these in my book *Llewellyn's Complete Book of Lucid Dreaming* as ranging from zombies and puppets to conscious equals and super-aware dream figures. While dream figures are usually symbolic, sometimes we may feel we are tapping into darker collective energies. If a super-aware dream figure, beast, or animal shows up in your nightmare as an aggressive presence, you can take various actions to protect yourself and respond creatively. See Practice 14: Creative Nightmare Responses and Practice 22: Create a Sacred Altar.

"Could I die in a nightmare or during sleep paralysis?"

Nightmares and sleep paralysis experiences take place in normal stages of sleep that we all move through each night. I have had thousands of sleep paralysis experiences and I'm still alive to tell the tale—why wouldn't I be? The truth is, anyone could die at any stage of waking or sleep. But if it was so easy to die during these experiences, we would find people dead in their beds all the time! The human body has a super-strong connection to life, and even when we feel extreme terror, unless we have a heart condition, our terror will not even come close to threatening our life. Why not be brave and—armed with suitable protections—walk towards our fears? It's not worth being dominated by them.

Ask yourself, "What is the worst thing that could happen to me in this state of consciousness?" And crucially, "What do I need to feel safe in this state?" (A superhero ally, a magic power …) Ask yourself how you feel about the natural transition we call death. Are you frightened of dying? What is that fear based on? Examine your beliefs and you may find it's easier to let go of fear than you imagine. Practice 39: Question Your Beliefs, Assumptions, and Expectations may help with this.

Lucid Dreaming and Its Connection to Nightmares

Other questions I often receive focus on lucid dreaming. Lucid dreams are dreams where *we know that we are dreaming while we are dreaming.* This awareness enables us to guide and shape the dream if we wish to, but lucidity is not synonymous with control: it's absolutely possible to go with the flow of the dream while lucid without actively trying to change events. Lucid dreaming can be a mind-blowingly fabulous experience, as you can fly to the stars, explore the fabric of consciousness, make love to sexy dream people, connect with deceased loved ones, and work directly within the dream for healing, creativity, and personal transformation.

Yet it's amazing how many people tell me they are scared of having lucid dreams. The common factor among these people tends to be that they suffer from frightening lucid nocturnal experiences, such as sleep paralysis or lucid nightmares. It's ironic, really, because there are millions of people out there who long to get lucid in their dreams and who would give a lot to have the kind of natural, spontaneous lucid sleep experiences that the others have. In fact, people often write to me asking how to trigger sleep paralysis, as they've heard it's a great route into lucid dreaming!

Many people successfully tackle their nightmares by becoming lucid and working directly with nightmare imagery in healing, creative, transformative ways. In my book *The Art of Lucid Dreaming*, you'll find many Lucidity Programmes and original techniques dedicated to helping you learn to have lucid dreams and increase their stability and frequency. In this book, I focus on the *scary* side of lucid experiences. We'll look at how to remain calm when frightening imagery seems to take on an ominous life of its own and we feel as if we've landed with full awareness inside a crazed horror movie. We'll also explore the wonderful ways in which lucidity can help us transform all manner of unpleasant sleep experiences.

But we don't need to be a lucid dreamer to heal nightmares! We can work in the same way when we reenter a dream imaginatively while awake, and this book gives you many techniques for doing this. However, if you're interested in having lucid dreams, the following practice gives you my top ten tips for waking up inside a dream.

practice 4
TOP TEN TIPS FOR GETTING LUCID
IN YOUR DREAMS AND NIGHTMARES

1. **Treat yourself to afternoon naps.** In terms of brain chemistry, a nap is an optimal moment for lucid dreaming: the body is tired but the brain is alert, and we are usually quick to enter dream-rich REM sleep, a state in which dreams are vivid and surreal—all the better for realising that we are dreaming.

2. **Do creative visualisations.** These can be thought of as beautiful, positive messages for your unconscious to absorb and react to. When we create a vivid "waking dream" in our mind's eye, we speak directly to our unconscious in its own language of symbolism and powerful imagery. Visualise yourself realising "this is a dream!" and going on to enjoy wonderful lucid experiences within the dream space. This primes your mind to get lucid.

3. **Practise meditation.** Meditate for just a few minutes before you sleep, and gradually build up to longer sessions. Try a simple meditation such as the one in Practice 6: Pre-Bed Meditation to Calm the Mind. Meditation is a wonderful mindfulness technique that brings us into the moment, stabilises the mind, and leads us to our calm, still centre. All of these things are great for training the brain towards stable lucid awareness.

4. **Label your states of consciousness.** Sleeping and waking are by no means the only states we experience, yet many people take this either-or approach to conscious experience. "You're either awake or asleep, right?" they say. Well, actually it's really not that simple. In fact, there are many states of consciousness, and a lot of overlap and twilight zones between them. To train your lucidity skills, practise labelling your state of consciousness whenever you can: daydreaming, wide awake, tired and struggling to remain mentally alert, deep relaxation, etc. Try labelling your sleep states as you enter them, such as the hypnogogic state (when pre-sleep imagery pops up as you're nodding off) or stage-one sleep (which is easy to identify, as this is when you're resting and your head lolls—always embarrassing when it happens in a business meeting!). Get used to doing this (labelling your state of consciousness, not falling asleep at work), and you'll find it easier to identify when you are dreaming, and become lucid.

5. **Keep a dream journal.** This opens the lines of communication between you and your dreaming mind. The better you recognise your individual dream images and recurring themes, the easier it will become to notice when they next appear in a dream, prompting you to realise, "This is a dream!" Follow the tips in Practice 2: Keep a Nightmare Journal.

6. **Observe pre-sleep imagery.** A fabulous practice to help you become lucid in a dream is to observe your weird and wonderful pre-sleep imagery and sensations. Known as *hypnagogia*, this state arises during the transition between waking and sleeping (and also when we emerge from sleep, when it's called *hypnopompia*). Relax in bed and instead of releasing your awareness, simply wait for points of light, imagery, and moving pictures to appear in your mind's eye. This is the

beginning of dreaming, and if you can stay aware and not get sucked into the imagery, you can sail straight into a fully lucid dream from this state!

7. **Tune into your body.** The body is one of the best lucidity triggers. Our dream body feels different from our physical body. It is light, flexible, stretchy, floaty, and it can fly. These are important clues that we are dreaming! Tune into your physical body while awake and really notice how it feels to exist in this body. You may have aches and pains or itches; your hair tickles your face; your body is solid; you have the same number of fingers from one moment to the next; it hurts if you bump into something; your limbs remain the same length all day long; and you have a weight and solidity to you. Feel the breath travel coolly in and out of your lungs, and remind yourself to recognise the difference the next time you find yourself in a dream body.

8. **Do reality checks.** Whenever you see something strange, beautiful, or ugly, or whenever you carry out a habitual action such as walking through a door, ask yourself if you are dreaming now. Expect to find that you *are* dreaming. After all, how do you know you aren't? Carry out a reality check, such as trying to put a finger through the palm of your other hand, or pinching your nose to see if you can still breathe through it. (Hint: if you can, you're dreaming!) The more you carry out reality checks while awake, the more likely you are to remember to check your reality in a dream … and discover that you are in fact dreaming.

9. **Wake early, then read, sleep, and get lucid.** There's a technique known as "Wake Back to Bed (WBTB)" where you wake yourself up around 4–5 hours into your night of sleep (that's the hard bit), then get up for about 15–30 minutes, write down your dreams, read a bit of a lucid dreaming book, or meditate. If you are a deep sleeper who usually falls asleep within seconds, you could try watching a YouTube video on lucidity (screen light can prevent some people from falling back to sleep, so only do this if it's easy for you to get back to sleep afterwards). Then you return to bed and visualise yourself becoming lucid in one of your dreams. As with afternoon naps, this is a great time to get lucid in terms of brain chemistry, and you can glide calmly

into sleep while repeating a lucidity mantra such as this one: "Everything I see and touch is a dream." Suddenly, that mantra will come true and you'll be lucid in your dream. It's best to use techniques that disrupt your sleep sparingly, and not on consecutive nights. Sleep is precious; it revitalises and heals us, giving us vital energy with which to face life, so skimping on it is not advisable.

10. **Incubate a lucid dream.** When we incubate a dream, we simply ask for one. It's helpful to ritualise this to solidify our intention and get the message through to our dreaming mind. You could write a letter to your dreaming mind, asking it to help you get lucid, and put it under your pillow, or you could sleep with a "lucidity pebble" in your hand and try to hold onto it all night—this is possible and has triggered lucidity in people on my retreats, so even if it sounds like a funny thing to do, give it a try! The pebble symbolises your lucid intent, and you may even find yourself holding it in a dream and then understanding that you are dreaming now. You can also shout out to your dreaming mind as you fall asleep, "Help me, please, to get lucid in my dreams!" This one often works for me. Feel gratitude (this is a powerful force) and fully *expect* that your awareness will increase enough in your dream for you to understand that you are dreaming.

The Sacred Elixir of Sleep

So often in these hectic days, sleep is viewed as an inconvenience—ah, if only we didn't have to sleep, we could just keep working and working like maniacs every single hour of the day! Wouldn't that be brilliant? Well, no. The fact is, without sleep, we would all become gibbering wrecks within a short amount of time. A lack of sleep kills our mental agility, crushes our creativity, stomps on our short-term memory, and brutalises our basic responses to the people around us. When we are sleep-deprived, we become short-tempered, unable to think clearly, and prone to depression and worry. This less-than-optimal mental state may well infiltrate our dreams, turning them into unpleasant nightmares.

Even if you are a severe nightmare sufferer and fear falling asleep, remember that there is more to sleep than dreaming! We enter deep, recuperative spaces during our night of sleep that help us heal. Hormones that stimulate cellular repair are released during sleep, immune system replenishing takes place, and an immune factor that is a potent killer of cancer cells increases tenfold. Unconsciously regulated bodily functions such as our circulation and endocrine systems are overseen by the autonomic nervous system, which has an intimate relationship with sleep.[2] We need our sleep to heal us. If you delay bedtime because you're scared of having nightmares, you wind up turning into a sleep-deprived insomniac. Now you have not just one problem but two! These turn into the even more impactful problem of feeling unable to cope with life because you're constantly exhausted.

The good news is there are easy steps we can take to have a happier dream life and healthy sleep. This book looks thoroughly at ways of working beneficially with nightmares so that you no longer feel plagued by them, and in the meantime, it's a good idea to change your perspective of sleep to embrace its deeply nurturing and healing function. Let's see what happens when we give the health-bestowing state of sleep a little of the reverence it deserves through the simple power of ritual.

practice 5
CREATE A SOOTHING BEDTIME RITUAL

When we dread sleep due to nightmares or resent it because we have other, more important things to do, we cut ourselves off from a vital source of healing and distance ourselves from the amazing journey that sleeping and dreaming can become. We spend a third of our lives asleep. This is such a huge chunk of time, so why not make the most of it? When we welcome sleep, we open the gates to a vital and sacred state of being.

- From this day on, make the healthy decision to view your night of sleep as a glorious mini-vacation. You may prefer to focus on the physiological benefits of sleep or how vibrant and alive you feel when you've had a good sleep. You might think of sleep as overnight soul therapy at a place of deep healing, or as a spiritual refuge or a visit to a world of great beauty and mystery. Word it however you want, but try and fix in your

---

2. Cortelli et al., "Autonomic Dysfunction in Sleep Disorders."

mind a firm and very positive vision of this "other world" you'll visit when you lie down to sleep.

- Sleeping is sacred. How do we prepare to enter this sacred, healing state? Do we overeat, smoke, or get a bit drunk, then flop into bed and start snoring immediately? It's fine to do this now and then! We don't have to become sleep zealots. But on the nights when we're not party animals, let's make a real effort to greet and welcome sleep. Start by preparing your bedroom for this nightly treat. Turn your bedroom into a peaceful, inviting space, with warm, dim lighting. Is your mattress comfy? And your pillow? If street noise keeps you awake, use ear plugs. If a street light shines into your room all night, consider installing blackout blinds. Keep your bedroom cool; studies show we sleep better with a cool head, and this can help with insomnia.[3]

- Create a ritual to encourage a night of blissful sleep. This might include any of the following: take a bath with candles and bubbles, listen to relaxing meditative music, or put a few drops of essential oil on your pillow (sleep-promoting ones are lavender and chamomile, and another favourite of mine for its warmth and comfort is sweet orange). Throughout this ritual, be aware that you are nurturing yourself, which is a very good thing to do. You deserve a restful night and a peaceful mind. Once in bed, meditate for a short while. (The next practice shares a simple pre-sleep meditation.)

- Keep an eye on the effects that your pre-sleep ritual has on your sleep and on your life. Try it for a few weeks at first, adjust it as you go along, and see how it makes you feel. Does it improve your sleep? Do you feel brighter when you wake up in the morning? How are your dreams? Write down any dreams you recall, as well as the way you feel when you wake up. Gradually you are building up a clear picture of yourself as a sleeper and dreamer, and this is an excellent first step towards a healthier, happier life.

....

The final practice in this chapter is designed to help you enter the right state of mind before you cross the threshold into sleep.

3. Goodwin, "Sleeptime Head-Cooling Cap Eases Insomnia, Study Finds."

practice 6

PRE-BED MEDITATION TO CALM THE MIND

Our state of mind as we enter sleep has a great influence on the kinds of dreams we have. When we take time to really calm down, release the stresses of the day, and welcome sleep as the healing refuge that it is, we have a far better chance of experiencing a peaceful night.

- Sit in bed in dim light or darkness and take deep, calming breaths.
- With every inhalation, bring peace and light into your body. Let this flow around, reaching every part of you, from your inner organs to the skin on your face.
- With every exhalation, consciously release the thoughts and worries from the day you just had.
- When you feel you have cleared your thoughts and worries, begin a simple mantra, such as breathing in while thinking, "I am ...," and breathing out while thinking, "... peaceful."
- As you settle into this gentle breathing rhythm, there will be moments when you feel as if you are floating in peaceful space. Relax and let these precious moments expand; they are golden moments of pure awareness and are to be treasured and prolonged whenever they occur.
- When thoughts arise, just notice them without worrying or judging yourself for "not meditating properly." Thoughts are natural. Don't engage with them; instead, use them as a reminder to continue with your breathing and mantra. Be ready for another golden floaty moment.
- Embrace the beautiful rhythm of mantra ... golden moment ... thoughts, mantra ... golden moment ... thoughts ...
- When you feel completely serene, lie slowly back in bed and smile, knowing you will have a wonderfully restful night's sleep.

In this chapter, we have explored what nightmares are, why we have them, and how dreams turn into nightmares. We've looked at what happens when we ignore nightmares and how to release excess fear. We've seen the four major steps in healing, transformative nightmare work (remember dreams, uncover their meaning, release emotions, take positive action). Keeping a nightmare journal is an excellent first step towards the art of transforming nightmares, and a relaxing pre-bed meditation sets us on the right path to a peaceful night's sleep. We've discussed lucid dreams and how to trigger them, and clarified that we don't need to be a lucid dreamer to heal nightmares since we can reenter a dream imaginatively while awake. When we walk bravely to meet our nightmares, we open ourselves up to receive their wisdom and their powerful healing and creativity.

In the next chapter, we'll explore the tantalising and often obscure symbolic language of nightmares, and how to decipher our wildest dreams.

CHAPTER 2

understanding the symbolic Language of Nightmares

How do nightmares speak to us? They communicate in an intoxicating mixture of imagery, metaphors, symbols, and visceral emotions. They paint a cinematic, high-stakes picture of our lives, our relationships, and how we really feel deep down. We are stars in the super-vivid movies of our nightmares! Nightmares reveal to us the state of our soul. They are supremely honest mirrors that reflect the darkest shadow sides of ourselves and illuminate our deepest fears, yet they can be surprisingly hard to understand. In this chapter, we'll look at how to decipher the symbolic language of nightmares, and I'll share some key practices for unwrapping their meaning.

The beauty of nightmare work is that nightmare images zing and sparkle with life: they have a powerful living energy that we can tap into. This energy is incredibly concentrated because of its emotional and personal nature, so it is extremely transformative. Its transformative power can be used for healing, creativity, and change in all areas of our lives. It's a curious thing, because when we unwrap a nightmare using the techniques in this chapter, we are fully awake, but since we are engaging imaginatively with dream images, we are simultaneously working on a deeper unconscious level.

Unwrapping nightmare images, symbols, and storylines can be instrumental in illuminating unhelpful beliefs we hold about ourselves, unhealthy relationship patterns we cling to, and old attitudes that have been holding us back. We know when we've hit gold because the results can be felt viscerally within our body as tension falls away, and there is often a jolt of understanding, an aha moment. We simply know when we have found the wisdom or insight we need to receive from our nightmare. We'll look at the symbolic language of nightmares in this chapter, and explore common nightmare themes, but first I'll say a few words about the ethical side of helping someone else understand their nightmare.

The Dream Belongs to the Dreamer

The way that personal dream images arise and how they fit with the dream story reflects each dreamer's unique life experience, memories, desires, and associations, which is why we should never tell someone else what their dream means. I'm honoured to be past president and current board director of the International Association for the Study of Dreams (IASD), and our code of ethics emphasises that *the dream belongs to the dreamer*; that is to say, the dreamer is the ultimate authority on their own dream.

Interpreting someone else's dream for them can be an aggressive act, leaving the dreamer feeling powerless and exposed. "Oh, if you dreamed about a sexy naked woman in your marital bed, it means your husband is having an affair!" How is this going to make the dreamer feel? If the dreamer were left to explore that dream in their own way, they might realise the sexy naked woman is symbolic of themselves at a younger age and the dream is in fact inviting them to get back in touch with their passionate side. Or whatever. Who knows which associations would come up for them? The point is, this dream belongs to the dreamer, so ultimately only they can truly know what it's about.

It's lovely to help others unwrap their dreams and nightmares if they'd like us to, but we should do so with the greatest kindness, because the dream is a piece of their soul, a fragment of their psyche.

Any remarks we make about someone else's dream are at least partially based on the inner visions, emotions, and associations that their dream invokes within us as we hear it. Whenever we listen to someone tell us their dream, we engage with *our own inner vision of that dream*. A cave or tree will appear very differently in your imagination than it will in mine. If someone shares a dream in which they are with their brother, the word *brother* will inevitably create different gut feelings in a listener whose brother died recently, or a listener who has never liked their brother, or a listener whose brother is their favourite person in the world. Because of this, in a sense every dream we listen to becomes *our* dream.

We offer the dreamer respect and compassion when we acknowledge the subjectivity of our listening experience by prefacing any comments about their dream with the words "If this were *my* dream…"[4] This reminds both ourselves and the dreamer that our comments are merely projections that reveal as much about our own psychology as they do about the dreamer's. In the case of the thoughtless remark about the dreamer's husband having an affair, this tells us more about the person who made that comment (their lack of trust in relationships or a loss of belief in fidelity, perhaps?) than it does about the dreamer. The following practice gives tips on how to help someone unwrap the message of their nightmare.

practice 7

THE NIGHTMARE REFLECTION TECHNIQUE

- When someone shares any dream or nightmare with you, listen all the way through without interrupting. Extend warmth and compassion to the dreamer; they are entrusting a piece of their soul to you. When they have finished, it can be good to empathise with how real and upsetting the nightmare was, using the words they used: "When the cave collapsed, I imagine that must have felt very frightening." This allows the dreamer to feel heard and to clarify their emotions: "Well, now that I think about it, I wasn't really frightened for myself; I was just dead worried about not being able to reach my son."

- Ask the dreamer clarifying questions about their nightmare: "How high was the demon's wall? What exactly did the weird bumps on your tongue look like?"

- Ask them, "Do you have any thoughts so far on what this nightmare might mean?"

---

4. American psychiatrist Montague Ullman created the "If this were my dream" approach within his group dreamwork method.

- Check with the dreamer: "Would it be okay with you if I shared my own associations with your dream?" When we offer our associations or gut reactions in a nonjudgmental way, we might trigger an aha moment in the dreamer, which is why group work on a dream can be so powerful when it's done respectfully and with love.

- It's good to use this respectful phrase to preface your comments, as it makes you as vulnerable as the dreamer: "If this were my dream/nightmare…" or "In my dream/nightmare…" For example, "I'm really scared of snakes, so if this were my nightmare, the snake would symbolise my fear." Or, "In my dream, I feel very helpless and insignificant when the king sentences me to death." Be careful not to label a dream as "a nightmare" unless the dreamer uses that term. As discussed in chapter 1, sometimes dreams that have a storyline or imagery that disturbs the listener are *not* in fact experienced as nightmares by the dreamer.

- If there is clearly fear or other difficult emotions around the nightmare, and if it feels right for the dreamer, you could ask them, "What would you need to feel safe in this dream?" (A strong friend, a magical power such as flying or invisibility, a healing potion, a rescue helicopter…) Or, "If you could go back into your nightmare and change the storyline, what would you change?"

- Nightmares may take several goes to unpack; don't expect an instant solution or push the dreamer to wrap things up with a neat conclusion. I've found that nightmares can be very dense, and sometimes days, months, or even years later, we can find further meaning in them that is highly relevant for our lives. In creating this book, many of the generous people who shared nightmares with me said that in writing down their nightmare and life context for me, they discovered new insights and incredible resonances that made them appreciate the gifts of their nightmare all over again.

- If it feels right, you could ask the dreamer, "What do you think this dream wants you to know?" and "Is there any action you could take in your life to honour its message?" Thank the dreamer for sharing their dream with you.

....

Now let's get to grips with the symbolic language that dreams and nightmares use to communicate with us.

The Symbolic Language of Nightmares

The true gift of a nightmare often lies hidden underneath some pretty nasty wrapping paper. Imagery of people getting shot, abandoned babies, or plane crashes can make us feel we'd rather not get involved with this dream at all! It's worth it, though, I promise. In order to unwrap this gift, we need to become familiar with the symbolic nature of not only the dream images themselves but also the actions that occur. For example, a dream of driving a car depends not only on the nature of the car (battered? brand-new?) but also on the way the car is being driven (wildly? with confidence?) and by whom (you? your dead mother?) and with what degree of success (is this a smooth and easy ride, or have the brakes failed?). In the case of you, the dreamer, driving a car fast and the brakes failing, this may indicate that you are being reckless in an area of your life, driving yourself too hard, or racing so fast that although you need to slow down, you cannot stop. The dream could be saying, "Danger! Slow down!" A dream car may also represent the body, so failing brakes could indicate failing health. The only way to know for sure is to unwrap the dream further.

Context is also very important for understanding dreams, since a person's current or past-life issues are often key to shedding light on the imagery. This is why dream dictionaries that offer one meaning for one image are sadly inadequate. How can a dream cow mean the same thing for a butcher as it does for a Hindu, for whom cows are sacred animals? A dream moth will have a very different meaning for an insect enthusiast than for someone who is moth-phobic. I do think that the deeper, more soulful dream dictionaries can be useful in helping people gain insight into the way that dream symbolism might work. It's often illuminating to explore how archetypes (universal images, symbols, themes, and archaic mythical characters) crop up in dreams and nightmares. It can also be fun to look up an obscure dream image, such as an ostrich feather or a balaclava, to see if anything resonates with you. The main thing is to trust your own gut feelings and associations around your nightmare imagery, and give due attention to its context and possible meaning in your own life.

Let's look at some different examples of nightmares and their meaning so you can see for yourself how nightmares speak to us symbolically through violent or upsetting imagery to get their message across, and how examining context can reveal insight into why a particular nightmare occurred.

> My very beloved cat has been beheaded. Someone has taken his severed head and hung it in my home as a chandelier—over the dining table!!!!!

This was the nightmare of a woman whose husband had been diagnosed with a mental illness and refused to take medication. She recognised that the severed head symbolised the shocking split between his former beloved self and the way he was after he "lost his mind."

> I walk into the bathroom and find my boyfriend swinging dead from a rope.

This was a nightmare I had after ending a relationship with my boyfriend in my early twenties. Upon waking, I panicked briefly that this highly realistic dream meant he might kill himself over our breakup. But death in dreams is usually not a prediction of a person's actual death. Death is a transition from one state to another, and in dreams it often symbolises transformation: the dying of an old way of life. I also worried that the dream meant my ex would soon be "dead to me." But even today, he and I are the best of friends. My nightmare was symbolic of the huge and difficult change we were undergoing.

The following two examples are from Stase Michaels's book *Nightmares: The Dark Side of Dreams and Dreaming*.[5]

> A large spider whose sac is swollen and about to burst is going to spawn many more scary creatures and create a horrible mess. I know I have to kill it.

---

5. Michaels, *Nightmares: The Dark Side of Dreams and Dreaming*, 88 and 57.

The dreamer's boyfriend was a bully who often had temper tantrums. She realised that this nightmare, which portrayed him as a spider and his tantrums as scary creatures, was a warning to leave him, to avoid a future filled with many more ugly outbursts.

> I watch as my friend sits motionless. Then he picks up a hammer and sharp tools and gouges himself, creating extreme pain.

This teenage dreamer was experiencing enormous pain as his parents went through an acrimonious divorce, but he hid his pain under a calm, polite exterior. This dream helped him realise that he needed to express his pain before it led to depression. (Depression is portrayed in the dream by the friend's passive, motionless position.)

Were you able to follow the dream logic of the symbols these nightmares chose to express themselves with? If so, you're well on the way to grasping the art of understanding the symbolic language of nightmares! Isn't our dreaming mind clever to come up with such fascinating stories to show us how we really feel and what we need to change? Each of these nightmares reflects pivotal emotions in the lives of the dreamers, showing in highly visual, shocking metaphors how the dreamers really feel about situations. Dreams show us what is happening in our heart, mind, body, and soul. Dreams act as emotional, physical, and spiritual barometers, and when they become nightmares, it's time to sit up and listen and to create positive change in our lives. This might take the form of taking steps towards self-care by acknowledging our wounds and ensuring we get the support we need, or it might mean we need to mend (or leave) a relationship or talk to a counsellor.

There are taboos around nightmares that I hope this book will help to break. Nightmares with extreme imagery and murderous or psychopathic actions are generally not shared outside of a therapist's office because people fear they'll be dismissed as crazy. In this book, I hope to illustrate the symbolic and emotional power of nightmares, to help readers understand that just because they have a shocking nightmare does not mean they are losing their mind. Nightmares can be incredible drama queens! If we aren't aware of how we truly feel about something, they escalate our emotions and set them on a lit stage, with the intention of shocking us into changing our ways.

One dreamer shared a nightmare in which a manipulative man forced him to use a pair of scissors to cut the head off a woman.

> I love this woman profoundly. My hands quiver and tears stream as I pick up the scissors. Doing as I am told, I cut the woman's head with these tiny shears from back to front, beginning with a cut through the cheek. I feel every visceral cut as the blades work through flesh and bone. The scissors crunch through the vertebra and I feel everything. Each cut devastates me emotionally, yet I do not hear screaming from the woman … I feel immense resistance. I am horrified at what I've done to this living, beautiful girl whom I love. The guilt is overwhelming. And yet, she seems to understand that I have no choice, and in fact, tells me to keep going.

This nightmare had a dark energy that haunted him, and he worried that his actions in the dream made him look like a psychopath, even though when he worked with it, he realised it was symbolic of the overly emotional and anima-possessed part of himself. It is valuable to work with the symbolism of nightmares and also explore the dominant emotions. In this nightmare, resistance and guilt seem particularly strong.

Let's have a look at common themes that emerge in nightmares—common nightmare stories and what they might mean—while remembering that every dreamer is a unique individual and has different memories, associations, and emotional reactions.

A Quick Guide to Nightmare Themes

There are so many possible nightmare stories. Here I'll cover only a few, just to give you an idea of some of the most common themes and what they might (or might not!) signify. Please forgive the generalisations in this section. As I have explained, every dreamer is unique in terms of their life experience and emotional responses, so this can only be a rough guide, its main purpose being to help you to understand the language of nightmares and how they might depict violent emotions, psychological shifts, physical illness or pain, spiritual impasses, and reactions to major life changes.

It's also good to bear in mind that dreams and nightmares may not be personal but rather collective and social—in other words, a nightmare about mass death and destruction may be a reflection of the state of the world or be linked to a current war or pandemic rather than being purely an amplification of the dreamer's emotions. An excellent example of socially influenced nightmares are those that emerged from the COVID-19 pandemic. These dreams around the common theme of a deadly virus emerged in the form of nightmares about ferocious bugs and invisible monsters, having difficulty breathing in a dream, or sensing that one has been infected by the virus. Other pandemic dreams focused on social distancing stress or were saturated with death imagery: corpses sit with the dreamer on a bus; deceased relatives show up to take the dreamer away with them, or the dreamer orders a taxi and a hearse arrives instead. A global crisis impacts dreams and reflects our unconscious response to threat. Researchers found that dream recall rose by 35 percent as the pandemic started to spread in earnest, as detailed by Harvard psychologist Dr. Deirdre Barrett, who collected over nine thousand COVID-19–themed dreams and described her findings in her book *Pandemic Dreams*.

The quick guide that follows focuses only on personal nightmares.

Feel free to absorb what resonates for you and then use the practices in this book to deepen your personal understanding of your own nightmares. Remember, the worse the nightmare, the greater its transformative potential, because the need for healing is more urgent and you are ripe for change.

- **Being trapped or unable to move.** Nightmares commonly involve being trapped in a burning building or in a plane that's about to crash, or in a confined and suffocating space, or paralysed and unable to act. The dreamer might scream, but nobody hears. These scenarios are often linked to feelings of helplessness, an absence of emotional support, and a belief in the dreamer's inability to change bad things. If you have a nightmare with this theme, ask yourself, "Where in my life do I feel trapped, paralysed, or powerless, as if there's no way out?" and "Where in my life do I need to take action?" Physical paralysis in dreams can also be linked to sleep paralysis nightmares; see chapter 7 for how to navigate these experiences.

- **Attacked, shot, wounded, or killed.** Violent attacks and killing are common nightmare themes. Killing may reflect unwelcome changes that are being forced on the dreamer. Scenes of mass shootings could reflect current news events, but on a personal level they may hint at a plethora of unpleasant situations, outbursts of aggression, or enforced changes. When the dreamer does the killing, they may be trying to rid themselves of unwanted shadow aspects of themselves. While shooting people in her nightmare, one woman experienced a moment of lucidity when she realised they were aspects of herself that she hated and wanted to finish with forever. When you are wounded or shot in a nightmare, pay close attention to the site of the wound, as it may be a reference to a health issue. Attacks are displays of anger and seem connected to confrontation, aggression, or being overpowered. Ask yourself, "Is there aggression in my life?" and "What's my own temper like, and how well do I express myself when I'm upset?" Chapter 3 explores the dark shadow side of ourselves that often rears up in nightmares.

- **Disaster and apocalypse nightmares.** "A giant tsunami wreaks havoc on the land, and there is death and destruction everywhere." Dreams of hurricanes, fires, floods, or other natural disasters may reflect our global relationship to our planet, but on the personal level, such nightmares and also scenes of war zones or other human-made disasters such as shipwrecks or plane crashes can indicate feeling overwhelmed during an extremely challenging time. Such nightmares can flag up emotional upheaval and feelings of helplessness and terror in the face of unwanted changes. Drowning in dreams often seems linked to feeling overcome by emotions or a life situation. To discover how to take positive action in your life through working with a nightmare, see Practice 17: The Nightmare Transformation Technique.

- **Animals in nightmares.** Dream animals are wonderful to work with because they have wild, intuitive, instinctive energy that we often don't tap into enough in our lives, and they can be very helpful in revealing our hidden shadow sides, our conflicts, and who we aspire to be. They may have a shamanic element, connecting us to the spirit world and reminding us of our soul's journey. When dream animals want our attention, they may chase us, bite us, attack us, or even rip us to pieces.

Nevertheless, they are soul allies! They take on threatening roles to wake us up to empowering action we need to take in our lives, and to help us towards psychological wholeness and spiritual advancement. Ask yourself, "Which qualities does this dream animal embody for me?" A snake may be the wise healer within you, while a lion might represent your powerful voice. A squirrel hides away what is important to him; a dinosaur lives in the past. Ask yourself, "What is my dream animal trying to teach me?" Practice 43: Turn Mythological Beasts into Protective Allies looks at how to work with animal nightmares.

- **Sex-themed nightmares.** Rape nightmares can relate to the misuse of power. It can be helpful to ask yourself, "Where in my life do I feel violated, disrespected, or overpowered?" When we dream that our loving partner is having hot sex with somebody else, we may wake up feeling betrayed, upset, and suspicious. Mostly, such nightmares won't be pointing to a literal infidelity. People in our dreams may symbolise an aspect of ourselves. Ask yourself, "Am I being untrue to myself in some way?" or "Where in my life do I feel cheated right now?" If you feel the dream is related to your partner, ask yourself, "Do I feel unsupported by my partner? Are we happy together? Do we need to change anything about our relationship?" Reenter your dream imaginatively and interview your cheating partner. Ask them why they are behaving this way. Practice 24: The Lucid Writing Technique for Nightmares can help you explore sex-themed nightmares. If you're interested in learning more about what sex dreams can symbolise and how to work with them, a great book is *Sexual Dreams* by Dr. Gayle Delaney.

- **Heavy emotional nightmares.** "I see a funeral procession on the street. My mother is in that coffin and I know I killed her." In any nightmare where heavy emotions such as guilt, shame, grief, disgust, dread, terror, or despair dominate, this can be seen as an invitation to begin healing the deep wounds and unresolved situations that may have caused them before these feelings cause further damage to our health and wellbeing. However, if your nightmares are very strong, please remember that you don't have to face them alone. In extreme cases, it's better to get a therapist or dreamworker to help you work with them. Chapter 6 explores ways of moving through deeply emotional and traumatic nightmares.

- **Nightmares with archetypal, mythical, and spiritual elements.** "Through a veil of mist, a phoenix appears. Its feathers are luminous green and it breathes a stream of golden fire that burns me until I'm nothing but ashes in the wind." Mythological dream beasts, hybrid animals, and fairy tale dream plots such as "trapped in the cabin in the woods" or "fleeing from the evil witch" are imbued with the ancient power of timeless stories and archetypes. They are cosmic yet personal. Often, such nightmares seem to reflect major periods of psycho-spiritual growth where we depart from a previous way of life and recreate ourselves anew. It can be a painful process, but such dreams invite us to examine our spiritual life and reveal the shifts taking place deep within us. Chapter 9 shows how to work with these nightmares.

- **Horror movie nightmares.** This encompasses zombie invasions, psycho-thriller dream plots, violence and murder, and nightmares with decapitation or dismemberment themes. Why does our dreaming mind sometimes create such disturbing stories? Because it's crying out for our attention and telling us we need to work towards wholeness and balance. Getting killed in a dream may reflect an unwanted change that someone else is trying to impose on the dreamer. Killing someone else may mean that part of you seeks major change, either within yourself or in waking life. Dying may symbolise the death of an aspect of the dreamer, and death in dreams is very often not a literal warning of future events, but rather a symbol of change and transformation. Dreaming of deceased loved ones is discussed in chapter 8. Dismemberment can be symbolic of feeling torn apart, while decapitation often registers a split between our mind and our heart. The emotions in horror movie nightmares can point us to the heart of their message. Unwrap your dream to find out, with Practice 12: Ten Key Questions for Unwrapping a Nightmare.

- **Vomiting, ingesting something, or choking.** When we vomit in dreams, there may be something we need to express, something we're sick of, or something impossible to digest. One woman was shocked by the suicide of her friend and unable to accept it. She had recurring nightmares about vomiting uncontrollably. When we ingest something in a dream, this might symbolise that we are trying to assimilate something. Such dreams can also be shamanic, as we absorb new energies. In one dream,

I watched a man very consciously eating his dead father's ashes so that his father would live on inside him. This dream came at a time when I was assimilating the mortality of my parents and others in their age bracket. Choking may indicate unexpressed emotions. One woman had recurring nightmares of choking and eventually realised these were an indicator of grief that needed to be faced and healed. Sometimes we cry buckets in our dreams, which may show that we are overloaded with sadness and have much to release. Practice 32: Forgive and Release can help with this.

- **Running away.** Are you being chased or running away from something you saw that upsets you? Ask yourself, "Is there something I'm terrified to face?" or "What am I running from (or turning my back on) in my life?" Threatening figures in nightmares can indicate shadow sides of ourselves that we have repressed or do not want to own. Chapter 3 shows how to work with shadow energies.

- **Monsters, ghosts, devils, vampires, and other supernatural figures.** Monsters and supernatural figures are often our worst fears incarnated as powerful nightmare figures. They demand our attention, and the bottom line is that they want change, integration, and healing. Ghosts might be seen as past psychic energy that's still hanging around, past issues we haven't confronted, or someone who has transitioned (been through a major spiritual change). Ask yourself, "Which ghosts from the past am I holding onto that need to be released?" Vampires or other parasites feeding off the dreamer may reflect people who are feeding off your energy in waking life, or flag up a health issue: one man dreamed there was a parasite filled with dark energy stuck to his neck. Soon afterwards, he was diagnosed with stage-four throat cancer.

  Devils may represent powerful limiting beliefs we have imposed on our psyche, or an inner struggle between good and bad. Ask, "Who does this monster/devil/ghost remind me of?" and "Where in my life do I need to transcend fear?" "What action can I take to move forward spiritually?" Supernatural nightmare figures have a strong link to the spiritual aspects of our lives. Try asking yourself, "Am I at an impasse in my spiritual life?" "Is there a spiritual conflict within me?" It may also be useful to consider your worldview and how it creates your reality, using Practice 39: Question Your Beliefs, Assumptions, and Expectations.

• **Naked in public.** Most of us have had some variation of this dream, which is not always a nightmare by any means! It can be liberating and sensual to be naked in public in a dream. It can feel brave and affirming. In dreams, I have put my chin up and danced naked in public with a sense of, "Okay then, who cares how it looks. This is me. Let's just do this!" (This is possibly a reflection of how it feels to publish books with my most personal and transformative dreams and life stories in them!) Nightmare versions involving horror and embarrassment tend to point to vulnerability and exposure: a sense of not being able to hide our true self or true feelings, or not having the right "clothes" (attributes, social skills) to fit in, or making a social blunder. Practice 13: The Lucid Imaging Nightmare Solution (LINS) is a creative and positive way of engaging with such nightmares for transformation and empowerment.

• **Black void nightmares and falling.** Many people write to me in terror of nightmares in which they fall or are sucked into infinite dark space and experience strange sensory sensations. The luminous black void is discussed in chapter 9 and is a space of infinite creative potential. It is really not something we need to fear! In fact, it's an excellent space for liberating ourselves from fear and opening up to spiritual adventures, as shown in Practice 42: How to Navigate the Lucid Void. Nightmares about falling off cliffs or high buildings may be linked to feeling unsafe or losing our emotional balance. Ask, "When do I not feel safe?" and "Where in life am I heading for a fall?" We "fall" asleep every night, and dreams of falling may also be linked to the sensory changes we experience when we fall back to sleep after a mini-awakening in the night.

• **Teeth falling out and other losses.** A dream of losing teeth is often linked to feelings of insecurity, instability, life changes, and loss, or to a sense that we can no longer hide how we really feel—we can't smile and pretend all is well because we have no teeth to smile with! We need to speak our truth and dissimulate no longer. Ask yourself, "Am I doing what I really want to do with my life?" "Do I feel insecurity or loss anywhere in my life?" Many nightmares focus around loss—we lose our phone and spend the rest of the dream searching high and low and freaking out ("Where am I unable to communicate?" "What am I searching for in my life?"), or we miss a train (an opportunity?). These can be seriously stressful dreams that often recur. The good news is they can be calmed, resolved, and rerouted through a simple, fast dream reentry technique such as Practice 17: The Nightmare Transformation Technique.

Now let's look at the way that physical pain can appear in nightmares.

How Pain Creates Nightmares

Dreams and nightmares can be intimately linked to the body. The dreaming mind automatically translates sensations, sounds, and other sensory stimuli directly into streams of vivid imagery. Physical pain during sleep is often directly translated into imagery, and excruciating pain can be experienced during nightmares, as in the following examples. Bernie dreams:

> I am in a building and I know I need to get to the other side. As I try to do this, figures holding swords attack me as I push forward across the room. I feel every cut and the pain is like being cut with a thousand razor blades. I become aware and realise I can wake myself up. I do this to escape.

Bernie realised this nightmare reflected all the physical pain he suffers in waking life. He has suffered from migraines all his life, has had nonstop pain for about 30–40 years, and also suffers badly from depression.

Natalie had the following lucid dream:

> A demonic creature appeared that was incredible to look at but really scary. This creature came up to me and towered over me. I was frozen (like with sleep paralysis, which I have had). The creature stuck one of its pinchers straight into my side and ripped the flesh and I felt every moment of it. The pain is impossible to describe. After doing that, the alien reptilian creature had sex with me. I had multiple orgasms which totally destroyed the pain in my side. The creature said pain and pleasure are very similar and both very powerful. They should be harnessed.

Years after this experience, on a lucid dreaming ocean retreat with me, Natalie experienced an insight into her nightmare. As the group worked with the Lucid Imaging Nightmare Solution, she could clearly see that area of intense pain where the demon reptile had stabbed her, and realised it was exactly where she'd had terrible pain for 33 years. She reports:

> Only a few months ago, a new doctor sent me for a scan I should have had decades ago and diagnosed me with adenomyosis. Now I know what is wrong with me, it actually makes sense.

Keith had a nightmare about being attacked in the woods by a headless horseman:

> With a swift slice to the back of the neck, my head comes off…I am now in a small cabin with a group of fellow victims; we have all had our heads cut off. Somehow, we are all still alive with heads reassembled, but we all bear a scar.

Keith reports:

> This dream came during the worst time of my life. I've had chiropractic problems with my head and neck for years, but this felt life-critical. My atlas vertebra was hypermobile, and surges of energy flowed up the base of my head; I felt like I could die at any second. I lived this way for weeks, with a feeling of impending doom. Every time I closed my eyes to go to sleep, I would feel the energy surge in my head and neck, and it felt as if I would die unless I kept the energy at bay with all my willpower.

Since dreams use a highly metaphorical language, nightmares involving intense physical pain can also represent emotional or spiritual pain. Through unwrapping the nightmare, we can reach its heart and hear its message. Let's look at some quick and easy ways of reaching the heart of a nightmare.

Core Techniques for Reaching the Heart of a Nightmare

These core techniques can be used whenever needed to help you unpack a nightmare and gain insight into its metaphorical meaning, or reenter it to reexperience it with full awareness.

practice 8

REENTER THE NIGHTMARE

This is a technique that we'll use throughout the book, based on "active imagination," which was developed by Swiss psychiatrist Carl Jung, the founder of analytical psychology. Any inner imagery, such as a memory, a fantasy, an emotion, a mood, or a dream, can be conjured up and imaginatively reentered for discovery, insight, and resolution. Here's how to reenter a nightmare so you can explore the imagery and actions while remaining in control, knowing you are in charge of the process and can stop it whenever you like. When working with very difficult nightmares, it's important to feel in control, especially when we decide to experience the emotions of the nightmare.

1. Sit or lie down and relax with closed eyes. Breathe slowly and deeply.

2. Create a golden space in your mind, a safe space.

3. When you feel ready, bring your nightmare into this space. Look at the images, knowing you are safe and can stop this process at any moment by opening your eyes. Notice the colours, the emotions, the action of your nightmare. Run the nightmare like a movie.

4. If it feels safe to do so, relive the emotions you experienced and feel them in your body. This helps the work to go deeper, but it's not essential, so if you prefer not to engage too deeply with major emotions such as disgust, guilt, and dread, that is fine; you can retain as much distance as you need from the nightmare movie.

5. Now you're ready to engage with your nightmare in any way that feels right; for example, by sending love and light to scary figures, or asking them why they came into your dream, or changing the nightmare story (as in Practice 14: Creative Nightmare Responses), or by using other techniques from this book. Be brave and trust your instincts! There is magic in this process, and working directly with nightmare images forms a strong bond with your unconscious mind so that healing and resolution happen naturally, without the need for us to push to get there.

practice 9

CONNECT YOUR NIGHTMARE TO WAKING REALITY

1. Reenter your nightmare as described in the previous practice, and keep your eyes closed.

2. Connect to the most powerful emotion in your nightmare. This might be shame, terror, grief, sadness, desperation, loss, loneliness, or any other feeling. It can also be a mixture of different emotions.

3. Feel these emotions in your body. Are they making your heart heavy or your gut tense? Are they stuck in your throat, or do they turn your legs to jelly? Bring your attention to them without getting too sucked into them, and remember you can stop this process whenever you like.

4. Breathe calmly as you remain present to these emotions. Sometimes an image will emerge from the part of the body that is holding the emotion. Notice what comes up.

5. Now ask yourself when in your life you have previously experienced this emotion or mix of emotions. Feel your way back, using your memory of the emotions and your bodily awareness of them to guide you. You might find yourself way back in the past, in your childhood, or you may find yourself feeling these emotions yesterday at work.

6. The point of connecting your nightmare emotions with your waking reality is to get clarity on the life context that this nightmare might be referring to. When we know which situation the nightmare reflects, we are much closer to understanding its message.

....

practice 10

**EXPERIENCE YOUR NIGHTMARE
AS AN ALIEN FROM OUTER SPACE**

1. You can do this practice on your own in your head or with a friend who is willing to turn into an alien for a few minutes! Dr. Gayle Delaney, author of *Sexual Dreams*, created the "pretend I'm an alien" technique for dreams, and it can be illuminating. Retell your nightmare as if you're sharing it with an alien from outer space who doesn't know what a vat of acid is, how pizza tastes, or how scary a pterodactyl can be.

2. Pause at key nightmare images and explain them to the alien with-out thinking too much—be spontaneous in your associations. If you have to explain to the alien what bread smells like, you might say, "The smell of freshly baked bread is the magic of childhood for me, but in my nightmare that smell gets swallowed up by black flames. Flames are destructive; they destroy what used to exist." Your descriptions of key words and images will be different depending on how they appear in the nightmare.

3. Make the link to your life. When you have to explain to the alien what a cockroach is, your answer might be, "It's a bug. It's something unpleas-ant I don't want near me." Using those same words, ask yourself, "Is there something in my life right now that is unpleasant and that I don't want near me?" Often this will result in an instant answer: "Aha! My coworker—she's been bugging me so much lately!" Dreams love puns. They love wordplay and idioms. If you dream of a bug, ask yourself what's bugging you.

4. After gleaning some insights into the language and metaphors of your nightmare, you can move things along further with a transformative technique such as Practice 14: Creative Nightmare Responses in the next chapter.

....

practice 11

FREE ASSOCIATION À LA FREUD

Austrian neurologist Sigmund Freud was the founder of psychoanalysis, and one technique he used was free association with dream images to explore the unconscious.

1. Choose the main figure from your nightmare, or the central image (the most emotive or disturbing one), or anything that shocked you about the nightmare, such as an out-of-control windmill or a dead bunch of flowers.

2. Relax with a pen and paper at hand, and bring your chosen nightmare element into your mind. Jot down any associations, memories, thoughts, or emotions that arise in relation to this. No judging or critical thinking

allowed! Even if you think the words you're writing make no sense, keep going. If you get stuck, return to the image or figure and begin again. Ask yourself about the image to get back on track: "What is a 'haunted house' to me?" Then jot down further associations, or choose a different element and play with that instead.

3. When working on a nightmare about trying to drink a glass of water but ending up with a mouthful of glass fragments, you might end up with something like this: water—elixir of life—thirst—nourishment—chewing glass—biting—bitten off more than I can chew!

4. Finally, look over your associations and see if anything causes you to go, "Aha!" Free association is a nice way to get more intimate with your nightmare images, but it's usually best done in combination with other techniques such as the following practice, in order to get the full experience of unwrapping a nightmare.

....

practice 12

TEN KEY QUESTIONS FOR UNWRAPPING A NIGHTMARE

After you've written down your nightmare and given it a title and sketched any images, if its meaning remains opaque to you, consider the following questions. A dream version of this practice first appeared in my book *Dream Therapy: Dream Your Way to Health and Happiness*.

1. Who are you in this nightmare? (An observer, an older/younger version of yourself, an animal, a different person, or you as you are today?)

2. What is the core image or scene in this nightmare? ("Core" means the central, most energised and powerful image.)

3. What are your associations with this core image? Quickly write them down without pausing to think or analyse.

4. Imagine that every part of this nightmare represents an aspect of yourself. Which part of you might the core image represent? Use your keywords and associations to connect with the image.

5. How do you feel in this nightmare? What are the strongest emotions?

6. Are these emotions present in any past, current, or upcoming life situation? Consider what was going on in your life at the time this night-

mare appeared; it could be mirroring your feelings about a current situation.

7. If you ask the most frightening or disturbing part of your nightmare if it has a message for you, what might it say?

8. Is there anything positive, light, loving, or beautiful in your nightmare? Close your eyes and ask it, "What do you want me to know?"

9. What does this nightmare want? View it as a movie and consider the possible meaning of the plot, characters, and any resolution or climax. Be alert for surprising plot twists and try to sense the message behind the imagery.

10. If you could experience your nightmare again and change the ending, what would happen?

When you have a clearer idea of what your nightmare wants to tell you, ask yourself, "What action does my nightmare want me to take in my waking world?" For example, imagine you have a desolate dream about a friend you haven't seen in a while, where she's standing far away from you in a desert. The waking-life action to take might be to close the distance between the two of you and check if she's okay by giving her a call. Or if you dream that you eat loads of candyfloss and ice cream and get sick, take action in your life by cutting down on sugar. Once we become familiar with the symbolic language of nightmares, it gets easier to grasp their message and work out how we can create helpful change in our lives.

....

In this chapter, we have explored the symbolic language of nightmares and seen that the dream always belongs to the dreamer. We've explored how to listen when someone shares a nightmare, and how we might help them to unwrap its meaning if they wish. We've examined common themes of nightmares to understand how they communicate with us, and I've shared some core practical nightmare techniques to help you to discover the valuable messages that your nightmares bring and begin to uncover their vast healing potential. In the next chapter, we'll take a look at the power of the shadow and how it emerges in our dreams to challenge us and to light the way to health and wholeness.

PART TWO

Illuminating the Darkness of "Bad" Dreams

CHAPTER 3

Exploring the Dark Shadow for Healing and Transformation

Now that we understand the symbolic language of nightmares, it's time to move into truly exciting territory: that of transformation! When we work and play with our nightmares, we enable transformation in the form of healing, creative inspiration, and spiritual growth. We raise our lucid awareness of life, in all states of consciousness, from sleep to waking and from nightmares to moments of peace and beauty. Doing shadow work with a nightmare increases our compassion for ourselves and others, helps us to become whole and happy, and shows us where we are on our journey through the cosmos.

What Is the Shadow?

The shadow is everything within us that we repress, ignore, are unconscious of, or deny—and that doesn't only mean feelings like anger, shame, and jealousy that nobody ever really wants to own up to. It includes unlived energies and desires. It includes memories we have pushed away, such as experiences or events from childhood that we didn't have the resources to cope with at the time. We may also deny or repress our higher potential, our spiritual connection, and our talents. The shadow is all of the parts of us that are not yet embraced and illuminated. It's shadowy simply because the light hasn't entered yet. We can illuminate our shadow very effectively through working with nightmares, because they have such strong, clear shadow energy. The shadow is not "bad"; in fact, it has immense potential to help us transform our lives on every level. In this chapter, we'll look at the *dark shadow*—this encompasses all the traits we view as negative or harmful, such as selfishness, spitefulness, or greed. At the end of the book, there's a chapter on the *luminous shadow*, which explores the way that a single nightmare can simultaneously destroy unneeded parts of ourselves and bathe us in spiritual light. Although terrifying, such nightmares reinforce our connection with the divine and reveal our innate capacity for enlightenment.

The shadow can reach out via a nightmare to protect us by showing us the truth about a relationship or how we really feel about a situation. It can trigger astonishing creativity. It can switch the spotlight on something that needs urgent healing and push us into incredible transformation. When we illuminate the hidden, unconscious, or rejected parts of ourselves and work on integrating them into our hearts and our lives, we accept powerful gifts from our psyche.

The Shadow as Archetype

Archetypes are universal images, symbols, themes, and archaic mythical characters that appear in all cultures throughout time. They appear in myths, legends, fairy tales, and dreams, and they embody human experience and universal meanings. Archetypal figures that everyone recognises include the Hero, the Trickster, the Warrior, the Wise Old Woman, the Judge, and the Lover. Symbolic archetypes include Light, Dark, Spiral, Circle, and Fire. Archetypal settings include Home, the Mountain, and Wasteland. Archetypal stories include the Quest, the Battle of Good and Evil, and the Initiation. There are many more examples in each of these categories. When we work with nightmares, it can shed light on their meaning when we identify archetypes in the story, characters, and symbolic imagery.

The shadow archetype is famously represented in its most severe form in Robert Louis Stevenson's 1880s story of Dr. Jekyll and Mr. Hyde. The respectable Dr. Jekyll transforms into a shadow side of his personality, an evil alter ego in the form of the murderous and unrepentant criminal Mr. Hyde. In the early 1900s, Carl Jung brought into public consciousness the concept of the shadow as a universal archetype. Since the dark shadow represents aspects of the self that are not socially or personally acceptable, such as envy, prejudice, and hate, it might appear in dreams, daydreams, and visions as a monster, a threatening person, or an aggressive animal.

These shadow aspects of ourselves emerge in nightmares and tend to plague us until we summon the courage to face them by working constructively with our nightmare to release its transformative potential. The archetype of the shadow manifests in our collective waking reality in the form of division, fighting, and war. The good news is that when we do our own personal shadow work, by resolving our nightmares and working with their transformative creative energy, we are helping to heal the collective psyche.

But shadow work isn't always a barrel of laughs, as it tends to present us with unsavoury aspects of ourselves or show us the uncomfortable truth of our situation, and thus force us to take action and change our lives. And that sounds like work, right? Wouldn't it be easier to just slam the lid on all that nightmare stuff and carry on sleepwalking through life? Jung said, "People will do anything, no matter how absurd, in order to avoid facing their own souls."[6] One of the ways we avoid our soul is by forgetting our dreams and ignoring our nightmares. These inner worlds are direct expressions of our soul, and by working with them, we illuminate our soul and deepen the connection with ourselves and with the cosmos.

It was also Jung who said, "There is no birth of consciousness without pain."[7] But we're not wimps, are we? We won't let that stop us! Anyway, it's a good kind of pain, the sort of pain that indicates a shift to better health, like muscle aches after sport. When we do shadow work, we exercise our awareness muscle, we raise our consciousness, and we look at truths that may be hard to face but that ultimately liberate us from old patterns, fears, hang-ups, unhealthy obsessions, and attitudes that have been holding us back. We integrate lost or discarded parts of our self and learn to transcend fear. Yes, we sometimes need to be brave for this work, but it's far more painful long term to lug around our unresolved traumas, our unhappiness, our frozen energy,

---

6. Jung, *Psychology and Alchemy*, 99.
7. Jung, "Marriage as a Psychological Relationship."

and our damaging relationship patterns. And it's a fantastic feeling to make a breakthrough and feel yourself soar towards new possibilities.

Let's look at different ways in which the shadow archetype emerges in nightmares, what it can teach us, and how to work with the shadow for healing and integration.

The Shadow Emerges as a Threatening Animal Nightmare

Chris Hammond had the following scary lucid dream encounter with a goat that turned out to be the essence of his shadow self.

> I step out of bed. My room is perfect, but there's a dreamlike quality to it, so I know this is a lucid dream. I decide to open my bedroom door and explore the house. As soon as I open the door, I see it: a hideous goat staring up at me. Its wool dirty and matted, its eyes black and shrivelled. It resonates evil and malignancy. I am paralyzed by fear. There is something so innately repugnant about this goat. I do not know why. I am so shocked, awed, and utterly terrified by this hellish image that my very soul wants to flee. I wake up immediately.

Chris explains:

> It took me some time to figure out the significance of the goat. The image had been so powerful that it would keep coming back to me for months afterwards. In fact, I was afraid to lucid dream again for some time. There were questions. Why had I been so repulsed by the goat? What was it about this creature that was so terrifying? It had not been the sight of the animal itself that was terrifying, but its presence.
>
> I eventually realized that I was afraid to confront the goat because the goat was the part of myself that I was afraid to confront. It was a part of my shadow. It represented toxic ego and narcissism that had been subconsciously driving my behaviours in life. It was literally the devil. I am now grateful for this nightmare because it helped me to understand that I had been heading down a bad pathway in life and that I needed to open my heart more to love.

When we encounter the shadow in a lucid dream, we are given an even bigger gift because we illuminate the shadow with full conscious awareness and have an opportunity to work with it directly in that dream—as long as we don't allow fear to get the better of us, which isn't always easy! It can be terrifying to stand face-to-face with something so repugnant, because lucid dreaming can feel more real than waking reality.

The Shadow of Pretending to Be Someone We're Not

Jan's account below shows that when we manage to turn things around while lucid in a shadow dream, this can result in an epiphany of sorts.

> In my dream I'm in a large crowd of people and acting rather bizarrely, but no one is really paying much attention to me. Then I become lucid and I'm standing outside of the crowd watching myself acting in a way I think is inappropriate and very embarrassing in front of all these people. I scream out loud to myself, "Stop it! Don't you care how others are looking at you and what they're thinking about you acting so crazy?"
>
> Myself in the crowd yells back to me, "No, I don't care at all anymore what people think. I'm going to be me and I just don't care. I'm just so tired."
>
> I then woke up and sat up in bed and felt this rush of lightness and ease wash over me.

Jan explains:

I actually could feel what it would be like if I was no longer overly concerned about how I portrayed my image to other people. It felt as if a huge weight had been lifted off my shoulders. Something inside of me had shifted. It was an epiphany of sorts. I have spent my entire life concerned about how I appear to others, worrying whether I was going to be accepted or liked. I have been a chameleon, changing my appearance to whatever would fit in with my current surroundings, never really feeling like myself.

But when I saw myself in that crowd not caring about how I appeared and saw that others didn't really notice, I realised that I had been taking myself much too seriously, that other people had their own stuff to think about, that I could be myself and still be part of the crowd. I could fit in and stop sweating all the small stuff. I am now sixty-six years old. This has been many years of work and introspection. I was raised by an alcoholic mother who was never there, and if she was, she was always yelling at me about how stupid and crazy I was. Now I lead meditation classes for a cancer organization and I study constantly.

Having had my career in law enforcement as a deputy sheriff, I never let my insecurities show, always putting on a tough persona. I've spent my life looking for the "real" Jan, and who would have thought I would discover this courageous part of myself in my dream; but now for some reason I feel like I can do this!

The split between the shadow aspect of Jan and the rest of her is clearly represented by two Jans having a shouting match: the censorious one and the defiantly free one. Jan managed to change the dream story: instead of feeling ashamed and acquiescing to the part of her that wanted to inhibit her self-expression, she did whatever she liked for once! This is so beautiful and courageous, because Jan managed to liberate herself from damaging beliefs about "acting crazy" that were rooted in her mother's verbal abuse, and the effects in her life were immediately felt.

Lucid Dreaming to Alleviate Depression

Darkness can seep into our hearts and minds in the form of depression, and it can become a constant struggle. When we illuminate a dream with lucid awareness, we are able to bring healing intent, love, and light into the dream state in a highly aware manner that can be beneficial. Simply becoming lucid in a dream can result in the instantaneous, spontaneous transformation of distressing dream imagery. The nightmares of people suffering from depression often reflect themes of destructiveness, hopelessness, or being badly treated. Psychiatrists Aaron Beck and Clyde Ward list these common depressive dream themes: "being deprived, disappointed, mistreated; being thwarted, exploited, disgraced; being rejected and abandoned; being blamed or criticized, ridiculed; being punished or injured; being lost or losing."[8]

Nightmares reflecting depression can be worked with using the practices in this chapter, and you can increase your healing and protective forces with Practice 28: Bring Soul Dreams and Healing Imagery into the Body and Practice 36: Invoke Protective Powers: Ball of Light. Lucid dream healing can also provide effective relief. In a conversation with me, psychologist Elliott Gish shared his story of using a mantra in a lucid dream in an attempt to heal his depression:

> I've struggled with chronic depression for over ten years, trying many different treatments and experiencing little relief. Some of the most significant relief I've experienced came from using a mantra in a lucid dream (around a 30–50 percent decrease in symptoms overnight, lasting several weeks). I decided to try using a mantra within a lucid dream because other people have reported improving various ailments with this strategy. However, I should mention that I did not expect it to work for me, so I don't feel like placebo was the primary reason for my results.

Lucid in his dream, Elliott repeated his mantra: "I will be depression-free for a month of three." Here is his dream:

> I put my hands over my head and close my eyes for a second. I recite the mantra out loud and feel a rush of energy hit my head, like a strong gust of wind from behind. I open my eyes and say it again and another wave of energy rushes into my head. I can feel it building. I say it again and another, stronger rush of energy hits. I say it two more times and two more waves hit me in the head, each one progressively stronger. By this time, I'm beaming with energy and feel ten times lighter and happier, so I put my hands down and stop reciting. It feels as if whatever I was doing was "complete." I'm so full of energy that I have to move, so I start running around, feeling like a kid just having fun again.

8. Beck and Ward, "Dreams of Depressed Patients."

Elliott reports:

Results were instantly noticeable when I awoke. The lightness and happiness I felt in the lucid dream certainly carried over into the waking state. It seemed like nothing could faze me for several weeks. This did not last for three months, but it did last for approximately three weeks, which is one of the longest and most significant periods of relief I've experienced since the depression's inception.

We Don't Have to Be Lucid to Create Healing Change in Our Nightmares

Don't worry if you rarely—or never—become lucid in your dreams. You really don't need to get lucid to transform your nightmares in empowering and life-affirming ways. All you need are powerful tools you can work with while awake. I'm going to introduce you now to one of my core nightmare techniques. We'll see the results it gives throughout the book as people share how they managed to transform different kinds of nightmares with it. The Lucid Imaging Nightmare Solution (LINS) combines elements of Carl Jung's active imagination, Barry Krakow's imagery rehearsal therapy, and my own Lucid Writing technique.

The beauty of this technique is that although it was designed to be used the very moment we awaken from a nightmare, it can also be used while awake, when we begin by relaxing our bodies and our breathing, then close our eyes and mentally reenter the nightmare story. I've taught this technique in workshops with wonderfully transformative results, and it only takes a few minutes. When the Lucid Imaging Nightmare Solution is carried out intuitively, with an open mind and the hope of healing, the effects can be startling and long-lasting. Recurring nightmares can be resolved and no longer need to keep ringing on our doorbell, and we can gain insight into the weirdest and least pleasant dreams. It's an empowering practice that I hope will help you, too, as you dive into the luminous darkness of your nightmares.[9]

---

9. The material in practice 13 previously appeared in *Llewellyn's Complete Book of Lucid Dreaming*.

practice 13

THE LUCID IMAGING NIGHTMARE SOLUTION (LINS)

1. Attend to your body.

As soon as you wake up from a nightmare, do whatever you need to calm yourself and make yourself comfortable. Some nightmares result in hefty physical reactions, like a wildly beating heart or sweat-drenched pyjamas. Drink water if you need to, and take deep, calming breaths. Then lie comfortably, close your eyes, and breathe calmly. Ask yourself if you want to work with this nightmare now or not. If the answer is yes, remind yourself that you are relaxing safely in your bed and can stop the process whenever you want to, simply by opening your eyes and sitting up.

2. Reenter your nightmare.

Recall the dream imagery as far back as you can. What were you doing before the dream grew unpleasant? Knowing that you are now safe in your bed, allow the imagery to resurface in your mind's eye. If you have difficulty summoning mental imagery, you can use the storyline of your nightmare as a way in. Notice any associations you have with the dream images and events, but don't agonise or obsess about possible meanings. If at any point in this process you feel very frightened, upset, or unsafe, stop immediately. Some nightmares are simply too strong and disturbing to face alone.

3. Identify the "tipping point."

Pinpoint the moment when feelings such as fear, guilt, or anxiety grew strong, or when the monster reared its ugly head. This moment is like the tipping point on a pair of scales. It is the moment that your dream turned into a nightmare. Your task now is to restore the balance. Decide where in the dream action you want to begin to change events or your attitude towards them. Beginning just before the tipping point usually works well.

4. Imagine this is a lucid dream.

Rerun the script to resolve the dream crisis. Watch the imagery as it unfolds and reacts responsively to your thoughts, questions, needs, and guidance. This is a highly creative state of consciousness because the mind is alert yet your body is relaxed and close to sleep. In lucid imaging, you can be a film director, rewinding the action and replaying different outcomes. Now that you are playing at being "lucid in this nightmare," you have many options. You could ask a frightening dream figure why they are following you, or actively change the nightmare story so that something harmonious or amusing takes place; you could introduce help into the dream in the form of a strong friend, a magic tool, or a healing mantra. You could try passively reliving the nightmare free from fear and observe how this affects the imagery and events. The best nightmare solutions are not forced; allow the imagery to develop spontaneously in response to your initial guiding thought or question. You'll know when you've found the right nightmare solution, because your tension around the dream will greatly diminish and you'll feel safe and calm.

5. Programme yourself to get lucid.

When you are happy with your nightmare solution, you are ready to return to sleep. This is an excellent time to watch as your hypnagogic imagery builds up into a moving dream, and set a firm intention to fall asleep consciously. As you fall asleep, try repeating, "I am lucid, I am lucid…" or "The next thing I see will be a dream." It's useful to use this post-nightmare work to programme yourself to become lucid the next time you have a nightmare. Simply repeat, "The next time something bad happens, I'll recognise that I'm dreaming." When working with a recurrent nightmare, remind yourself that the next time you are confronted with its particular imagery, this will trigger lucidity.

Why Is It Helpful to Transform the Nightmare Story?

A lot of the nightmare solutions we'll explore in this book involve engaging with the nightmare story from a fearless standpoint, claiming our power as the dreamer, utilising inner resources to react in empowering ways, and enabling the nightmare to fully reveal its healing and transformative gifts. It is extremely powerful to *transform the nightmare story*—but not in such a way that we attempt to force the narrative into something "healing." Forcing unconscious imagery never works; we need to be intuitive, spontaneous, and open so that our unconscious produces the transformed nightmare story for us. Let's explore why this works and how it's done.

Psychologically, it can feel vital to know that we have options. There's nothing worse than feeling that there is no way out and that we are helpless to act to change something. Sleep researcher Dr. Barry Krakow has worked with chronic nightmare sufferers and finds that rehearsing a happier nightmare outcome often has the effect of decreasing nightmare frequency.[10] This is because when we work directly with the imagery of the nightmare, we are speaking to our unconscious mind in its own language, and when we change the nightmare story, we communicate the fact that there are other options. For example, we don't have to put up with falling off a ski lift and breaking our leg every night! We can bring help into that nightmare scenario so that the accident never happens, or so that we do fall but land unhurt in the snow. We don't have to rerun the same nightmare story again and again. When we rehearse a different ending, it's like using the points on a railway to divert the train onto one track or another. We can divert a destructive nightmare into healing and empowering transformation by changing the story in intuitive ways that feel right to us.

In a 2006 pilot study by Dr. Victor Spoormaker and Jan van den Bout on the effects of lucid dreaming therapy on nightmares, participants created alternative endings to their nightmares.[11] They were also taught techniques for becoming lucid in their dreams. Overall, the nightmares of the participants decreased, but in some cases no lucid dream was reported, so it wasn't clear if the reason for the overall decrease in nightmares was due to lucidity or simply knowing that "bad dreams can be changed." When we work with our nightmares, sometimes just the realisation that we have options can be enough to effect transformation, because we feel freer and less fearful and more empowered. When we become lucid in a nightmare or when we do waking dreamwork, we bring awareness to the nightmare story and can react to it fearlessly, knowing that we can choose how to react.

10. Krakow et al., "Imagery Rehearsal Treatment for Chronic Nightmares."
11. Spoormaker and van den Bout, "Lucid Dreaming Treatment for Nightmares."

Different Imaginative Responses to Nightmares

There are so many different possible responses to nightmares when we bravely and fearlessly encounter them in the Lucid Imaging Nightmare Solution. For example, we might protect ourselves within an egg of light, or bring powerful allies into the nightmare scene with us. We might choose to send love and light to threatening dream figures, or give them a gift.

Many generous dreamers wrote to share their life-changing nightmares with me for this book. Let's look at a beautiful and healing nightmare solution that Kristin shared with me. In this account, Kristin actually falls back to sleep as she does the dreamwork but without forgetting her aim to face her nightmare. Note how she wisely protects herself so that she feels safe before she faces the nightmare, and notice her flexibility as she allows the dream to unfold spontaneously without much guidance.

In a parking lot, I feel like someone is watching me. I see an old man with a wrinkled and ghostly white face peering at me. He scares me. I sense he is going to rape me. I yell at him to go away, but he starts to approach. I struggle to say something, but no sound comes out. I try to tell him he is not allowed near me, but he comes in to attack, his hand reaching for my throat. I try to scream, but again, no sound will come out. Then I wake up in total panic and fear.

Awake in bed now, I feel angry about being attacked in my dream and not being able to protect myself. I decide to reenter the dream and find the old man. I start by going into my imagination and forming a bubble around me that I start filling in with all the things I feel supported by: plant allies, objects, and symbols. I'm taking my time to really build this bubble up, but at some point, I'm back in the dream, still completing the task. At this point, filling in my bubble takes on a life of its own, and suddenly the bubble starts moving. I'm pleasantly surprised because I have never flown by bubble before!

I am travelling through the dreamscape in my bubble, and I see the creepy ghost man still in the parking lot. I began to move in as if I'm going to destroy him when I hear a voice saying, "Remember to do it with love!" I think, "Oh right, I am supposed to be working with love!" As I approach him, I see a look of shock on his face. Then

I direct a bridge from my heart towards him. I tell him I am a being of light and invite him to step into love. I tell him this is the only way he can be with me. Then I watch as he begins to go from a ghostly ashen colour to white, then transparent, until he turns to dust and disappears all together. Bam!

When I woke up, I felt an incredible surge of energy and couldn't believe how easy it was to transform this terrifying experience. It felt like I finally learned how to take my power back. I took this sense of empowerment into my waking life from that day on. It was one of the most powerful dreams I have had.

When we encounter the right nightmare solution, it resonates within us on an incredibly deep level and can be very therapeutic, enabling us to release unhelpful psychological patterns and behaviours that have been holding us back. The empowerment of the dreamwork remains with us, and we notice positive changes in our waking lives. It can be so simple and so quick to make real changes! The Lucid Imaging Nightmare Solution can be helpful for any kind of nightmare. The following practice looks at the many different creative responses we can choose during nightmares, or afterwards, when we work with them while awake.

practice 14
CREATIVE NIGHTMARE RESPONSES

Imagine you have a nightmare in which you are lost in the woods, surrounded by a pack of vicious wolves. Let's replay this nightmare and see what might happen depending on the response we choose.

The more you practise this sort of imaginative nightmare reentry work, the more you are impressing upon your mind the fact that *you have a choice of how to react* in your dreams and nightmares. In any nightmare and in any waking dreamwork you do, the following creative responses (and many more besides) are always available for you to choose from. Anything can happen! See how your chosen response influences the nightmare.

1. **Offer a gift.** When we offer dream aggressors a gift, the energy of the nightmare changes. As the wolves circle you, snarling, you put your

hand in your pocket with the intention of finding a gift for them there. You pull out … a glowing ball of light. When you place it on the ground, it expands and emits gentle heat, warming the wolves. They lie down and relax, watching the ball dreamily. The sense of contentment is palpable and you feel you are in a circle of friends.

2. **Be an escape artist.** Sometimes removing ourselves from danger seems urgent. You feel very unsafe and want to escape from the pack of wolves, so you turbo-fly into the sky, leaving their upturned faces in your wake.

3. **Ask, "Do you have a message for me?"** You smile bravely at the wolves as you ask this question, and their response comes fast. An old, gray wolf steps forward and looks at you intently from wise, golden eyes: "We are here to help you become your bravest self."

4. **The aggressive, fearful response.** It can be psychologically freeing to defeat a nightmare aggressor. Having said that, a live dream friend is always better than a dead dream enemy! Still, sometimes we need to assert ourselves when facing threatening nightmare figures. You materialise a sword that glistens in the sunlight when you swing it in the air. Then you charge for the nearest wolf. The pack scatters, howling, their tails between their legs. You feel strong and free.

5. **Be present to painful emotions or physical discomfort.** Acknowledging our wounds and embracing our emotions can be psychologically freeing, as long as it is not too overwhelming. You decide not to change this nightmare but to be present to whatever the wolves have in store for you. One big wolf leaps up and knocks you right over, snarling in your face. Terror rises in you, but as it snarls and growls, you remain fully present to this terror and are able to identify it as your fear of death. As you explore this feeling, you sense this fear, which seemed so solid, dissolving away. Along with it, you feel old, unwanted patterns of behaviour being sloughed off. To your astonishment, when the wolf stops snarling and moves away, you feel like a new person—healthier, happier, and brighter.

6. **Hug the monster.** This can be a wonderful way of integrating shadow energy. You open your arms and seize the nearest wolf in a huge

hug. After a moment of growling resistance, it cedes and your bodies buzz harmoniously together. In a flash of insight, you understand that these wolves symbolise the artistic talents that you have denied and rejected for years. No wonder they were acting aggressively! As the other wolves come forward for a joyful group hug, you vow to embrace your inner artist again. The very first thing you'll draw will be this beautiful pack of wolves.

7. **Call for help.** We can call on anyone, anytime, both while the nightmare is happening and when doing dreamwork with it. As the wolves edge closer, you shout, "Help!" and to your relief, your power animal, a magnificent sabre-toothed tiger, bounds into the circle and roars at the top of its lungs. The wolves are gone in a flash. The sabre-toothed tiger raises its paw and you high-five.

8. **Fearless surrender.** When we reenter a nightmare free from fear, it can be enlightening to go with the flow and see what happens if we don't struggle or flee but instead remain open to whatever is happening. In some shamanic cultures and tantric traditions, it is believed that allowing oneself (the ego self) to be destroyed in a dream is an important part of a spiritual journey. People commonly report surrendering to being torn to pieces by wild animals or eaten alive in a dream, only to experience transcendence or be presented with marvels. Consciousness explorer Karim Bou Said from Dubai dreamed he was attacked by a black dragon, and fighting him off wasn't working. Fear triggered lucid awareness, and he allowed the dragon to swallow him up. Karim reports:

> As he swallowed me, I was transported to his belly that looked like a treasure room filled with golden objects. And there I spoke to a voice that gave me some excellent advice. We need to get past our fears to reach the gold.

You decide not to fight off the wolves. If they want to tear you limb from limb, let them! You know you will emerge alive and safe from this dream experience. To your surprise, as soon as you relinquish the desire to fight, the wolves transform into beings of light. They are utterly breathtaking. As you watch in awe, they transmit cosmic wisdom to you, revealing to you the mysteries of the universe.

9. **Develop magical powers.** Anything is possible, so why not gift yourself with superpowers? You could turn invisible, become telepathic, shapeshift into any animal, person, or object, or grab a magic sword and wield it to set yourself free. You decide to turn yourself into an ant and chuckle from a blade of grass as you watch the wolves' astonishment at your disappearance. They sniff around disconsolately for a few moments before heading back into the woods. With great glee, you turn yourself into a hummingbird and zoom skywards for an aerial view of their retreat.

10. **Send love and light.** Dreams and nightmares are thought-responsive environments, so this can change everything. You face the wolves and summon a feeling of love for these tired, hungry animals, understanding that they may represent neglected aspects of yourself. From your heart, you beam out love and light, and this actually becomes visible on the air as a glittering stream that envelops the wolves. As they feel it hit them, they purr like big cats and lie down, peering up at you with gratitude in their eyes. You feel a surge of euphoria as you realise how easy it is to transform their attitude simply by changing your own.

11. **Protective shield.** Never hesitate to procure protection for yourself when working with a nightmare. If you become lucid during a nightmare, any of the previous responses can be implemented directly within the dream, and any protections can be summoned. As the wolves crouch and snarl, you pull a protective circle of white light around you. The light shield removes your terror, and now you see that the wolves are not aggressively poised to attack you—they are scared of *you*! It was your fear that made them look so scary. They are like harmless puppies. Laughing, you crouch down and extend a hand, and allow these gorgeous wolves to come up and lick you.

12. **Ask for a gift.** When you ask the wolves for a gift, they amaze you by presenting you with an amber amulet. They convey that this amulet will protect you from danger in dreams and in waking life.

You may well find that as you engage in this type of imaginative night-mare work, quite naturally your habitual, fearful responses to frightening nightmare figures and situations will change, becoming more flexible, less fear-based, and more compassionate. This change of attitude will transform your dream life and positively impact your waking life, too. It may also give you some wonderful creative ideas for fiction and artwork. The essential thing to remember is that *you can change your response to your nightmares.* When we do Lucid Dreamplay to experiment with different responses, we train the brain to recognise that fear is not the only possible response. We gift ourselves with creative resources. We open ourselves up to real change!

Nightmares Help When the Shadow Manifests in Our Lives

When the shadow manifests in waking life in the form of abusive, drain-ing, or unpleasant people, it can be difficult to know how to act to protect ourselves. Have you ever heard the term *energy vampire*? It's not a pleasant term, but it paints a clear picture. Now and then, there will be people in our lives who suck our energy. This is usually an involuntary, unconscious act on their part, and so blaming them isn't really fair. They may not intend to be vampire-like; often they are desperate and are not grounded enough to receive the energy they need from other sources, so they seek a person who gives them energy in the form of kindness, sympathy, or whatever type of attention they need. But whether or not it's intentional, when we have an insatiable person like this in our lives, we need to set boundaries and protect ourselves, or else things can get out of control.

The easy way to tell if a person is sucking your energy is to gauge how you feel after spending time with them. Exhausted and drained? Then that per-son has sapped your energy. Of course, if a friend is going through a tough time and needs to talk about it, we may feel tired on occasion after listen-ing to them and trying to help, but with an energy vampire, we *always* feel drained or less happy after spending time with them.

Sometimes nightmares come to show us the unhealthy truth about a friendship or relationship. Many years ago, I had this nightmare:

I walk into the bathroom and to my horror, I see X lying in the bath, covered in blood! In a panic, I rush to her and try to help her. She is almost unconscious and must be bleeding to death. I am desperately worried, but as I help her out of the bath, I realise she is strong enough to stand alone and I suddenly notice that the "blood" is in fact tomato ketchup! I'm deeply shocked—why would she cover herself in fake blood and pretend to be dying?

I woke from this nightmare feeling confused and tricked. But within moments of mentally replaying the dream movie, I understood what it was telling me. For several years, this person had been lurching from one crisis to the next in her life with an attitude of martyrdom, and I was one of the main people she turned to for support. The lengthy long-distance phone calls and discussions where I listened to her grievances and tried to help her feel better about her life had become draining for me, but I cared deeply about her and wanted to help.

My nightmare enabled me to understand the unconscious manipulation behind this person's behaviour: she wanted my undivided attention. Creating drama to lead me to believe that she was in dire straits was her guaranteed way of securing it, as it made me feel so worried about her. Until the nightmare came along and opened my eyes to the truth, I hadn't understood the extent of her unconscious emotional manipulation. I also had two further insights: first, I realized that I needed to take steps to protect myself from this person whose needs were exhausting me; and second, I grasped on a deep level that I cannot create another person's happiness—they have to do that for themselves.

I acted on this nightmare by purposefully becoming less available to her and I switched my tactics: instead of providing an endless pool of sympathy whenever she bewailed her life, I remained kind but said things like, "Take charge of your life. Nobody else can do that but you. Only you can create your happiness. Stop looking for validation from the outside—look within. Get in touch with the deepest part of yourself and align yourself with that part. Then everything in your life will flow in the direction you hope for. You are the *only* one who can change your life!" This no-nonsense attitude, combined with my new protective boundaries, changed things fast. As the nightmare had shown, this person was in fact strong enough to stand alone and no longer needed me as an emotional crutch. She began to get her act together and her life finally changed for the better. Once I began to actively protect myself from being sapped by her neediness, our relationship became healthier, and we both benefited from this. In the end, we became even closer.

Now let's suss out the nature of our own personal shadow. Here's a simple practice to help you do this.

practice 15

HOW TO IDENTIFY YOUR SHADOW SELVES

Who are you? How well do you actually know yourself and how honestly can you assess your own shadow? Sometimes we are not the least bit aware of a shadow aspect of ourselves, while other aspects will be blindingly obvious to us. This is a writing exercise, so grab a notebook and pen.

1. How do you like the world to see you? Write down your own character traits that you identify with positively.

2. Which parts of you would you prefer the world not to see? Write down any negative character traits that you know are part of you.

3. Who are you definitely *not*? These can be both positive or negative traits (not a leader, not a coward, etc.). Write these down.

4. Jot down the character traits that you particularly revile in others—what really winds you up? (People usually find this the easiest part of this exercise!)

5. Who do you aspire to be? Write down the characteristics or talents you would love to have or feel envious of in others.

6. And now I ask again: Who are you? The answer is, you are all of these things, dark and unpleasant sides, hidden and luminous sides, and aspirational qualities waiting to be brought into the light.

7. Review all of these different traits and see which ones have a particular charge for you. Circle three positives and the same number of negatives. These may be the qualities to focus on illuminating (in the case of positive hidden qualities and talents) or integrating (in the case of unwanted parts of the self) at this point in your life.

The purpose of this practice is definitely not to depress ourselves with how many "negative" qualities seem to be part of us! Take it lightly, playfully. It's just designed to give you an idea of possible shadow aspects, that's all. Send loving compassion to all of the varied parts of yourself and trust your dreams and nightmares to help you explore, integrate, and heal.

·······················

Shadow work is about bringing our awareness to the hidden and unexpressed parts of ourselves. No matter how in tune with ourselves we are, life is filled with unexpected challenges that can throw us off balance and cause an internal split. Nightmares can direct us to what needs healing within us by bringing us straight to the shocking core of a shadow side. In the following section, I describe a nightmare I had in which I encountered a rejected part of myself during a difficult time in my life.

Shadow Sides Revealed: Rejected Parts of Ourselves

Who are you? Me, I'm an optimist, full of hope. I see kindness and beauty all around. I'm playful, empathetic, joyful, strong. I'm at ease dreaming up creative solutions to any problems that happen along, and I wake up happy every day. Pretty cool, huh? Well, it's all true … but it's not the full story. How could it be? We all have shadow sides. I'm just as flawed as the next person: impatient, emotional, impulsive, with a rebellious streak and a hot temper. (I like to blame the temper on my red hair—surely it can't be my own fault?!) Seriously, though, how in touch are we with the parts of us that we'd rather not own? And what happens when we suppress and ignore them?

One hard winter, during a very challenging time in my life, a nightmare burst through to force me to pay attention to a part of myself that I had neglected. My default mode of optimist had been wearing thinner than I knew. My little girl had been diagnosed with a serious disease, and although we were following the treatment plan, there were no signs of improvement yet. On top of that, since her immune system was compromised, she had bronchitis and the doctors said it looked as if it was developing into pneumonia again. Do you know who the least interesting person in my life was at that time? It was me. I barely existed for myself. I was 100 percent focused on my five-year-old, who had always been so bright, energised, and joyful but now was asking me why her bones hurt and why she had no breath left after climbing a few stairs. All of my energy went into taking care of her and pouring love and smiles and fun her way, and that felt right.

Then I had the following nightmare.

> In a big public building, I find the bathroom, but when I open a cubicle door, I see a woman sitting slumped over on the toilet. She has been completely squashed by the lid and her face is forced down into the toilet bowl. Her long blond hair and her arms dangle to the ground.
>
> In horror, I realise this woman has drowned in the toilet!
>
> Instinctively, I back out of the cubicle fast and dash into the next-door one. My heart is going crazy. I'm so shocked that I become lucid. As I stand there trying to calm down, I know I should return to the disturbing dream scene I just witnessed, to discover what it means. But I'm aware of a deep reluctance to go and face it. I wake up.

I've had thousands of lucid dreams in my lifetime, and due to my early "baptism by fire" into nightmares and sleep paralysis, and all the work I've done on releasing fear, I'm usually pretty brave when I come across an upsetting image in a dream. So, when I woke up, I was struck by my reluctance to face the drowned woman. This told me that I absolutely had to work with this nightmare to discover its message. I was sleep-deprived, and to be honest, I didn't feel like doing any dreamwork right then, but I made myself do it. I used my Lucid Imaging Nightmare Solution and imaginatively reentered the dream just before the tipping point when I first saw the woman. Here's what happened in that imaginal space:

> I lift the woman off the toilet and lay her gently on the floor. Next to me is a healing salve, and I apply it to her neck and mouth. Somehow this revives her and she comes back to life. I realise she hasn't died; she only fainted. She sits up and we hug. I help her to stand up and as I do, my gaze falls on a speck of blue light inside the toilet. It's a piece of jewellery—a ring. I pick it out and wash both it and my hands in the sink, then I hand it to the woman. She had lost it down the toilet and had been looking for it when she lost consciousness. We leave the cubicle and the building together and cross the road into a green park.

I look at the bright, beautiful ring, which she is wearing again now. I ask her what it means to her.

She answers, "Hope."

I think, "Oh! She lost her hope down the toilet!"

Suddenly, the meaning of the nightmare is so clear to me. In these past months of serious health issues with my daughter, part of me had lost hope and had almost drowned or got shut down or trapped from the loss of hope. In this dreamwork, I have rescued that unacknowledged part of me and recovered my hope.

There was only a time span of a few minutes between waking from my nightmare and finding healing resolution through the Lucid Imaging Nightmare Solution. Yet this was deep work; it felt huge to finally accept the toll that the previous months had taken on me and acknowledge my unwanted and unexpressed feelings of hopelessness. No optimist likes to admit that there isn't always a solution in sight! My dreaming mind was being very blunt with me. It was saying, "Hey! Just look at the state of you! Stop pretending you can cope with this—you actually feel as if you've drowned down a toilet. It's not healthy, Clare, so sort it out!"

It's not easy to acknowledge the hopeless, trapped part of myself. Who wants to admit to an uninspiring shadow part of the self? I'd much rather be Supermum, able to heal all illness with a flick of my sequinned cape and cope with strength and resilience in any situation. But when we ignore our true feelings, we actually lose resilience because of the tension of suppressing how we really feel. We end up at a breaking point. Nightmares are powerful gifts that smash through our inner walls to show us where healing is urgently needed. When we do dreamwork to enable nightmare imagery to change spontaneously into a new story, we can resolve deep issues with amazing speed.

What I loved about my nightmare solution was the spontaneous appearance of the sparkling blue ring of hope. When new symbols arise in a nightmare reentry, it's always fascinating to see what insights they bring to the story. I had rejected my pitiful, hopeless shadow self so determinedly that the poor thing drowned in a dream toilet, but now I had a healing symbol to remind me to take care of that part of me that had lost hope. The symbolic ring also showed me how vital it was to recover my hope and learn to trust that my child would respond to the treatment and get well again, which thankfully she soon did!

The Shadow as the Rigid, Controlling Part of the Personality

This nightmare and the healing work that resolved it was shared by Charmaine, a young woman I met at an IASD dream conference.

> A throng of women in grey combat uniforms barge into the condo and order us to sit in a circle and hold hands. The bulky leader of the pack eyes us like an eagle. Suddenly, she thrashes the butt of the gun into my head. I collapse, letting go of the other hands. Then I'm on my knees facing a window ledge, with my hands tied behind my back, as if I'm the victim of a terrorist beheading video. The leader yanks my head towards her and sticks the gun muzzle at my nape. She pulls the trigger. What felt like a bullet was actually a blast of compressed air. She plucks my limp body back up, thrusts the muzzle into the same spot, and hisses, "This is what it feels like to die." She shoots again. I see my lifeless body floating in a bathtub of blood from above.

Charmaine explains:

> The nightmare emerged during a period when I was incredibly anxious about my future and experiencing inner conflicts. I felt stuck, alienated, and terribly unhappy in my job. I kept thinking about moving from Toronto to Berlin, where I felt freer and more comfortable in my own skin than ever. After waking up from the nightmare in a fit of sobs, the terror from the dream followed me everywhere that day.
>
> Some weeks later, with the remnants of the nightmare still lingering, I was still determined that a change needed to happen in my life, and so I booked a one-way flight to Berlin and made it my new home. During Clare's Transformative Lucidity workshop, while entering into this nightmare again in my mind's eye, I decided to turn toward the woman in the grey uniform and face her. I realized that throughout my nightmare, this woman, this person embodying terror, was always

situated *behind* me. I had always felt her presence hovering over my shoulders and the terror she evoked, but I had never *seen* her.

The act of turning toward her, facing her head-on, seeing her human face, somehow relinquished her power over me. It seemed to me that she might embody the rigid and controlling side of me that was immensely afraid of uncertainty and the unknown. The fact that I could turn toward her during the Lucid Imaging Nightmare Solution experience made me aware of how I've grown to become more comfortable with uncertainty, and seeing her face reminded me that my desire to control is natural and part of the human experience. The increased awareness of this side of myself and the acceptance of it felt new and profound to me.

I love Charmaine's brave example because it shows in a very literal way that the simple (yet at times terrifying) act of turning to face our fears can instantaneously reduce their power. Nightmare work can help us identify the shadow sides of ourselves that we sublimate so expertly that we barely recognise them as part of ourselves until they burst into consciousness in the form of a terrifying dream.

Next, an artist friend of mine, Walter, shares what happened when he worked with a nightmare in which Adolf Hitler tried to force him into sex.

I am living with a beautiful, caring woman in the very center of Berlin, Germany. It is after World War II and everything around us is burned out and destroyed. We have a pretty isolated but good life. The one huge difficulty is that Adolf Hitler is living with us. It is a secret that Hitler lives here, and neither of us is happy about it, but hell, he is the Führer after all and he does what he wants.

Hitler declares that he will have sex with me.

Yikes. Gulp. I consult with my companion and she tells me I better do it. One call from Hitler and both of us are dead.

Holy hell, I have no choice. I am resolved that I will have to do this, climb in bed with Hitler and kiss him and make love with him. Yuck. I go into our bedroom and take my clothes off and prepare myself mentally for this horrid event.

Hanging over the bed is a giant piece of art that is rough black paint on the left side and rough white paint on the right. Maybe I can use this to concentrate on as Hitler has sex with me. Hitler enters. He is naked and menacing. I start to sweat and panic. He climbs on the bed and crawls towards me, baring his teeth like a wolf. He is about to enter me and I just can't do it! I start to fight him, knowing this will mean the death of me, but I can't! He grips me firmly and I hit him. I scream and wake up on the floor with the covers strewn everywhere and my heart racing.

Walter's dreamwork experience with the Lucid Imaging Nightmare Solution:

In Clare's workshop, she had us reenter the dream. As I sat inside the dream, a thought came to me: "Wait a minute. If it is after the war and the Allies have won, my god, Hitler has no power here. He is a fugitive!" And with that knowledge I entered the bedroom scene and confronted Hitler. As he approached, I stood up and told him I would have none of this. "This is my home and my body and you have no power over me. You can go fuck yourself." That enraged him, but I was taller and stronger than him and threw him up against the black-and-white painting. He suddenly realized I was right and settled down onto the bed in a funk.

"Could we still have sex, please?" he asked in a sheepish voice.

"Maybe," I replied. "But it will be on my terms and my companion will be present."

"Agreed," he said, and we shook on it.

Walter's insights after the LINS dream reentry:

None of these are thoughts I had until after I did the Lucid Imaging Nightmare Solution. I think this dream taught me more about my relationship to the shadow part of my soul. I tend to be very optimistic and avoid conflict to a fault. I think Hitler represents that angry, controlling, dark part of me that I sublimate so well. What if I face that part and not just succumb to it but expose it to the light of day outside the confined apartment of my soul and have a relationship with it that is of equal footing? The Hitler in me will always exist but now can play a smaller and more integrated part in my journey.

If you want to take one step further and actually *become* the shadow figure in your dream to gain insight into their motivations, their perspective, and their vulnerability, here's a practice showing how it can be done.

practice 16

BECOME THE MONSTER

When we reenter a dream in our imagination, the possibilities for action within that imaginative space are many. This "become the monster" technique is based on Gestalt therapy, which was developed by Fritz Perls in the 1950s. The idea behind it was that we are the makers of our own dreams, so every element of the dream is a part of us. The method was for the dreamer to speak with the voice of that dream element, moving from his own chair into an empty one to do so, and creating an entire conversation between himself and this dream element. The dreamer might "become" his deceased father and speak from his father's perspective. He might "become" a dream frying pan and speak with its voice. This therapeutic dreamwork technique was developed to help people to become whole and integrated.

My variation can be done on your own if you're curious about the dream figures or imagery in a dream or nightmare and want to discover more, but if you have a seriously disturbing nightmare, it's better not to work on it alone—ask a friend or see a therapist who is trained in dreamwork. I refer playfully to "the monster" here, but you can illuminate any element of your nightmare with this method, from objects to landscapes to dream people and animals.

1. Sit and relax with your eyes closed. Calm your thoughts. After a few deep breaths, bring your nightmare into your mind's eye. Conjure up the nightmare as vividly as possible, and experience the emotions and imagery anew, knowing that you are safe and can stop this process whenever you need to.

2. Try "becoming" the main nightmare image or the threatening or disturbing figure by speaking from the point of view of your personal

monster. You may want to try Perls's technique of moving to an empty chair to do this, but it's not necessary. All you need is imagination and empathy. Begin with "I feel…" or "I want to …" This can have surprising results—perhaps the terrifying figure is itself terrified … of what? Speak without judgment or expectation, and find out. You can speak aloud or silently in your head.

3. Now reply to the monster as yourself. Ask it any questions you wish: "Why are you in my nightmare?" "Do you have a message for me?" "How can I help you?" "What is your greatest fear?" "Why did you turn into a flying horse at the end of the nightmare?" Each time, to receive a response, mentally inhabit the monster and speak with its voice. Keeping your eyes closed throughout allows you to observe the way the monster and the nightmare imagery morph and change in response to your inner conversation.

4. You can do this with as many nightmare elements as you wish. It can be fascinating to gain insight into geographical features in nightmares, such as raging rivers or frozen mountains.

5. Remember, you are totally free to engage imaginatively with the nightmare, and its story is not set in stone! Roles are fluid and anything can change during this process—it might help to think of it as improvised theatre. It can be revealing and enlightening to gain a deeper understanding of the elements of your nightmare, and this technique often yields surprising results as we grasp how our nightmare monster *really* feels!

Sometimes people find it hard to do this imaginative roleplay work. They say, "But aren't I just making it all up?" They doubt their inner experiences because they can't classify them neatly as "a dream" or "a nightmare." Yet we are the co-creators of our nightly dreams! Since dreams are thought-responsive environments, they reflect our beliefs, expectations, and thoughts. Think of it like this: everything we imagine emerges from our psyche. Our imagination is born from the same place where dreams are created, so when we engage imaginatively and intuitively with unconscious imagery, we co-create new imagery hand in hand with our unconscious mind. We become lucid dreamers while awake. This mix of awareness with unconscious imagery is a fantastically creative state of consciousness, one that fuels writers and artists all over the globe. Would an artist look at her fabulous sculpture and think, "Well, I just made it up, so it means nothing and can have no impact"? No—she would understand that this creation emerged from the intuitive symbiosis between her unconscious and her conscious mind. During this emergence, the creation took on its own unique energy and power.

The litmus test for any kind of imaginal dream reentry work is to ask yourself, "How does it feel?" If it feels wrong, forced, unimportant, false, or uninspiring, then the process has not been helpful. If it feels emotionally real, liberating, profound, surprising, or healing, then you have done some deep work. The best advice I can give is this: Don't worry too much about who or what is doing the creating, and resist the urge to analyse and judge. Just dive in and go with the flow. Listen and react intuitively. Trust that you have the ability to reach the deeper, wiser part of yourself anytime. It is not under lock and key; it is an intrinsic part of you!

....

Here's a technique that uses imaginative responses to bring you quickly to the beating red heart of your nightmare.

practice 17
THE NIGHTMARE TRANSFORMATION TECHNIQUE

This quick technique helps you to understand and transform your nightmare and then find a way to take action in your life to honour its message. You can do this in just a few minutes while waiting for your morning coffee to brew. It combines asking key questions with the serious play of changing the nightmare script, then taking concrete action in waking life.

1. **Replay the nightmare movie.** Bring your nightmare clearly into your mind's eye and allow it to play like a movie. Fast-forward to the core image or place of deepest emotion. This might be the moment the monster bit your head off, or the moment you realised your car was spinning out of control.

2. **Label the core emotion.** Is it fear, loss, a sense of being tricked, anger, guilt, despair? Remember, the most intense emotions may not belong

to your dream self, but to another dream person or animal. You might dream of a sad, neglected owl sitting in a cage, in which case, you might focus on the owl's sadness and sense of being trapped. It can be helpful to view every part of the dream or nightmare as representative of part of ourselves.

3. **Bridge to waking life.** When did you last feel this emotion in your life? Does this nightmare seem linked to any life situation, past, present, or future? Some insight might arise, but if not, continue to the next step anyway.

4. **Play with the nightmare.** Now close your eyes and step back into your nightmare movie in the role of film director (one who enjoys improvisation and surprises), armed with tools such as a powerful animal to protect you, a magic sword, or the ability to fly. Replay the nightmare with a different outcome, experimenting with different responses until you find one that resonates with you and feels satisfying or healing. (You open the owl's cage and it flies free; you befriend the monster before it bites your head off.) Never force a "positive" ending. This isn't about forcing the nightmare to play out as you wish; it's about empowering your dream-self to try out different responses, and seeing what comes up spontaneously. Practice 14: Creative Nightmare Responses earlier in this chapter shares an exciting array of possible responses.

5. **Take action in your waking life.** Perhaps when you played film director with your nightmare, you realised the monster bit your head off because you are separating your head from your heart too much with regard to a particular situation. Action to take might be to bring more heart and compassion into that situation. In the car crash nightmare, perhaps the message was to slow down your workload or put the brakes on an unhealthy relationship before it spins out of control. When nightmares come to warn us of unhelpful behaviours or poisonous situations, taking action based on their message can help to turn our life situation around. Action can also be something comparatively small, such as dreaming of a jewel-eyed snake and drawing a picture of it to honour its power and bring it into our waking lives.

....

In this chapter, we've begun the exciting process of transforming nightmares. We've looked at archetypes and examined our own shadow aspects. We've explored the healing value of changing the nightmare story, and we've heard the nightmares and resolution process of several dreamers. I've shared my Lucid Imaging Nightmare Solution as a key transformative technique that can be used either while lying in bed directly after a nightmare or while awake. In the next chapter, we'll explore the fascinating and creative realm of childhood nightmares and mythical dreams.

CHAPTER 4

Rediscover Your Inner Child Through Nightmares

This is a particularly magical chapter. We're going to dive into the mythical, archetypal, animal-rich world of childhood nightmares and explore how magic works both during dreams and during waking dreamwork. We all still carry our younger selves within us—our three-year-old self, our five-year-old self, our eight-year-old self, and all of the other selves from our past. These younger selves have not disappeared; they are an integral part of us, and sometimes their fear and vulnerability are so strong that even today, they infect us and cause us to act in limiting ways. Never forget the child that you were! That small person needed love and protection back then and still does today. Through working with childhood nightmares, and by taking care of the babies and children who appear in our current nightmares, we can heal ourselves on profound levels and tap into our creative, playful, and wide-open child mind.

In this chapter, we'll explore the world of the child mind to reconnect with the younger selves we all still carry within us. We'll discover the possibilities of lucid dreaming and how to become a magician both in and out of dreams. Lucid Dreamplay—working with dreams and nightmares while awake—is a waking version of lucid dreaming. It increases self-awareness, empathy, mental flexibility, resilience, intuition, and resourcefulness. I call this mixture of skills "dream intelligence." It becomes a tool for empowerment in waking life. This book is filled with Lucid Dreamplay techniques and we'll discover new ones in this chapter. We'll look at nightmares that have their roots in what our childhood was like and how we dreamed as children. These include mythological nightmares, lucid and recurring nightmares, and those that are set in our childhood home.

Humans are capable of suppressing traumatic memories for many years, with no conscious memory of them at all. In one of my workshops, a man used my Lucid Writing technique (practice 24) to explore a childhood nightmare image of his grandmother swinging dead from a rope in the family barn. To his shock, he realised that this was no nightmare: it was an actual memory of a true event that he had repressed for over fifty years! At the age of eight, he had found his grandmother hanged, but the family kept her suicide a secret and never spoke of her again. This recovered memory was like a missing jigsaw puzzle piece for the man, who suddenly understood many things about his family.

Working with a nightmare rooted in childhood can bring up disturbing memories. If you find that a nightmare or the emotion it evokes in you is too extreme or too distressing, please do not work on it alone. Instead, find a psychotherapist who is experienced at dreamwork. There is also a resources section at the end of the book. Nightmares reflecting childhood abuse are discussed in chapter 6.

We were all children once, and we are still intimately connected with those younger selves. This connection emerges most powerfully through memories, through contact with childhood friends and family, and through dreams and nightmares. Our childhood contains the essence of who we are today. When we feel ready for self-discovery, we can reclaim, heal, and recover the lost or damaged parts of ourselves that we left behind along the way to adulthood. Working with nightmares helps us do this important work.

Mythological Nightmares

Children often dream of mythical beasts, cartoon monsters, skeletons, ferocious animals, evil fairies and witches, cannibals, ghosts, zombies, shapeshifters, or strange hybrid creatures such as a lion-bird or a monkey-ogre. When Carl Jung was around three or four years old, he had a terrifying nightmare of a king's throne that had something standing on it:

It was a huge thing, reaching almost to the ceiling. But it was of a curious composition: it was made of skin and naked flesh, and on top there was something like a rounded head with no face and no hair. On the very top of the head was a single eye, gazing motionlessly upward … The thing did not move, yet I had the feeling that it might at any moment crawl off the throne like a worm and creep toward me. I was paralyzed with terror.[12]

This dream haunted Jung for years, and it was only decades later that he understood the thing in his dream was a ritual phallus. The phallus has deep mythological roots and is an important aspect of male development. Children dream big and they dream deep. In *Sleep Monsters and Superheroes*, a book I co-edited on children's dreams and nightmares, psychologist Dr. Kelly Bulkeley remarks:

Some dreams of childhood are experienced as intensely frightening because they suddenly open up dramatic new dimensions of the unconscious mind, dimensions that seem completely alien to the waking self yet are filled with tremendous energy and emotion … The dreams are pointing toward a future of psycho-spiritual development that will be difficult, frightening, and painful, but also tremendously joyful and fulfilling when the dangers are overcome and the new growth is achieved.[13]

At around the age of five, we become aware of death—the fact that we will die one day, and so will our parents and everyone we love. Death begins to show up in our dreams. The following is a nightmare that mythologist, artist, and animator Keith had when he was five years old. Since childhood, Keith has felt that he is awake to an archetypal, mythical realm that others are unaware of. In this nightmare, he dreams that he wakes up to hear a creepy sound …

CHINK-CHINK! CHINK-CHINK! It's a skeleton, and I'm petrified. I can't let it know that I'm awake. I understand that one is safe if asleep … But if Skeleton catches me awake, it will come for me. In

---

12. Jung, *Memories, Dreams, Reflections*, 11–12.
13. Johnson and Campbell, *Sleep Monsters and Superheroes*, 22–23.

a panic, I lie back down, stiff as a board, and pull the covers over my head.

Too late. It knows. Somehow, Skeleton can detect my consciousness. And it approaches. CHINK-CHINK!!! I shut my eyes into a tight wince, praying it will go away.

I feel Skeleton standing close by, and then, with a WHOOSH, the covers are pulled back. Completely exposed now, I brace myself. A bony thumb and finger reach for my eyes, prying them open with a POP! Skeleton forces me to look at its toothy grin, now inches from my face. I wake up in terror.

Sometimes mythological nightmares persist into adulthood and carry with them an archetypal power that can be highly transformative to work with. Keith had the following nightmare with its compelling shapeshifting and life-or-death battle theme in adulthood.

I notice an ominous creature far off in the night sky. It's a huge dragon-like Nazgul steed from Lord of the Rings. Then it's upon me and my friends, circling like a shark, as if swimming through the air above us. I see it leap out into the open, revealing its true self as a mythical chimera. Its primary head is that of a male lion with a voracious appetite. Goat and snake heads move about on either side. Its wings and tail are those of a dragon. Locked in its gaze, I realize there is nowhere to run. We are cornered and defenseless…

[Scene shifts to an open field.] As I turn to my left, I notice a cloud of chimera, thundering in stampede toward my group. They shapeshift into sharks, and I see about a hundred of them swimming overhead…I am now wrestling with one of them, its features more specifically lion than chimera, as it stands with its forepaws on my shoulders. We are equally matched, locked in each other's grip. Then I break Lion's neck. The day is mythologized. I glimpse a parade with floats and streamers. I am being honored as the hero who slays Chimera. The scene changes and I see its head mounted on the wall of my living room.

Keith told me that this nightmare reflected his inner conflict as he sought a balance between a calling for inner work and a "real" life—he had been feeling as if a force within was sabotaging his romantic relationships, keeping him alone for another purpose. Holding this tension was tearing him apart. It's symbolic that Keith manages to turn the nightmare around by taking control and slaying the beast, before being feted as a hero. He sees the chimera's head mounted on his living room wall in true triumphant hunter style, as if the nightmare is showing that he has defeated his inner monsters and reached a turning point in life. However, as things turned out, this nightmare was but the initiation into a long cycle of brave internal struggle.

Lucid Nightmares

Have you ever experienced a nightmare where you knew you were dreaming yet you felt powerless to act or change anything? These are lucid nightmares. They can happen both in childhood and in adulthood. In these nightmares, it's key to consciously release fear to prevent the powerless feeling, because this feeling infects the dream and increases its scariness. Once we have released fear, it's normally possible to guide the nightmare towards resolution. When children are empowered through lucid dreaming, they can interrupt the cycle of recurring nightmares and discover inner resources. Prolific lucid dreamer Line has had many thousands of lucid dreams, and here she shares her initiation into guiding nightmares towards positive resolution when she was just six years old. Notice how at first, these are lucid nightmares, since Line is aware that she is dreaming but doesn't realise that she can change the nightmare story, so she wakes herself up instead.

> I started having recurring nightmares where I would be in the car with my parents, just driving along. After a while, my parents would vanish, and I'd be alone in the back seat, the car still moving forward. I'd be terrified, even though I knew that I was dreaming because people don't just disappear and cars don't move on their own. When I first started having these nightmares, I would wake myself up.
>
> At the age of six, I started realising that I can change and manipulate dreams, and one night while having this nightmare, I imagined two of my friends from preschool were there with me, and they then

appeared in the front seat! They stopped the car, and I woke up, happy that it ended well. I only had this dream a few times more, and I summoned my friends each time. I never had this nightmare again after that.

Sometimes we have no choice but to face our nightmares alone. Children can experience terrifying nightmares, and if the adults in their lives are not interested in dreams, it can take a long time for these children to realise that instead of suffering the nightmare over and over, they can wake themselves up from it or change the dream by interacting with the imagery when they become lucid.

When I sent out a call for nightmares to enrich this book, Manuel was one of the people who kindly sent me an account explaining his approach to lucid dreaming, which is rooted in his desire to escape the nightmares he had as a small child.

I have been having lucid dreams since I was around five years old. It all started as a way to escape nightmares. I used to be followed by dark entities and suddenly I couldn't run, my legs couldn't move fast, it was like trying to run under the water. And the feeling of fear was immense. The "monster" that used to follow me was … the best description I can give you is that it was a bunch of newspapers in the form of a human.

Since then, I do not have nightmares. Well, strictly speaking, I do have them, but as soon as something starts to go wrong, something inside me reacts to whatever is happening (lions or dogs surrounding me, "evil" people trying to kill me, or even "dark entities from hell") and I become LUCID, which means I can defeat ABSOLUTELY EVERYTHING. I throw people as if they are light backpacks; it's like becoming Superman inside the dream. I can also fly and have any superhero power I can think of. Defeating the "dark entities from hell" is easy unless they are (sort of) "the devil itself." In this case, the dreams become very complex, the narrative very complicated and intense, but I never experience fear. I just follow the narrative in the way I know I have to follow it to finally defeat the "supreme evil."

The interesting thing about lucid dreaming is that we don't have to wage epic battles and defeat dream people and animals with brute force in order to resolve a nightmare. Manuel's nightmares haven't gone away; they have simply become lucid battlegrounds. Everyone has their own preferred way of reacting in lucid dreams, and each dreamer is free to work out the most helpful approach for themselves. It can be wonderful to experiment with different reactions while lucid, as described in Practice 14: Creative Nightmare Responses. Responding to menacing dream figures with love and patience, or calmly asking them what they want, can have marvellous and surprising results.

One nine-year-old boy, Giovani, had a recurring nightmare of being chased by a bear. His dream therapist, Ann Wiseman, author of *The Nightmare Solution*, had given him some tips on what to do the next time the bear turned up. He then reported this nightmare where he turned things around spectacularly:

> I felt desperate and thought I was going to die, so I woke up. Then I remembered what you said about drawing the dream and talking to the monster. Next time I went to sleep [the bear] came back and instead of running, I asked him why he was scaring me. He said he was just trying to get some attention. "Every time I go into someone's dream," he said, "they run away … You are the first person who stood up to me. I have no one to talk to so I get very angry, now we are friends." [14]

This is a heartwarming result: Giovani now has a powerful dream bear as a friend! I often say that a live dream friend is worth more than a dead dream enemy. Whether we are nine years old or eighty-nine, befriending our nightmare monsters instead of fleeing from them or slaying them is an integrative act that empowers us and makes us aware of our internal resources. It creates resilience and helps us to feel braver because we feel we have protection and know that when we fall asleep, we are going to a realm where we have powerful friends.

---

14. Wiseman, *The Nightmare Solution*, 14.

practice 18

LUCID DREAM MAGIC

There are many options available to us when we become lucid during a nightmare. Here are some fun ones to try.

- **Create a magical object in the nightmare.** Look for it in your pocket or behind a dream tree. Expect it to be there, and expect it to work really well. Expectation is a powerful force in lucid dreams. You might find a carved wooden eye that can see into the heart of your attacker, an ancient sword that can beat any foe, or a thimble-sized, live golden eagle that bestows you with the power of flight.

- **Create an escape route.** If things get too intense and you can't handle this nightmare right now (perhaps preferring to work on it while awake instead), here's a trick. Paint a circle on the ground (or in the air) with your finger. This is a portal. Dive through it with a rock-solid intent to get into a different dream.

- **Summon help.** If you find yourself in a sticky situation in a lucid dream, request help calmly and with power in your voice. You might want to summon a muscular superhero, a magical being such as a unicorn or a griffin, a family member, or your pet dog. Don't worry if they turn up not looking too like their usual selves—it's all part of this crazy dreamworld. If you *expect* them to help you, they will.

- **"Om" your way to a peaceful dream.** The voice carries its own peculiar magic in the dreamworld; it can cause deep shifts in the dream scene. Try taking a deep breath and chanting "Om" on a long exhalation. Watch the nightmare respond to the peace and connection in that richly vibrating sound.

- **Shapeshift.** In lucid dreams, it's possible to change yourself into anything, such as a rainbow-scaled fish, a tree, or a ball of white light. Simply will yourself into that form with focused intent, or announce aloud, "I become a sabre-toothed tiger!" and see what happens next. (Heads up: you may turn into something totally different, but just go with it!)

- **Play at being a lucid dream magician.** It's fun to practise magic in lucid dreams. You could levitate a dream monster with your mental focus or make an unpleasant object shrink or expand by pointing at it. Do somersaults in midair or create a vortex and spin away into a different dream. For beginners, this lucid dream magic may not have much effect at first, or curious things may happen (the monster melts instead of obediently levitating). Experiment and work out the rules of your own dream or nightmare. As you get better at lucid dream magic, you can use it to heal yourself, create beauty in the dream, dissolve into light (an incredible and deeply healing experience), or offer fabulous gifts to anyone who menaces you.

Also available to us in lucid dreams are all of the possibilities in Practice 14: Creative Nightmare Responses, as well as everything we do during dream reentries and in Practice 24: The Lucid Writing Technique for Nightmares. The possibilities are in fact endless! It's wonderful to experiment with all manner of healing, creative responses to nightmares, and accept the gift of transformation. The next practice explores various artistic ways of engaging with a nightmare.

practice 19
ARTISTIC NIGHTMARE OPTIONS FOR ADULTS AND KIDS

Remember, you are powerful both in and out of your dreams and can transform your nightmares! Art helps us to reclaim any power we feel a nightmare has robbed from us. We become the all-powerful creator. Just as important as this empowerment is the insight we gain from working closely with our inner imagery and exploring our nightmare story.

- **Make an artistic nightmare book.** Use acrylics, watercolours, or collage materials to recreate your nightmare. On thick paper, use wool for fields, wood chippings for trees, sequins for stars, blue ribbons for the ocean, acrylic diamonds for pirate's treasure, or pointy stickers for the fangs of the monster you met in your nightmare. Have fun with it. It doesn't have to be perfect by any means; indulge your inner child with a totally free creativity session! You could write the nightmare story around each page of your book in circles, or write the main words within the picture. For major nightmares, try creating a stand-alone collage on canvas.

- **Draw help into your nightmare picture.** Drawing a dream is a creative and empowering way of engaging with its energy. When we depict not only the nightmare monster but also add help and resources, such as a friendly sorceress, a force field, a strong parent or ally, or a trap door that the monster falls through, any feelings of powerlessness we have dissolve. You are free to change the nightmare through your artistic and imaginative engagement with it. Make the terrifying monster pitiable or hilarious, create a new ending to the nightmare, or light up the dark cave to discover what lies within.

- **Create a "nightmare zoo."** This is a fun activity for children and adults. If you have a variety of scary dream figures, animals, or monsters, create images or models of them and enclose them in a dream zoo made of cardboard boxes or Legos. You're the zookeeper, so you get to make up the rules.

- **Interview your nightmare figures.** Lie down and imaginatively reenter your dream using Practice 8: Reenter the Nightmare. Summon your nightmare figure and have a calm chat with them, knowing that you can stop the process at any time you choose by opening your eyes. Ask, "Why are you in my dream?" "Why do you have a beard made of rat's tails?" "Do you have a message for me?" "Why did the snake eat the baby and then transform into you—an ancient man?" "Why do you chase me in my dreams?" It can be enlightening to find out how nightmare figures feel and why they act the way they do. If you're a writer, this can produce gripping material for stories and poems.

- **Act out or dance your nightmare.** You can do this with or without music. Recreate the way the monster lumbers, or become the thrashing branches of the tree in the storm. Move, speak, sing, or dance your nightmare in any way that feels right. You may find some power or unexpected beauty as you embody the imagery.

- **Send love to a dream monster in a nightmare reentry.** Love is the most transformative force in any state of consciousness. Reenter the nightmare in your mind's eye, then summon a feeling of love by placing your hands over your heart and imagining warm pink light there. Then open your arms wide and send that love to whatever is frightening you in the nightmare. You can also pull a circle of white light around you for safety and protection, or experiment with the effects of power words. Any power word will do—it could be *abracadabra* or a prayer, a Harry Potter spell or your own invented power word. If you become lucid in a nightmare, try this for sure! When we shout or sing in dreams, the sound reverberates around the dream scene with transformative effects; it can be quite astonishing. See how these actions transform your inner movie of the nightmare, and draw or write down any changes you notice.

- **Create a magic dream box** and fill it with objects and sketches from your dreams and nightmares. Dreams are full of gifts and beauty. Even nightmares contain treasures. Don't focus only on the terrifying elements—was there anything strong or inspiring in your nightmare? A chocolate wrapper cut into a circle could be the golden sun you saw, or an orange ribbon cut into flaring strips could symbolise the gorgeous colour of the flames that shot out of the fire-breathing dragon. Our dreams and nightmares are choc-a-bloc with intense creativity. Look at your objects or drawings before you sleep to remind you of the treasures your dreams bring. Tonight will bring even more treasure!

It's easy enough to work in creative and empowering ways with imagery-rich nightmares. But how can we make sense of terrifying sleep events that we have no memory of? Episodes that cause us to scream and flail, waking up the household, but then vanish without leaving any trace on our memory? Let's have a look at how to deal with night terrors, or *pavor nocturnus*, also known as sleep terrors.

Sleep Terrors

Children sometimes suffer from nocturnal episodes where they scream and scream in their sleep, often with their eyes wide open, and don't recognise or respond to their parents. They may thrash around, sweat, and tremble alarmingly for around twenty minutes or so before they fall into a calmer sleep. The next morning, they usually have no memory of the event. Although sleep terrors are harmless, they can be frightening to witness. They are most common in children under the age of seven, but teenagers can have them too, and so do around 2 percent of adults. Children usually grow out of sleep terrors, but anyone who experiences them on a regular basis should consider consulting a sleep specialist to rule out any underlying medical condition. The next practice gives tips on how to reduce sleep terrors and how to respond to someone who is having one.

practice 20

COPING WITH SLEEP TERRORS

1. Research shows that sleep terrors often happen at the same time each night, so it's helpful to note the time of episodes and wake the sufferer fifteen minutes before one is due to happen. Keep them awake for five minutes or so, then allow them to sleep again, as this scheduled awakening interrupts and resets the sleep cycle.[15]

2. Sleep terrors tend to occur in slow-wave sleep, so it's best not to try and wake the person up, as they will be hard to awaken and probably very confused and disorientated if you force them out of deep sleep. If a child does awaken from a sleep terror, it's important to give loving reassurance and a sense of safety and peace, so stay calm yourself! Sleep terrors are not dangerous, but if there is flailing, you may need to ensure the person doesn't hurt themselves on the bedframe or wall.

3. If you have sleep terrors as an adult, please see a sleep specialist who is board-certified in the field of sleep disorders medicine. Some medications used for depression or PTSD can trigger sleep terrors, so you'll need professional medical advice. You can also try to find out more about your sleep terrors by asking questions during deep relaxation or if you become lucid in a dream: "What do I experience that makes me so frightened?" "What do I need to change or face up to for these episodes to stop?" "What was happening in my life when these episodes began?" Work with the nightmares you do remember to see

---

15. Frank et al., "The Use of Scheduled Awakenings to Eliminate Childhood Sleepwalking"; Lask, "Novel and Non-Toxic Treatment for Night Terrors."

if you can discover a root psychological cause for these disturbances. Are these episodes flagging up something you need to act on to heal your life in some area? Do you feel spiritually undernourished, are you unsupported by your partner, or are you grieving? A psychotherapist or hypnotherapist could help you to investigate any possible underlying issues, such as repressed trauma.

4. Try to view sleep as a restful and revitalising retreat into the sacred. Create a beautiful bedtime ritual, as in Practice 5: Create a Soothing Bedtime Ritual, and always combine it with a meditation such as the one in Practice 6: Pre-Bed Meditation to Calm the Mind. Make efforts to recall and write down your dreams to discover more about what is going on in the deepest part of yourself.

....

It's useful to consider all sleep events, from regular nightmares to full-blown sleep disturbances, as our psyche trying to bring something important to our attention. Sleep terrors are harmless compared with REM Sleep Behaviour Disorder, where people physically enact their dreams and nightmares, leaping out of bed and destroying furniture because they think the chest of drawers is an intruder, or jumping out of the window because they dream the house is on fire. Such disturbances may have a physical origin, such as obstructive sleep apnoea, when the throat muscles block the airways during sleep. There may also be a psychological component to violent moving nightmares, sleep terrors, and other sleep disturbances. The practices in this book provide ways of reaching the heart of nightmares, and we can help ourselves to feel braver and safer during sleep by enlisting protection and building a sense of empowerment, as shown in the following three practices.

Nightmare Protection Practices

We could all use a little extra protection at times, and when we have nightmares on a regular basis, the world of sleep can seem a frightening place. Here are my top protection practices.

practice 21
ENLIST A POWER ANIMAL FOR HELP AND PROTECTION

Native Americans, Aborigines, and other indigenous cultures have traditionally seen animals as spirit helpers. Animals appear to us in dreams, visions, and trance states … as well as in waking life, of course, where an encounter with a wild animal may also be viewed as a visitation, or an invitation to accept the wisdom, spiritual power, and protection of that animal.

We have all had animal dreams. Sometimes we let fear dominate us so that we chase off or fight the animal. If we stay calm and present to a dream animal, we open up the channel to its wisdom, its soul medicine, and we can take on its instinctive, wild nature to help us in our lives. My daughter once kindly freed a dream leopard from a zoo, because he told her he didn't want to be there. After that, her leopard showed up in her dreams to protect her and to help her save any small dream animals who needed help. When we help a dream animal, we may gain a friend for life! It's excellent on every level for nightmare sufferers to enlist the help and protection of a powerful totem animal, so this is an important practice.

- **Mythology, archetypes, and story.** Think about the role of this animal in mythology, fairy stories, and modern literature. Which qualities does it generally embody? How are those qualities represented in your nightmare? Are they the opposite of the norm, as with a ferocious killer rabbit or a meek and helpless crocodile? Considering an animal from an archetypal perspective can help us to find personal meaning in it as a universal symbol, for example, Bear as healer, Eagle as spiritual power, or Lion as courage.

- **Why this animal, and why now?** A nightmare is an urgent message from the unconscious mind. Why does this animal urgently need your attention? Why has it appeared at this moment in your life? Try reentering your nightmare in a relaxed state of mind and ask these questions of the animal itself.

- **Turn your nightmarish animal into an ally.** When my daughter, Yazzie, was about seven, she dreamed of a lush rainforest with delicious fruits. A gorgeous bird of paradise was sitting in a tree smiling, but then it turned towards her and gave her a really nasty look! Shocked, Yazzie woke up and called for me. I talked her through the Lucid Imaging Nightmare Solution (practice 13), and in her dream reentry, she walked bravely up to the bird, who still looked mean. She pulled a surprise gift from her pocket; this turned out to be a necklace of blue stones. The bird was amazed and touched. In a small voice, it said, "Nobody ever gave me a gift before!" It turned out that loneliness had made the bird of paradise mean and resentful. It put on the necklace and was truly happy. This nightmare came at a time when Yazzie was experiencing bewilderment because a child she'd thought was a friend had suddenly started to be mean to her at school. Her dream reentry helped her to understand that kids who act mean are often sad or unhappy inside.

- **Lucid Writing** (practice 24) can help you reenter your nightmare and play creatively with new outcomes while feeling safe and unthreatened. Is it possible to make friends with your nightmare animal, ride on its back, play a game together? Thank it for its presence in your nightmare. Ask it, "What powers do you bring me?" or let it know, "I have a gift for you."

- **Get to know your nightmare animal.** Which attributes does your animal have? Try a creative writing exercise: focus on your nightmare animal, then write from its perspective: "I am Monkey…I feel…My strengths are…" "The best thing about being a monkey is…The worst thing is…" "What I really want is…" This helps you access its energy, understand its message, and begin to bring some of its strengths into your life.

- **Imagine a nightmare protector.** If you could call on any animal or beast to protect you from nightmares, who would it be? A mythological creature, a hybrid, or any protector animal can defend us in nightmares and help us feel brave. They are manifestations of our inner resources. In *Sleep Monsters and Superheroes*, Martha Taylor reports what happened when she asked a group of children who their dream protector would be: "Each one had a very unique figure. Here are some: two lions, one on each side; the wind-spirit; a hippogriff; a dragon-unicorn; the family cat; an eagle; a black panther; a bear; and two pet dogs."[16] You can be

---

16. Taylor, *Sleep Monsters and Superheroes*, 117.

wild and free in imagining a special nightmare protector. Give it greater reality by drawing it, collaging it, or creating it from modeling clay.

- **Create a protective statement.** When you have a power animal, integrate it into your bedtime routine. Write a message from your power animal on a card: "I am a strong and powerful Bengal tiger. I bring you gifts of mightiness, keen instincts, and lithe grace. I am here to protect you and keep you safe always. You can sleep and dream with a happy heart, in total safety." Place the card by your bed, perhaps with a picture of your animal. Look at it before you go to sleep and carry the image of this power animal into your dreams.

practice 22

CREATE A SACRED ALTAR

Since she was around five, my daughter has spontaneously and without any prompting from anyone created sacred altars. A recent one she made when she was nine had an outer circle of animals made from many different materials: a dolphin from blown glass, an elephant formed from hardened lava, a snail she made herself from a twig and rolled felt, a wooden owl, and a turtle made of tiny shells. The inner circle was made up of seven sitting fairies with different-coloured wings, and in the centre were Yasmin's gemstones and crystals: chunks of amethyst, fool's gold, turquoise, with her newest magical stone sitting on a smooth, round granite pebble right in the centre. Whenever she acquires a new gemstone, she learns about its properties (such as intuition, courage, or an energy boost), decides which properties she needs, then holds the stone in her hand whenever she feels she needs them.

When children—or adults!—are suffering from nightmares, it can feel healing and empowering to create a sacred altar in your bedroom with photographs of loved people or places, precious objects, healing and protective symbols, and gifts from the natural world, such as leaves, pebbles, or mossy twigs. You can change it and add to it anytime a new healing symbol arises in your dreams or to reflect a new way of thinking or acting in your life. Placing a gemstone under the pillow at night can act as a totem to keep nightmares away and protect the dreamer.

practice 23

THE EGG OF LIGHT AND OTHER NIGHTMARE PROTECTIONS

Rehearse the following tricks to protect you in nightmares.

- **Create an egg of powerful white light around you.** Practise this during the day so you feel safe and protected. You can do this with arm gestures—stretch up high with both hands, then lower them to your sides, imagining protective white light encompassing you above and below. Then stretch both arms straight out in front of you and open them wide, imagining the light in front of and behind your body. Repeat this in any nightmare while breathing calmly, and remind yourself that you have powerful protection in this dream.

- **Create a protective mantra.** Use this whenever you feel threatened or fearful in a nightmare. When my daughter was four, I gave her a mantra to empower her in her scary witch dreams. Soon afterwards, I came across her jumping up and down on her bed, shouting it with great power: "I am Yasmin! This is MY dream! I am STRONG!" After that display of strength, the witches who had been upsetting her didn't dare come back as foes—instead, they became her friends and created magical picnics in the woods for her.

- **Sing or chant a power word.** Choose a prayer, spell, or word that has a powerful positive emotional significance for you, or try out the magical effects of an ancient word like *abracadabra* to transform the nightmare. Practise singing or shouting it while awake. Singing has a very strong effect on dreams and nightmares; it reverberates through them and they react to its power and presence. If you remind yourself of your power word before you sleep, you'll recall it when you need help in your dreams.

- **Fill your heart with love.** You can practise this while awake, too, as it is such a supremely beneficial and beautiful practice. Stand tall, place your hands over your heart, and summon a feeling of unconditional love. (Just think about your dog or a baby if you get stuck.) Bring a colour into your heart if it feels right—warm pink or glowing orange work well. Now send this abundant love to whoever needs it. In a nightmare, this may be a vulnerable dream figure, yourself, or a dream monster. Be prepared for astonishing transformation when you send love in a nightmare! A furious stallion might turn into a peacefully grazing pony; a menacing giant might shrink down to normal size and give you an apologetic smile; a Tyrannosaurus rex might roll over to have his tummy tickled.

- **Choose an empowering talisman.** This can be anything you love or admire that inspires you with confidence or transmits a feeling of safety and happiness. It could be a toy soldier from your childhood, a translucent seashell, a doodle of Popeye, or a string of mala beads. Imbue your talisman with the expectation that it will help to keep nightmares at bay, and help you to be strong and calm if a nightmare does come along. Then put it under your pillow or on your bedside table. Say goodnight to it every night and thank it for helping you have a happier dream life.

Animal and Insect Nightmares

Childhood nightmares often involve ferocious animals or predatory insects. My daughter's best friend, Imogen, had this nightmare when she was nine.

I'm in my bedroom with my brother when suddenly a giant rhino-spider bursts in through the walls and through the windows. We scream, but every time we scream, the rhino-spider gets bigger and bigger. We have to hide. We run to a force-field place where we're protected, but the floor isn't protected and the spiders dig their way in. My whole family is in there. If they bite you once, in one place, it doesn't really matter—nothing happens. If they bite you again in the same place, you get a scar. If they bite you a third time in the same place, poison gets into you and you die. We have to try and run away, but how? We manage to run and hide in a grassy cave. The spiders suddenly show up from behind us…

I hear Mum saying, "Imogen, Imogen!" I open my eyes. It's time to get up for school.

Imogen then had the idea of writing a story about a girl who goes into a nightmare land and has to try and find her way back home. She told me how the story begins: The girl finds a leaflet in her garden. She doesn't read the back of it, but just follows the instructions to read aloud some magical words and take two steps to the right, then move forward…She turns the paper over and it says, "Nightmare Curse!" Suddenly, she's in Nightmare Land!

My daughter also has a rich dream life, and mythical creatures and power animals have featured ever since the first nightmare she reported, at age two and a half: "Dragon—got sharp teeth!" At age nine, Yasmin wrote a mythic quest novella starring a plethora of mythical beasts straight out of her dreams and imagination. We don't have to be nine years old to tap into the boundless creativity of our dreaming mind and turn it into compelling, original fiction. The Lucid Writing technique in practice 24 later in this chapter can take you straight to the heart of an original story created from your own inner nightmare imagery, and nightmares can inspire creativity in any area of the arts, as well as innovative solutions to problems.

Nightmares Stimulate Creativity

Nightmares can be extremely useful for creativity and problem-solving, whether subtly or overtly. One night, the inventor of the sewing machine, Elias Howe, was stuck on the design of the needle and had a nightmare in which savages forced him at spearpoint to finish the machine immediately. "Suddenly he noticed that near the heads of the spears which his guards carried, there were eye-shaped holes. He had solved the secret! What was needed was a needle with an eye near the point!"[17] Such direct creative solutions can be found in all types of dreams, including lucid dreams and waking daydreams, but often the meaning is muddier and so we need to do a little more work ourselves before we can reap the benefits—yet another reason to spend time unwrapping a nightmare.

On the other hand, nightmare images can be so strongly emotive and strange that they are immediately ready to be painted, sculpted, or transformed into music. Some nightmares would make amazing surrealist paintings. One

17. Kaempffert, *A Popular History of American Inventions*, 381–382.

of my lucid dreaming ocean retreat attendees, Carl, dreamed he was in a dirty hotel bathroom and a prehistoric man was lying in the bath, asleep or comatose…or dead. Then Carl noticed that marijuana was growing all over the bathroom floor, and each spiky leaf had a human face! These freaky marijuana leaves leaped up into the air and landed on his body while he tried to pluck them off. Imagine that scene as a Dali-style painting! Nightmares can also be lifted directly into a story in progress. Novelist William Styron remarked, "I recall, after my mother died, having a rather ghastly dream of her coming alive in the coffin…That's why I put the dream in *Sophie's Choice*." [18] The economic framework of a poem also provides a great discipline for unwrapping a nightmare in a series of startling images.

When we reenter nightmares, it often happens that the imagery morphs into something else, generating new imagery that carries as much power, or even more. Once I had a nightmare that I was in my childhood home during a storm so violent that my bed collapsed and the walls fell in on me. When I worked on this image with Lucid Writing, as shown in the next practice, I was assailed with memories of my rebellious teenage years: escaping from home down a drainpipe, doors being slammed with such force that the walls shook. An image came up of a girl who had an arrow—shot by a family member—lodged in her third eye, a rivulet of blood splitting her face in two. Although the original nightmare image of the room collapsing was interesting, this new image carried more power for me. I knew that would be the one I would choose to collage, or the character I would focus a story around. In the end, I wrote a poem from that new image: "Making My Third Eye Weep."

I love this transformative movement from nightmare imagery through memories and associations to new imagery. For me, it lies at the very heart of the creative process. This is the magic of the technique—you have a kickoff point, but beyond that it's all mystery, as you never know where you'll end up!

Lucid Writing for Creativity, Healing, and Transformation

I'll introduce you now to another of my core practices. I created the Lucid Writing technique when I was writing my first novel, *Breathing in Colour,* as

---

18. Epel, *Writers Dreaming*, 275.

part of my PhD on lucid dreaming as a creative writing tool. As I sat at my desk daydreaming about my book, I would slip into a trancelike state where my vivid lucid dreams would mingle with my novel characters and magic would happen: whole streams of scenes would self-create in movielike fashion in my mind's eye, and all I needed to do was scribble down what I saw without judgment, without any care about spelling, grammar, or punctuation, and without censoring a word I wrote.

When I reread what I'd written, I would very often find that original images had spontaneously arisen—a cross between my lucid dreams and my imaginative engagement with my novel. Or I'd gain an electrifying insight into what made a certain character tick, or I'd see a new plot thread springing to life. Archetypal figures arose from the interplay between lucid dreaming and the waking creative trance, and these had huge presence and power in the fiction.

It was only when I started to teach Lucid Writing in international workshops, around 2005, that I grasped that it wasn't just a creativity tool but also a transformative healing technique. Not only were people dissolving creative blocks and unleashing creative energy in my "creative dreaming" workshops, but they were also resolving recurring nightmares with Lucid Writing. Others reported gaining profound insights into their relationships, integrating shadow sides of themselves, releasing trauma, and generating powerful healing imagery. The Lucid Writing technique can be used to work with nightmares for creativity, healing, transformation, and self-reflection, and it can also help us to understand the message behind seemingly "indecipherable" nightmares. If you have a nightmare that is horrifying or terrifying to an extreme degree, please do not work on it alone with any technique—instead, enlist the support of a friend or therapist.

A nightmare image can take you anywhere: it might morph into a childhood memory, pull you into a creative inner world, or empower you by enabling you to experience the nightmare without fear. The key to the transformative potential of Lucid Writing is that we give our nightmare image the freedom to change and morph spontaneously into something else.

practice 24

THE LUCID WRITING TECHNIQUE FOR NIGHTMARES

A "dream" version of this technique appeared in *Llewellyn's Complete Book of Lucid Dreaming.* This version focuses on nightmares, although any dream, sleep paralysis event, out-of-body experience, or even waking-life "nightmare" in the form of a challenging life situation can be used as a springboard into Lucid Writing.

1. Before you begin, consider which dream or nightmare you'd like to focus on. Focus on one core image rather than a long, convoluted plot. Nightmares are perfect as a lead-in to Lucid Writing because of their high energy, startling imagery, and emotional charge. If you have trouble identifying the core part of your nightmare, give it a title, such as "Running from Mr. Tickle" or "Stuck in a Pool of Tar." This helps to focus your mind on the main scene or event.

2. Have a pen and notepad close to hand. Sit comfortably on a sofa or armchair. Close your eyes and keep them closed throughout the next steps.

3. Breathe calmly and deeply several times, then let your breath rise and fall in its own natural rhythm. Observe the breath moving in and out, like the ocean breathing.

4. Inhale deeply, and as you do so, turn your head to the right. As you exhale, allow your head to move slowly back to the centre. Now inhale as you turn your head to the left. As you exhale, your head returns to the centre. Do this combined breath-and-head movement for a while, then return your head to the centre and relax.

5. Visualise golden light cascading slowly over your body, from head to toe. Consciously relax each part of your body as the light bathes it: head, shoulders, chest, belly, hips, legs, and feet. Focus all your thought and energy on making this bath of light come to life. Allow any unrelated thoughts to drift past without grasping onto them.

6. When you are completely bathed in golden light, create a space in your mind—a luminous, golden space.

7. Now bring your chosen nightmare image into this golden space. Feel it come alive with emotions, colours, and sensations. If at any point you feel very upset or unsafe, know that you can stop the process immediately by opening your eyes and taking a deep, calming breath. Otherwise, stay with the imagery. There is no need to be fearful, because you are safe. As you focus on your nightmare image, it may move and transform into something else, and you can let this happen. Stay with the flow of imagery as long as you like.

8. When you feel ready, open your eyes just very slightly, take up your pen, and write without stopping, without caring about spelling or punctuation and without judging what you are writing. Simply let it flow out without analysing it. You might find yourself writing about a waking-life memory, or extending and changing the dream story. All of this is good; let the writing go wherever it goes. Allow new imagery to arise. If you ever get stuck, simply return mentally to your nightmare imagery and continue to write without stopping until you feel you are done.

9. If you prefer to do a variation that doesn't involve writing, once you've done steps 1–7, continue with the medium of your choice, such as collaging, doodling, or speaking your observations aloud into a recording device. It can be wonderful to play around with different forms of creative expression when working on a nightmare.

Protecting Our Inner Child

Children and helpless animals in our dreams often represent vulnerable or neglected parts of ourselves. These can be thought of as aspects of our inner child—the younger self we used to be; our innocence, our pure and shining soul. Of course, there are also dreams about babies and kids we know in waking life, but when it comes to healing dreamwork, there's a simple rule of thumb here: whenever we work with a nightmare that involves children, babies, or vulnerable animals who are in danger, abandoned, ill, or attacked, it's important to protect, defend, and heal them. Snatch the baby away from the snapping jaws of the crocodile. Heal the wound of the little boy who got shot through the heart. Reanimate the dying teenager. Cuddle the abandoned toddler and give them food, warmth, and love. If you see a lost, crying little girl, take care of her. If children die in your nightmare, then in your Lucid Dreamplay you can bring them back to life.

The psychological concept behind this is that we all have parts of us that we abandoned, parts that broke and still lie in tatters somewhere in our psyche. We may have parts of us that died of loneliness because nobody ever tended them, or parts that we severed contact with because they were not valued or encouraged by the adults in our lives. When we take the time and care to give our younger selves the love, healing, and tools they needed back then, this is an integrative act that can be very healing.

Adults may have shut themselves off from their artistic, imaginative side long ago, because parents or teachers propelled them towards their rational, analytical side. That side has grown so powerful that they feel they have lost the way to their creative, joyful side. Dreamwork is a way to bridge the gap between our child selves and who we are today. The "saviour" rule of thumb in dreamwork also applies to less extreme dream scenarios, such as a dream child being unable to open a door—we can give the children in our dreams practical assistance or advice or help them to discover their inner resources.

Sometimes there may not be a child present in the nightmare, but the setting may indicate that this dream is connected to childhood. A particular place has certain associations for us. A setting can also pinpoint a particular time in our lives; if a nightmare plays out in the house we lived in between the ages of eleven and thirteen, this might mean that the nightmare is directing our attention to what happened during that time in our lives. It does this to help us release any lingering upset or rancour linked with those past events. Or it may be drawing a parallel between old feelings and a current situation—"Look! Your big brother is still bullying you like he did back then, even though you're an adult now!" Such nightmares remind us that it's never too late to change destructive relationship patterns and set healthy boundaries.

In extreme cases of abuse and criminal behaviour, working with a nightmare in therapy can be a vital step to healing. In *Sleep Monsters and Superheroes*, clinical psychologist David Gordon and psychotherapist Dani Vedros share the nightmare of a juvenile offender, Sam, whose mother's boyfriend was a convicted paedophile. Sam had this nightmare when he was six or seven.

We all heard a noise from my mom's bedroom. Some of the kids went to the door to find out what the noise was. Then a dark man jumped out and started shooting everyone. The other kids fell to the ground and they all died. Then, the man looked me in the eyes and shot me through the heart. In the dream I died and I woke up with a horrible pain in my chest.

David Gordon elaborates:

Sam's dream explains in visual terms how he was hurt with a shot to the heart—meaning metaphorically that his heart had been broken. With this broken heart, his openness to love and being loved had closed down by the time of the dream…It is reasonable, given the known history, to speculate as well that the man responsible for this was the pedophile with whom Sam lived.[19]

When Sam reexperienced this dream murder with his therapist, he was able to acknowledge how severely he had been hurt and begin to feel compassion for himself. For the first time, he was moved to work with his past trauma and abuse and embrace his own sadness, loss, and vulnerability.

practice 25
NIGHTMARE WORK TO PROTECT YOUR INNER CHILD

- Choose any nightmare you've had that featured a child, baby, or vulnerable animal in danger. Dolls can also symbolise the inner child. It doesn't matter whether or not you identified with being that dream figure during the dream.

- Close your eyes and focus on your dream child with love and compassion. Notice your emotions as you do so. Notice the action of the nightmare—what is going on? Now become your dream child, looking out at the world from their eyes. How does the child feel? Does the child need help or attention?

- You are all-powerful and can help your dream child in every imaginable way. You can raise the dead, heal the sick, bring deep solace, and

19. Gordon, *Sleep Monsters and Superheroes*, 133.

provide your dream child with any tool or magical power they need to help them. In your imagination, help and empower your dream child in whatever way intuitively feels right.

- Allow the inner nightmare story to change in spontaneous ways, always remaining aware of your duty of care to your dream child and your absolute power to help them. Find resolution in any way that feels natural and powerful to you.

- Does your dream child have questions for you? Does the child need a hug, either from you or from someone else in the dream?

- Complete this practice by creating an affirmation for your younger self, whatever makes sense to you, for example, "I am always safe and loved" or "I deserve respect."

- Finally, do something nice for your inner child. Go to a fair, visit a park, do some finger-painting, climb a tree, or slide down a really big slide. Reconnect with your playful, creative side and you'll feel more whole.

Variations on this practice include doing it with a pen and paper, as in the Lucid Writing practice. You can also try it with a waking-life situation: Choose yourself at any age, perhaps returning to a time in your life when you experienced great challenge or unhappiness. Reenter that time in your life as if it were a nightmare that you are gently working with for healing transformation. Offer yourself the same help, love, and powerful resources that you offer your dream children. After all, at every moment in our past, we were our younger selves! And those younger selves can always benefit from healing. Compassionately connecting with ourselves like this is a very nurturing and supportive act of self-care and a way of acknowledging hard times from our past in order to release any lingering damage and emotional residue. It brings us greater resilience and teaches us to draw on our powerful inner resources as we move through life.

In this chapter, we've looked at mythological nightmares, animal nightmares, and lucid nightmares. We've seen how to become lucid dream magicians and how waking dreamwork methods such as Lucid Writing help us to connect consciously with our nightmare imagery for resolution, creativity, and healing. We've explored the value of nightmare work in protecting and healing our inner child. I've shared nightmare protection practices so that you can choose the ones that resonate with you and incorporate them into your sleep routine. Now it's time for us to move into a cornerstone practice in this book: the Nightmare Quiz!

nightmare solutions for Healing & Transformation

CHAPTER 5

THE Nightmare Quiz and Nightmare solution programmes

Fear is the biggest obstacle to psychological and spiritual growth. When we find the strength to face our fears, this is the first vital step to releasing the power they have over us. This book is all about how to face our deepest fears and, in doing so, transcend them and remove the obstacles that stand in the way of our personal growth and happiness. But how do we go about doing this? Knowledge is power, but you'd be surprised how few people have a solid understanding of their own personal relationship with sleep, dreams, and all the weird and sometimes scary experiences that can arise from these states of consciousness.

A keystone of this book is the Nightmare Quiz, which I've created to help you deepen your understanding of your relationship with sleep and identify the type of sleeper and dreamer you are. Based on your quiz results, I'll show you how to identify the nightmare relief techniques that will be most effective for you. Then you can custom-make your own powerful Nightmare Solution Programme and fast-track yourself to a happy, inspiring dream life!

Everyone loves a good quiz, but why is there a need for a Nightmare Quiz? Well, there's no "one solution fits all" when it comes to sleep disturbances, nightmares, and upsetting nocturnal experiences. Each of us is thoroughly individual. This quiz is based on the questions I ask people when I give one-to-one mentoring sessions for sleep paralysis, lucid dream induction, nightmare relief, and dream therapy. I like to get a clear idea of the kind of dreamer I'm working with so that I can fast-track them towards the techniques that are most likely to work in their particular situation.

Sleeping may be universal and essential, but our relationship with sleep is highly personal and everyone engages with their night of sleep slightly differently. Some lucky people roll into bed and fall straight into a blissful sleep, with wonderful dreams. Others wrestle with the bedcovers, pummel their pillow, heave frustrated sighs, and check the clock all the time, finally working themselves up into a state of furious frustration that they STILL haven't gone to sleep! Yet others lie scared with a pounding heart because each time they drift off, they find themselves trapped in their body while horrifying visions accost them. And these are only the differences that might appear at the *onset* of sleep—we still have the entire night to get through! The more knowledge we have about the type of sleeper and dreamer we are, the easier it is to hand-pick the best, most effective techniques to improve our sleep quality and overall nocturnal wellbeing.

practice 26
THE NIGHTMARE QUIZ

By analysing the kind of dreamer and sleeper you are, you'll bring deeper understanding to your entire sleep and dream experience. You'll also have a far greater chance of success in freeing yourself from all manner of distressing sleep experiences, from recurring nightmares to the loneliness of chronic insomnia.

The best way to take the Nightmare Quiz is to set aside thirty minutes or so to sit quietly and write down your answers. If you're not keen on writing, you can speak your answers into a voice recorder. It can also be useful to get a friend to ask you the questions, because when we skim through a list of questions without really bothering to answer them fully, we miss out on a surprising amount of information. Make your answers as specific as you can. The quiz is divided into sections to make it easier to navigate, as it goes pretty deep.

This Nightmare Quiz is based loosely on my Lucidity Quiz from *The Art of Lucid Dreaming*, with a strong focus on nightmares, sleep disturbances, and your overall level of wellbeing during sleeping and dreaming. I receive many messages from people who have all sorts of major problems with their sleep and dreams. Some have repetitive, screaming nightmares, while others wake up in the middle of their sleep cycle with feelings of extreme dread and anxiety. Others have such hyper-real, uncontrollable lucid nightmares that they feel wrung out and exhausted the next morning. Still others take a tumble into the black void and are afraid of what might happen to them in this mysterious space.

The questions in this quiz attempt to reflect a diversity of nocturnal experiences. Part of the goal of the Nightmare Quiz is to increase your own awareness of yourself as an individual sleeper and dreamer. There are so many individual differences! We are all unique, and this quiz aims to help you identify the practical techniques that will be the most helpful to you personally in healing from nightmares, transforming sleep paralysis experiences, and coping with a range of sleep disturbances. The Nightmare Quiz may prompt you to look at the spiritual aspect of your own individual range of sleep experiences, and the Nightmare Solution Programmes that follow will give you deeper resources for facing whatever is happening in the night.

Depth and Quality of Sleep

- How long does it take you to fall asleep at night?
- Are you aware of pre-sleep imagery and peculiar sensations or noises that occur as you're falling asleep (hypnagogia)?
- How many hours a night do you sleep on average?
- How deeply do you sleep? (e.g., lightly, deeply, hard to rouse, feels like I barely sleep at all)
- Are you aware of waking up often during the night?
- What is your mood upon waking up in the night? Do you feel panicked, stressed, or fearful? Is there a feeling of dread or anxiety, or do you feel cosy and content?
- How do you feel physically when you wake in the night? Do you wake gasping for breath or feeling suffocated? Does it feel like there is a

weight crushing you into the bed, or are you soaked in sweat? Is there pain anywhere in your body?

- Are you aware of vivid imagery that seems to manifest physically in your bedroom as you transition from sleep into the waking state (hypnopompia)?

- In the morning, do you generally wake up feeling exhausted, energised, confused, clearheaded, depressed, or joyful? Find the right words for you.

You and Your Dream Life

- How many dreams do you remember each morning?
- Do you recall dreams during periods of wakefulness in the night?
- Do you mainly have happy dreams, anxious dreams, dreams of being chased or attacked, or action movie–type dreams? Highly conscious or lucid dreams? Confused, murky dreams? Quiet dreams of calm and light? Find the words that best describe your dream content.
- Do you think something that happens in a dream can affect your waking life in any way? (e.g., mood, physical body, emotional reactions, life events)
- Do you feel that dreams and nightmares have meaning? (symbolic, psychological, spiritual)
- On a scale of 1–10, how happy are you with your current dream life?
- What would you change about your dream life if you could?

Recurring Dream Themes

- Do your dreams or nightmares have recurring environments? Do you repeatedly find yourself in your childhood home or standing by a dark river? Jot down your nightmare haunts, as they can be helpful for nightmare solutions that involve lucid dreaming techniques.
- Is there a recurring emotion or state of mind in your nightmares, such as blind terror, grief, hopelessness, guilt, or rage?
- Can you spot common themes or stories in your nightmares, such as being chased, attacked, or killed; hiding from danger; escaping from

fire; being lost; missing the train you simply had to be on; fighting in a war zone; or finding a room full of atrocities?

Childhood Nightmares

- Can you still recall particular childhood dreams and nightmares?
- Did you grow up in a family supportive of dreams? Think back to how your parents responded when you shared dreams or nightmares as a child.
- Did you have any memorable consciousness-related experiences as a kid, such as sleepwalking, leaving your body, sleep terrors, sleep paralysis, lucid dreaming, sharing the same dream as another person, experiencing a sense of "expanded consciousness," knowing something you could not logically know, or dreaming about a future event that came true?
- Did you sleepwalk or sleep-talk as a child?

Nightmares

- Do you have nightmares (a) only as a child, never now; (b) rarely; (c) at least six times a year; (d) monthly; (e) weekly; or (f) nightly?
- How high is the anxiety level in your nightmares? (a) relatively low, (b) high, (c) unbearable, or (d) I'm scared to go to sleep because my nightmares are so terrifying.
- Do you have scary pre-sleep imagery or frightening lucid experiences where you feel consciously aware but are unable to wake yourself up?
- Do you have frightening dreams that then seem to come true (precognitive) or nightmares that seem telepathic? Do you have upsetting dreams of deceased loved ones?
- Have you had nightmares of annihilation or horror that spontaneously transform into luminous spiritual experiences of oneness?

Insomnia and Sleep Disturbances

- Do you suffer from insomnia (defined as lengthy periods of sleeplessness or an inability to fall asleep)?

- Does your brain feel super alert and wired during these periods of wakefulness and involve itself with obsessive worrying or vivid imagined scenarios?
- Do you sleepwalk, sleep-talk, kick out in your sleep, or physically act out your dreams? (Sleep kicking is a symptom of restless legs syndrome, and violent dream enactment is a symptom of REM sleep behaviour disorder.[20])
- Have you ever experienced sleep terrors (where you scream and thrash and generally don't recall anything afterwards)?
- Do you fall asleep involuntarily several times a day? (This is a symptom of narcolepsy.)
- Do you jolt awake in the night feeling like you are choking or cannot breathe freely? (This is a symptom of obstructive sleep apnoea.)
- If you experience periods of sleeplessness during the night, do you find this irritating and debilitating, or do you welcome this as time for creative thinking and fantasy?

Depression and Anxiety

- Have you ever experienced periods of anxiety or depression, and if so, how did this affect your dream life?
- On a scale of 1–10, with 1 being "not at all" and 10 "extremely," how fearful or anxious a person would you say you are at this point in your life?
- Are you currently taking medication for anxiety or depression? (Medications can have a strong effect on dreams, repressing or activating them.)

Physical Health

- Do you have a chronic illness?
- How would you rate your overall state of physical health on a scale of 1–10, with 1 being "perfect health"?
- Do you have any pain in your body, currently or long-term?

---

20. An excellent book on a wide spectrum of sleep disturbances is Carlos Schenck's *Sleep*.

- Do you wake in pain or discomfort in the night?
- Can you describe your attitude to any health issue or physical pain you have? Do you soldier on with it, is your health a burden to you and others, do you view it as having an intrinsic teaching for you, or are you open to different ways of working with it? Putting your relationship with your health into words can be very illuminating.

Imagination and Visual Thinking

- Would you consider your imagination to be (a) wild, free, and unstoppable; (b) vivid and inventive; (c) average; or (d) you don't consider yourself an imaginative person.
- If someone leads you through a guided meditation or imaginative journey, is it easy for you to follow this and does your mind produce accompanying visuals, or is it more like just listening and not seeing anything?
- If you close your eyes right now and visualise an apple, how clearly do you see it?
- Would you describe yourself as artistic?
- Are you a daydreamer? What kind of waking daydreams and fantasies do you indulge in? Are these similar to the kinds of dreams you have at night?

Awareness

- What is your most usual level of awareness in your dreams? (a) regular lucid dreams with stable lucidity; (b) occasional lucid dreams, with some difficulty staying lucid for long; (c) fairly aware but not fully lucid; (d) non-lucid; or (e) deeply non-lucid.
- Do you find you are *constantly* lucidly aware in your dreams to the point that you find sleep exhausting?
- Do you examine your state of consciousness while awake? And in your dreams?
- In non-lucid dreams, we assume we're awake until we wake up for real and realise we were dreaming. How do you know you're *not* dreaming right now?

- How conscious are you in your waking life? How often do you feel fully, gloriously alive?

Conscious Sleep Experiences

- During your night of sleep, do you ever find yourself floating bodiless in a vast black space, or in white light, or in imageless space of any colour? (the lucid void, or the Lucid Light)
- Are you ever aware of the sensation of shooting out of your body, possibly accompanied by loud buzzing vibrations, or simply the gentle sensation of floating out of your physical body? (out-of-body experience)
- Do you ever feel locked inside your body and unable to wake up (sleep paralysis)? If so, how often? And how does it make you feel—do you panic and struggle, or relax into it?
- Are you ever sucked forcibly out of a dream, or propelled through space, or swirled around by an invisible force? (The lucid void and out-of-body experiences can involve one or more of these sensations.)
- Have you ever experienced an attack or sexual assault in a conscious sleep state such as sleep paralysis?

Lucid Dreaming

- Do you have spontaneous lucid dreams?
- Do you think lucid dreaming is easy, hard, dangerous, or transformative? Find your own words.
- Have you ever experienced a lucid nightmare, where scary things happen and you know you're dreaming but you have no control over events?
- Do you want to get lucid in your dreams?
- What are your goals (if any) for practising lucid dreaming?

Insights

- Do you think there is a current triggering factor for your nightmares or sleep disturbances, such as overtiredness, alcohol, caffeine, or stress?
- Do you feel there may be an original triggering factor linked to the onset of your earliest unpleasant nocturnal experiences? For example,

did sleep paralysis or nightmares begin during a time of extreme emotional stress, the loss of a loved one, or other traumatic/difficult circumstances in your past? There may be no obvious triggering factor.

- How do your nightmares or sleep disturbances affect your waking life? (a) hardly at all, (b) I occasionally wake up tired or depressed from nocturnal experiences, (c) they often impact my life negatively, or (d) they make my life a constant misery.
- Is there anyone in your life, past or present, who supports you with your nightmares (perhaps simply by listening compassionately), or have you never had any support?
- How hopeful are you of finding a solution to your sleep troubles?

....

Well done for completing the Nightmare Quiz! I know it's a lot to think about, but this is a vital step to getting a really good handle on the kind of sleeper and dreamer you are. Above all, please don't worry if you feel that the outlook is bleak because you have so many seemingly unsolvable sleep and dream issues. *It is absolutely within your power to change your dream life for the better and to improve your night of sleep beyond recognition.*

Just the act of doing this in-depth quiz has helped you on some level, by laying out before you the colourful quilt of your own individual sleep habits and nighttime experiences. Look at how amazingly unique you are! See the richness of your nighttime world and all of its creative potential—this is a rich seam of your own consciousness that is full of promise and bursting with energy. No matter how blighted your sleep might appear to be or how unhappy your dreams are right now, the practices in this book will give you tools to help you explore your nocturnal world for healing, peace, creativity, and spiritual transformation.

Your highly individual responses to the Nightmare Quiz will form the basis of your Unique Nightmare Solution Programme: a customised set of techniques to fast-track you towards a happier, healthier dream life. I'll help you create your own programme, but first let's start by looking at these different sleeper and dreamer types, so you can see which categories you fit into. This helps us avoid wasting time on techniques that likely won't work for us.

Each sleeper/dreamer type is set up as a Nightmare Solution Programme, with my recommendations for the best techniques that are most likely to work well for that particular type. I've pointed to specific practices from this book so that you can always refer to this chapter when creating Unique Nightmare Solution Programmes for yourself as your path into sleep wellness deepens and transforms.

You will identify with more than one type of sleeper/dreamer and will probably fit into quite a few categories. Go through the following list and choose from the fifteen different types:

- The nightmare sufferer
- The traumatised dreamer
- The agitated sleeper
- The insomniac
- The lucid dreamer
- The anxious or depressed dreamer
- The visual and imaginative thinker
- The mythical dreamer
- The child prodigy dreamer
- The health-challenged sleeper
- The psi dreamer
- The out-of-body traveller
- The lucid void visitor
- The sleep paralysis explorer
- The spiritual dreamer

It's useful to write down your own unique combination of types. After taking the Nightmare Quiz, one person might identify themselves as "an insomniac sleep paralysis explorer and nightmare sufferer who was a child-prodigy dreamer." Another person might describe themselves as "a traumatised mythical dreamer and lucid void visitor with depression and health challenges." Again, don't worry if your personal combination of types seems daunting. The programmes in this chapter, and the practices through-out the book, will help you transform your nocturnal life for the better.

There is a large number of possible combinations of sleeper and dreamer types, and not enough space in this book to write a programme for every single combination. Instead, what I've done is provide you with three examples of Unique Nightmare Solution Programmes for common combinations of sleeper/dreamer types (see appendix II) so that you get the idea and can then create your own. You can do this quickly and easily by referring to the listed suggestions for the most effective techniques for each overall sleeper/dreamer type that you identify with, and combining them into a programme that reflects your individual needs. There's also a Unique Nightmare Solution Programme template in appendix I for you to fill out with your own tailor-made routine.

The aim of the Nightmare Quiz is simply to fast-track you to the best techniques for your specific sleeper/dreamer type. Your personal Nightmare Programme can and should be changed and expanded on at any time to reflect your progress, so it's helpful to keep a record of what works best for you. Never force yourself to continue with a technique that bores or irritates you, but instead gravitate to the ones that you find the most inspiring. If the first programme you create isn't optimal for you, throw some different techniques into the mix. It's always good to experiment with an open mind to discover the combination of techniques that suits you best at this point in your life.

Nightmare solution programme 1

THE NIGHTMARE SUFFERER

If you feel terrorised by your nightmares, suffer from recurring nightmares, or are fearful to the point of not wanting to go to sleep, don't despair! It is possible to turn this situation around and reduce your nightmare frequency, as well as harness the healing and creative energy of these strong dreams.

- It's a vital life skill to learn to release an overload of fear. When we live a fearful life, we are hampered and constricted in the very core of our being. We can't even breathe properly. Learn to let go of excess fear and calm yourself in waking life, and this will become a natural response in your nightmares, too. Practice 1: How to Release Fear and Become Calm, will help with this.

- Going calmly off to sleep is beneficial for nightmare sufferers. Try Practice 5: Create a Soothing Bedtime Ritual, and make a habit of Practice 6: Pre-Bed Meditation to Calm the Mind.

- Understanding your nightmares is a first step to healing the issues they may be flagging up. The core dream reentry technique is helpful; see Practice 8: Reenter the Nightmare. A quick way of gaining insight into a nightmare is given in Practice 12: Ten Key Questions for Unwrapping a Nightmare, and you could also try Practice 9: Connect Your Nightmare to Waking Reality.

- If you suffer from recurring nightmares, go to Practice 30: Imagery Rehearsal Therapy: Rewrite a Nightmare for Healing Resolution to help you change the nightmare story, and try Practice 31: Lucid Dreaming to Transform a Recurring Nightmare.

- Work with your nightmares to claim their power, create new allies, and initiate healing. Start with Practice 13: The Lucid Imaging Nightmare Solution (LINS) or Practice 17: The Nightmare Transformation Technique.

- If you feel you need protection above all at this point, check out Practice 23: The Egg of Light and Other Nightmare Protections and Practice 36: Invoke Protective Powers: Ball of Light. Remember to talk to a friend, therapist, or sleep medicine doctor if you feel your nightmares are out of control. There's no shame in asking for help, and if your nightmares are making you sleep-deprived and ruining your life, please do see a doctor and get help and support. The resources section and bibliography also list helpful books.

- Ask a friend to help by listening to your nightmare using Practice 7: The Nightmare Reflection Technique, or play around with Practice 10: Experience Your Nightmare as an Alien from Outer Space and Practice 11: Free Association à la Freud.

Nightmare solution programme 2
THE TRAUMATISED DREAMER

Past traumas can have a relentless grip on us until we take active steps to free ourselves. Nightmares are red flags, shouting out, "Healing is needed!" When we work with our nightmares, we can release old hurts, build up our inner resources, and forge new, healthy patterns in our relationships, bringing light into all areas of our lives. However, if you have a history of abuse or trauma, please go easy with the nightmare work at first. Working with dreams can unlock deep emotions for anybody, and you are particularly vulnerable. It makes sense to get support from a therapist as you begin your healing journey.

- Use your most wonderful dreams and most luminous images to fortify yourself as you begin to work with your nightmares with Practice 28: Bring Soul Dreams and Healing Imagery into the Body.
- Practice 2: Keep a Nightmare Journal will help you spot patterns in your dream life.
- Try nightmare protection techniques such as Practice 21: Enlist a Power Animal for Help and Protection and Practice 23: The Egg of Light and Other Nightmare Protections. Practice 22: Create a Sacred Altar can be a fortifying and calming ritual.
- Forgiveness can be deeply healing. See Practice 32: Forgive and Release.
- Another healing technique is Practice 25: Nightmare Work to Protect Your Inner Child. It's beneficial to return to our lost or abused child selves to offer them our help and protection.
- Transformative techniques for trauma-induced nightmares are Practice 29: How to transform a Post-Traumatic Nightmare and Practice 30: Imagery Rehearsal Therapy: Rewrite a Nightmare for Healing Resolution. It's wise to try these in the company of a friend or therapist if you are dealing with traumatic material that you've never worked with before.
- Check out the resources section and bibliography in this book for helpful books on dreams and trauma.

Nightmare solution programme 3

THE AGITATED SLEEPER

Do you flail and thrash around during nightmares or kick out in your sleep, disturbing your bed partner? If you suffer from disturbed sleep, violent nightmares, sleepwalking, or sleep terrors, or if you sometimes wake up screaming, this can make for a bewildering sleep experience and can seriously disturb your bed partner.

- Immediately upon waking from a disturbed sleep episode, try Practice 13: The Lucid Imaging Nightmare Solution (LINS). You can also calm yourself with Practice 6: Pre-Bed Meditation to Calm the Mind. (This can be done anytime during the night.) Practice 5: Creating a Soothing Bedtime Ritual is also important for agitated sleepers.

- If you have sleep terrors, when you thrash and scream but awaken with no memory of any nightmare content, see Practice 20: Coping with Sleep Terrors for ways of reducing these episodes.

- Are these nightmares different each time? When did they start? What happened in your life right around the time they began? Are these recurring nightmares? Once their root psychological cause is understood and resolved, they may no longer return. Techniques such as Practice 12: Ten Key Questions for Unwrapping a Nightmare and any of the practices in chapter 2 will help you to decipher any message your nightmares have for you.

- You can then move to a nightmare resolution exercise such as Practice 17: The Nightmare Transformation Technique.

- People with narcolepsy (excessive daytime sleepiness and falling asleep involuntarily) often report nightmares, sometimes mixed with high lucidity. If you have narcolepsy, you can benefit from any of the nightmare practices in this book, and in particular Practice 14: Creative Nightmare Responses, which focuses on the many different approaches available to us when lucid in dreams, to guide the nightmare story into resolution.

nightmare solution programme 4

THE INSOMNIAC

If you have difficulty falling asleep or spend hours wide awake in the middle of the night, you could put your alertness to good use and perhaps experience a wonderful lucid dream by using the following techniques.

- Practice 38: The Insomnia Freedom Technique can be super relaxing. Let sleeplessness become a golden gateway into the wonderful world of lucid dreaming.

- The simplest form of yoga is the relaxation pose, where you lie on your back with your legs and arms slightly apart and focus on your breath. Try doing this while imagining something peaceful, such as flying over an enchanting landscape. Practice 41: Yoga Nidra: Balance Between the Worlds, gives tips for entering and sustaining this state. When you use those sleep-eluding hours for meditation or beautiful visualisations, it replenishes you and is often so relaxing that you end up falling into a restful sleep.

- If you find yourself stressed and anxious during wakeful periods in the night, get out of bed. Sit in the dark with zero stimulus, allowing your thoughts to calm down. Return to bed only when you feel calm.

- Check your medicines and any hormones or stimulants you ingest. Consider their effect on your sleep. Consult with your doctor before making any changes.

- Practice 5: Create a Soothing Bedtime Ritual and Practice 6: Pre-Bed Meditation to Calm the Mind are both helpful practices to ease insomnia and help us wind right down and welcome sleep.

- If old resentments arise in your mind during periods of insomnia, or if you find yourself reliving upsetting moments from your past, try Practice 32: Forgive and Release to let go of some of the baggage you may be carrying. When we lighten our mental load, a good night's sleep becomes less elusive.

Nightmare Solution Programme 5

THE LUCID DREAMER

Having a raised level of conscious awareness in your dreams and nightmares is an excellent thing, because it enables you to do powerful healing and transformative work while the nightmare is actually happening. If you already have lucid dreams and would like to have more, try reading a few pages of a lucid dreaming guidebook every night before bed and watching videos on the subject. Experiment with creative lucidity induction techniques such as those in *The Art of Lucid Dreaming*, and create your own unique lucidity programme to help you wake up in your dreams.

- Practice 4: Top Ten Tips for Getting Lucid in Your Dreams and Nightmares gives some basic pointers for you to begin to implement in your daily life.

- Set the firm intention to become lucid the next time you experience fear or anxiety in a dream. This will help you to become lucid in any nightmare. Once lucidly aware, you have a huge array of options for responding to the nightmare story. Practice 14: Creative Nightmare Responses sets out some of these possible responses.

- If you wake up from a nightmare and want to reenter it to change it, Practice 13: The Lucid Imaging Nightmare Solution (LINS) is a useful technique and can spark dream lucidity.

- If you're excited by the idea of being a magician in your lucid dreams, check out Practice 18: Lucid Dream Magic. Levitate, shapeshift, create magical objects … Anything is possible when you are aware within your dream!

- Practice 31: Lucid Dreaming to Transform a Recurring Nightmare is a visualisation exercise to set an intention to change the dream story and create integrative healing.

- You could also hone your storytelling skills with Practice 30: Imagery Rehearsal Therapy: Rewrite a Nightmare for Healing Resolution. It's worth practising different nightmare endings while awake so that we have a whole array of possibilities at our fingertips the moment we become lucid in a scary dream.

- Rehearse your next lucid dream with Practice 45: Drumming Journey: Create Your Own Spiritual Dream.

Nightmare solution programme 6
THE ANXIOUS OR DEPRESSED DREAMER

Sleep can be exhausting for people with depression or anxiety. You might be too anxious to fall asleep, or wake up in a state of extreme anxiety during the night, or have awfully vivid nightmares, or have no dream recall whatsoever but wake up feeling depressed every morning.

- Check your medication. Some people's anxiety medication gives them nightmares, while others report zero dream recall. Discuss your sleep and nightmare frequency with your doctor to see if it makes sense to make changes in dosage or switch medications.
- Try Practice 5: Create a Soothing Bedtime Ritual and Practice 6: Pre-Bed Meditation to Calm the Mind to prepare yourself for a restorative night of sleep.
- It can be helpful to invoke protection. Practice 23: The Egg of Light and Other Nightmare Protections has a variety of examples. Try one each morning. Practice 36: Invoke Protective Powers: Ball of Light is one I teach in yoga classes. It can dissolve deep-seated emotional and physical blockages. Practice 22: Create a Sacred Altar is a calming protective ritual.
- Practice 28: Bring Soul Dreams and Healing Imagery into the Body is an empowering technique to try if you feel depressed or anxious. It should be done only with positive imagery.
- We are the creators of our own mental story of life, and we always have a choice in how to react to circumstances. Practice 14: Creative Nightmare Responses reminds us of how we can change our reality by reacting in different ways.
- Practice 45: Drumming Journey: Create Your Own Spiritual Dream can provide you with a soul-enhancing journey to return to in times of need.

- You are a unique, precious, and gifted person, and you belong here on this planet. You have the right to a life filled with happiness and joy. It can be enormously beneficial to send yourself love every day; try it the moment you wake up or whenever you look at yourself in the mirror. Practice 44: Meet Your Inner Light reminds us of our inner strength and beauty.

nightmare solution programme 7
THE VISUAL AND IMAGINATIVE THINKER

If you fit this description, you're lucky, because many powerful nightmare solutions involve visual thinking and a lively imagination. You are naturally close to your dreams and visions, so any imaginal journey you undertake is likely to lead you quickly into a space of transformation.

- Visualising in deep relaxation can be powerfully healing. Try Practice 41: Yoga Nidra: Balance Between the Worlds, and combine it with Practice 44: Meet Your Inner Light or Practice 28: Bring Soul Dreams and Healing Imagery into the Body.
- Practice 13: The Lucid Imaging Nightmare Solution (LINS) should be very easy and effective for you when working on a particular nightmare, as should Practice 24: The Lucid Writing Technique for Nightmares, where a stream of fresh, nightmare-resolving imagery can virtually be hallucinated onto the page. This can provide you with a wealth of original creative imagery and compelling new stories.
- If you want to work out the motivations of a threatening dream figure, try Practice 16: Become the Monster.
- Visual and imaginative thinkers will find it easy to enter entirely new worlds and perform healing magic in exercises such as Practice 45: Drumming Journey: Create Your Own Spiritual Dream.

Nightmare solution programme 8

THE MYTHICAL DREAMER

If your dreams and nightmares create powerful stories or have recurring themes or archetypal images, it can be both therapeutic and a creative boost to mythologise these stories and create art or fairy tales from them.

- Turn your nightmares into mythical stories to harness their power. I initially created Lucid Writing as a creative writing tool, before it naturally developed into a transformative and healing technique when I began to teach it in workshops. Use Practice 24: The Lucid Writing Technique for Nightmares to continue the story of a mythical or an archetypal nightmare.

- Practice 14: Creative Nightmare Responses can help you explore different reactions to frightening dream monsters and nightmarish hybrid beasts. Any art form can be used to depict nightmare stories and creatures, and it can be highly therapeutic to explore a nightmare artistically. Try collage, sculpture, storytelling, dance, or theatre. Practice 19: Artistic Nightmare Options for Adults and Kids gives some ideas for creative engagement with nightmares.

- Practice 31: Lucid Dreaming to Transform a Recurring Nightmare is also one to play with for insight and creativity.

- Practice 43: Turn Mythological Beasts into Protective Allies can be a great exercise to play with if you wish to harness the powerful energy of nightmare aggressors.

- Envision a fairy tale from your nightmare while listening to inspiring music by modifying Practice 45: Drumming Journey: Create Your Own Spiritual Dream. When we channel our most disturbing sleep encounters into art, we unleash our creativity and enjoy the therapeutic benefits of working closely with our unconscious material.

Nightmare solution programme 9

THE CHILD PRODIGY DREAMER

If you had an inclination towards memorable consciousness-related experiences as a child, such as flying lucid dreams or out-of-body experiences, sleepwalking episodes, sleep paralysis, dreams of the future, dream visitations from deceased loved ones, experiencing the same dream as another person, and so forth, then you fall into the category of "child prodigy dreamer." Perhaps you want to reclaim these "lost" abilities, which are never completely lost. We all have our younger selves within us and can reconnect with them anytime, through visualisations, imaginal journeying, and lucid dreaming.

- Some of your past dream-related experiences may have terrified you. Close your eyes and travel back in time. Reassure your child self and give them the help and support they needed back then. Try Practice 25: Nightmare Work to Protect Your Inner Child. You can do this practice by focusing on your actual past self rather than a dream child.

- Rediscover your inner child. Make a conscious effort to reconnect with that vibrant, innocent, amazing past self. Practice 24: The Lucid Writing Technique for Nightmares can be helpful here: summon a mental image of your child self, then begin your writing with "I am seven years old …" and allow your child voice to spill onto the page, sharing fears and telling stories about how life felt at that age. Extend compassion, love, and support to your child self.

- Practice 19: Artistic Nightmare Options for Adults and Kids can be used when exploring your own fearful childhood experiences as another way of getting closer to the child you used to be.

- Take fun action to honour your inner child: climb a tree, bomb down a hill on your bike with your arms flung wide (this is one of my favourites), go to a waterslide park, colour in a picture, go to sleep with an object that reminds you of childhood, or do whatever you feel connects you to the little kid you once were. When we support and integrate our younger selves, we experience new freedom and joy.

Nightmare solution programme 10

THE HEALTH-CHALLENGED SLEEPER

Nightmares can have physical causes: the dreaming mind translates physical sensations directly into imagery. We're thirsty and have a nightmare about crawling through a desert. We need to pee and have stressful dreams of hunting for a bathroom. Going to sleep with a headache could provoke a dream of being tortured with a steel band being tightened around our head. Stabbing menstrual cramps during sleep could lead to nightmares of being stabbed. Pain and discomfort in the body can and does directly affect our dreams, and the natural response of our dreaming mind is to turn this pain into streams of vivid imagery.

- Working with healing mental imagery can be highly effective as a response to physical health issues and has been shown to help health issues ranging from asthma to chronic pain.[21] Practice 28: Bring Soul Dreams and Healing Imagery into the Body is a good place to start.

- Practise healing during waking dreamwork in any way that feels right. Working with a specific nightmare can release repressed emotions and blockages that impede healing. Practice 30: Imagery Rehearsal Therapy: Rewrite a Nightmare for Healing Resolution is a useful one because you can create your own healing imagery and then bring it into your body every day by reliving it in your mind's eye.

- Use pain-induced imagery as a lucidity cue and do something healing as soon as you get lucid in a nightmare, such as creating a healing pool and diving into it with the affirmation "I heal myself from …" or sending healing light to yourself.

- Go on a healing journey with Practice 45: Drumming Journey: Create Your Own Spiritual Dream. This practice can easily be modified at the intention-setting stage to focus specifically on resolving or relieving a current physical health issue.

---

21. Kohen, "The Use of Relaxation–Mental Imagery (Self-Hypnosis) in the Management of 505 Pediatric Behavioral Encounters."

- Practise being bodiless with exercises such as Practice 41: Yoga Nidra: Balance Between the Worlds, as this is a powerful state of mind from which to invite healing.

Nightmare solution programme II
THE PSI DREAMER

If you have frightening dreams that then seem to come true (precognitive), upsetting dreams of deceased loved ones, nightmares that seem telepathic, or out-of-body experiences in which you feel you receive communications from another source, then you are a psi dreamer. While most psi dreams are usually low-key synchronistic happenings and can also focus on happy events, it can be terrifying to dream of an accident or death only to find it then actually happen.

- It's valuable to reflect on your worldview whether you have these types of nightmares or not. Practice 39: Question Your Beliefs, Assumptions, and Expectations gets you thinking about the nature of time, space, dreams, and reality.
- Sometimes a psi dream may carry both precognitive or telepathic elements and also have a personal message for us. When we familiarise ourselves with the symbolic language of nightmares, it becomes easier to work out if this is a psi nightmare or a personal one, or a little of both. Practice 9: Connect Your Nightmare to Waking Reality and Practice 12: Ten Key Questions for Unwrapping a Nightmare can help with this.
- If you want to try a little reality creation, check out Practice 13: The Lucid Imaging Nightmare Solution (LINS) and see what happens when you reenter the nightmare and guide it in a new direction. Dreams often seem to show us possible realities: nothing seems set in stone.
- If you feel blasted by psi nightmares, try Practice 23: The Egg of Light and Other Nightmare Protections.
- Reconnect with your inner strength with Practice 44: Meet Your Inner Light.

Nightmare solution programme 12

THE OUT-OF-BODY TRAVELLER

Out-of-body experiences (OBEs) can be such wondrous and inspiring events, but if we carry too much fear with us, the OBE can become another frightening realm where we feel out of control and very alone. If you are suffering from fearful OBEs, the first thing to do is to reduce your fear levels. The following practices can help with this.

- Practice 1: How to Release Fear and Become Calm. When we bring feelings of calmness and safety into our waking-life stress responses, we will find it easier to recover this calm when faced with some of the strange sensations connected with OBEs.
- Practice 40: How to Release Fear During an OBE focuses specifically on the out-of-body experience. The nightmare protection practices in chapter 4 are helpful for building confidence and a sense of safety during an OBE.
- It can be beautiful to become adept at yoga nidra to familiarise ourselves with the sensation of releasing the physical body, as in Practice 41: Yoga Nidra: Balance Between the Worlds.
- It's empowering to know that we have many different available responses to us in any state of consciousness. For some ideas, check out Practice 14: Creative Nightmare Responses.
- When we become aware of our inner strength, it can be helpful to connect to this during an OBE. Try Practice 44: Meet Your Inner Light.

Nightmare solution programme 13

THE LUCID VOID VISITOR

The void is a space of infinite potential and an absolutely fascinating space to experience and explore. But it can be supremely frightening to be sucked forcibly into endless blackness and spun around willy-nilly or shot down twisting wormholes! The wonderful thing is we are effortlessly lucid and alert in this state, and that is a gift. When we learn to transcend fear and turn our time in the void into an adventure in consciousness, we lift off into amazing and liberating experiences.

- Practice 42: How to Navigate the Lucid Void gives tips for reacting in this at times bewildering space.
- You can practise being aware and fearless in the lucid void by engaging in imaginative techniques such as Practice 45: Drumming Journey: Create Your Own Spiritual Dream, or by floating on the cusp of sleep, as in Practice 41: Yoga Nidra: Balance Between the Worlds.
- If fear is getting the better of you in the lucid void, try Practice 36: Invoke Protective Powers: Ball of Light. You could also do the core day-time calming technique as described in Practice 1: How to Release Fear and Become Calm.
- The fear-releasing techniques in this book can help in any state. Try Practice 33: How to Release Fear in Sleep Paralysis; this works very well for the void, too. Also try Practice 40: How to Release Fear During an OBE.
- Above all, remember that you will wake safely from this experience, so you might as well enjoy being lucid, bodiless, and free while you can!

Nightmare solution programme 14
THE SLEEP PARALYSIS EXPLORER

It can be terrifying to feel locked inside your body and unable to wake up while scary things are happening. But sleep paralysis is a state where we are naturally lucid and aware, and this gives us the huge advantage of being able to explore and utilise this state as a springboard for fabulous lucid dreams or as a meditative space for healing. The first step is to release our terror.

- While awake, try Practice 1: How to Release Fear and Become Calm so that you can sink more easily into a peaceful frame of mind in any state of consciousness.
- Do Practice 6: Pre-Bed Meditation to Calm the Mind each night to relax you and remind you that you are safe.

- Check out the nightmare protection practices. Practice 36: Invoke Protective Powers: Ball of Light and Practice 23: The Egg of Light and Other Nightmare Protections can help you decide on a protection strategy to implement as soon as you find yourself experiencing sleep paralysis.

- Practice 33: How to Release Fear in Sleep Paralysis should help to prepare you for sleep paralysis, while Practice 34: How to Discourage Sleep Paralysis Episodes helps you to bypass sleep paralysis.

- Once you have tackled the fear factor, sleep paralysis can be a gateway to amazing dream experiences. See Practice 35: Sleep Paralysis as a Springboard for Lucid Dreaming.

- Work on changing the story of your fearful experience—you have the power to do this! Practice 37: Change Your Sleep Paralysis Story shows how.

Nightmare solution programme 15

THE SPIRITUAL DREAMER

Sometimes nightmares turn into the most luminous, transformative experiences quite spontaneously. We may find ourselves in mortal danger or actually be killed in a nightmare, but find that this then leads to an experience of deep understanding or spiritual awakening within the dream. Such experiences are gifts that can bring solace and nourishment during very difficult times in our lives. It can take a long time before we grasp every layer of meaning of such powerful dreams, and it can be helpful to work with them.

- If a spiritual nightmare remains opaque, work with it to open up its deeper significance with Practice 9: Connect Your Nightmare to Waking Reality or Practice 12: Ten Key Questions for Unwrapping a Nightmare. You can revisit your nightmare with Practice 8: Reenter the Nightmare, and explore it afresh to discover more about it.

- If your spiritual nightmare involves a terrifying animal, person, or object (such as a golden dagger or a deadly laser beam), Practice 16: Become the Monster can help you explore this energy.

- Spiritual nightmares sometimes help us discover our luminous shadow. Practice 15: How to Identify Your Shadow Selves can give us insights into the parts of ourselves that we suppress, including our aspirations and hidden talents.

- When honouring a spiritual nightmare, it can be beneficial to integrate the nourishing energy or wisdom it has brought to us by doing Practice 28: Bring Soul Dreams and Healing Imagery into the Body.

- Relive any parts of your spiritual nightmare that you wish to using Practice 45: Drumming Journey: Create Your Own Spiritual Dream. When we mingle the imagination with powerful dream experiences, surprising insights can emerge.

- Do something in waking life to act on the message of your spiritual nightmare. This might be anything from forgiving someone who hurt you in the past (Practice 32: Forgive and Release can help with this) to freeing yourself from an unhealthy relationship or job situation, or pledging to take better care of yourself.

As you work actively with your nightmares and other scary sleep experiences, you'll find that your sleeper/dreamer type changes; in fact, your entire dream life may change. You may no longer consider yourself an agitated sleeper or an insomniac, and the term *nightmare sufferer* may no longer fit once you have released the worst of your fears and reached a new understanding that your nightmares are gifts that come to help and heal you. It's worth revisiting the Nightmare Quiz every now and then to check in with your current status, notice any changes, and see if your Unique Nightmare Solution Programme needs to be revised. It's generally a good idea to switch regularly between different practices, just to keep things fresh as you discover what works best for you.

In appendix I, there is a blank programme template that you can fill out. Appendix II has three example Unique Nightmare Solution Programmes for common combinations of sleeper/dreamer types to give you an idea of how it works. The following practice gives steps for creating your own programme.

practice 27

HOW TO CREATE YOUR OWN UNIQUE
NIGHTMARE SOLUTION PROGRAMME

A tailor-made programme is a wonderful thing, as it will resonate with you mentally, physically, and emotionally, reflecting your unique cognitive style, your personal sleeper/dreamer type, and your deepest needs.

1. Take the Nightmare Quiz, giving it your full care and attention—everything else rests upon you doing this thoroughly!

2. Here is the list of the fifteen different sleeper/dreamer types: the nightmare sufferer, the traumatised dreamer, the agitated sleeper, the insomniac, the lucid dreamer, the anxious or depressed dreamer, the visual and imaginative thinker, the mythical dreamer, the child prodigy dreamer, the health-challenged sleeper, the psi dreamer, the out-of-body traveller, the lucid void visitor, the sleep paralysis explorer, and the spiritual dreamer.

3. Read the list and pick the types you identify with the most. You'll end up with your own unique combination, for example, "lucid void visitor, child prodigy dreamer, anxious dreamer." If you fall into a large number of categories, try to whittle them down to three or four.

4. Check out the Nightmare Solution Programmes in this chapter that correspond with the sleeper/dreamer categories you most identify with. Note the techniques that especially appeal to you, using your intuition to choose.

5. If many techniques appeal to you, you'll need to whittle these down too, so that you have a tighter focus. You can save the others for future use!

6. Use the template in appendix I to fill out a personal programme for yourself. Decide on the duration—how long do you want to use these practices for, to give them a decent chance of changing your dream life? If you get stuck creating your programme, look at the three example programmes in appendix II for inspiration.

7. Begin your Unique Nightmare Solution Programme tonight! Good luck.

In this chapter, we've tackled a cornerstone practice of the book by doing the Nightmare Quiz to assess what type of sleeper and dreamer we are. This raises awareness of ourselves as individuals with our own way of dreaming and our own specific challenges when it comes to scary sleep experiences. We've seen how to create a Unique Nightmare Solution Programme for ourselves to fast-track us to the practices that are most likely to be beneficial to us in our current sleep situation.

Now comes the exciting work of implementing the best nightmare solutions for us so that we begin to see some real change in our dreams. The second half of the book provides further healing and transformative practices as we dive into the major nightmare types, starting with recurring and traumatic nightmares.

CHAPTER 6

Healing from Recurring and Traumatic Nightmares

Nightmares can be prickly bedfellows. It can feel deeply unfair when they keep bothering us! There we are, valiantly trying to get through life ignoring our wounds and sadness, and what happens? Our nightmares rear up while we sleep and bellow at us again and again until we receive their message, which is generally along the lines of, "Healing is needed!" or "Change is needed!" or "This is how you *really* feel!" With wicked visual detail, charged emotions, and astonishingly apt metaphors, our nightmares create this wild theatre to show us how much they care. On a mission to help us become whole, they shine a spotlight to show us where healing or transformation is needed.

However, despite their good intentions, nightmares can wreak havoc on our lives. Nothing destroys a peaceful night of sleep as effectively as a bone-chilling nightmare. In the case of recurring nightmares, it can feel as though we are being repeatedly kicked in the teeth or being punished for something we don't understand. People write to me saying, "Each time I go to sleep, I feel myself falling into my recurring nightmare, so I force myself awake. This happens again and again. I am exhausted." Or they write, "How can I stop this nightmare that's been haunting me for twenty years?" or "I am too frightened to go to sleep, so my sleep quality is terrible and I wake up depressed and anxious." At this level of interference, nightmares are not doing us any good because we have reached such a state of fear and exhaustion that our health, mental state, relationships, and job may be severely compromised. We are more likely to develop chronic health issues when our sleep quality is eroded, and become emotionally unstable, as well as more vulnerable to anxiety and depression.

Sleep is a wonder. It is an elixir of health. While we sleep and dream, our bodies carry out a wealth of restorative activities, including cellular regeneration and the regulation of blood pressure, the endocrine and circulatory systems, and more. Memory consolidation takes place during sleep, and sleeping well increases our social intelligence and emotional empathy.[22] The immune system is strengthened during sleep. Dreaming takes place during sleep, and when we dream, we process experiences, incorporate new skills, create solutions to problems, release strong emotions, and bring healing to the psyche. Healing is one of the main functions of sleep. Studies indicate that getting adequate sleep could help us reduce depression[23] and suicidal tendencies.[24]

Anything that regularly prevents us from getting a good night's sleep is a threat to our health and wellbeing. Yes, there will occasionally be times in life when we have to get through a period of inadequate sleep, such as that magical and exhausting time when we welcome a newborn baby into our lives, but factors such as stress and worry can cause long-term insomnia by stopping us from falling asleep and waking us up in the night. So can recurring nightmares. If nightmares regularly disturb our sleep, they need to be worked with for resolution and healing so that they no longer "need" to visit us to flag up our festering wounds and unresolved issues. I cannot overstate the importance of a good night's sleep for health, vitality, and living an empowered life. Practice 5: Create a Soothing Bedtime Ritual gives tips on how to welcome the healing power of sleep into your life. Now we'll explore how to work directly with recurring nightmares for healing transformation so that we become empowered and more joyful both in the dreamworld and in waking life.

---

22. Guadagni et al., "The Effects of Sleep Deprivation on Emotional Empathy."
23. Hayley et al., "The Relationships Between Insomnia, Sleep Apnoea, and Depression."
24. Bernert et al., "Association of Poor Subjective Sleep Quality with Risk for Death by Suicide."

What Are Recurring Nightmares
and Why Do We Have Them?

A recurring nightmare is a distressing dream that returns again and again. Some recurring nightmares return only during times of stress, or they happen in a short burst around a triggering event but then stop of their own accord. Other nightmares return again and again over an entire lifetime! Sometimes a nightmare repeats in exact detail, like watching the same movie a second time (and a third, and a fourth...), but often there are slight deviations within the dream story: "I had the 'monster in the attic' dream again last night, only this time the monster wasn't hiding behind the curtain; it jumped out of the closet!" There are also recurring nightmare themes, such as "hiding from danger," "falling to certain death," "intruder in my home," and so on.

A recurring nightmare indicates that we have an unresolved issue, an ongoing challenging situation, or a moment in our past when we didn't have the inner resources we needed to get us through it without fear, shame, stress, embarrassment, or pain. In the case of recurring nightmares rooted in traumatic past events, part of us remains "stuck" at a particular moment in our life and our nightmares revisit that moment to flag it up, so that we can actively find resolution and move into a happier, more peaceful way of living. Recurring nightmares can range from the well-known "stress" ones, such as missing a train or sitting an exam and realising we know none of the answers, to nightmares rooted in specific personal trauma, such as the war veteran who repeatedly dreams of being wounded or killed in combat.

When we look closely at how the brain works, we see that recurring nightmares are also learned behaviours.[25] Like a broken record, the brain slips into a groove it recognises, and the nightmare story or theme replays multiple times, sometimes for years on end. The good news is we can change learned behaviours. We can change the nightmare story so that the brain slips into a different groove. In this chapter, we'll look at the power of changing the nightmare story, and I'll share different practices for working with any recurring nightmare, as well as dedicated practices for people suffering from post-traumatic stress disorder (PTSD).

---

25. Krakow, *Turning Nightmares into Dreams.*

Let's look at an example of a recurring nightmare to see how the dreaming mind translates feelings of deep unease and dread into visual imagery. In this nightmare, the storyline is attached to a well-known horror story by Stephen King. One lady who responded to my call for nightmares for this book, Kris, shared this recurring nightmare with me. It occurred at a time when her husband had been diagnosed with a mental illness.

I am so utterly horrified by the realization that we have purchased a home that has the history of the murdered twin girls from the movie *The Shining*. I know we need to list this house for sale as soon as possible, but I don't believe it will sell because it will be discovered that there has been this awful murder in the home and no one will want to purchase it. We'll just be stuck living here!

In my mind's eye, I can see where there would have been blood splatter on the walls. Now it is cleaned up, but the psychic imprint of the blood and the murder remains. I feel horrified to think of these twin girls being axe-murdered by their crazy father. I must keep this a secret from my guests, so as not to terrify them. I wonder if I can just stay away from this part of the house? It feels there is so much evil in that room, and like I will never be able to escape living here.

Kris comments:

I had this dream in so many different ways and formats. It's always pretty much the same in that there is a room that just absolutely terrifies me where these girls have been murdered. Sometimes the twins themselves morph into something evil! Sometimes they appear as skeletons, very scary ones, with creepy grins, and in one version of the nightmare, one was wielding a butcher's knife. She was stabbing at her twin's pelvis bone. Both had the biggest, most evil skeletal grins! Interestingly enough, after my husband and I got divorced, the dream became less and less and I finally quit dreaming it all together. The reason we got divorced was he became very ill with mental illness. He chose not to medicate. I find it interesting that the main character who was the axe murderer in the movie also lost his mind and was mentally ill. Was this the reason I was having this dream?

The dreaming mind is incredibly gifted at finding parallels for our personal situation in movies, mythology, art, fiction, historical and current events, and the situations of friends, family, or the famous. A recurring nightmare may fixate on a particular story to tell us that we are in fact living a similar story. This can be baffling at first ("Why do I keep dreaming about Stalin/ the Minotaur/my friends Sue and Bob?"), which is why it's helpful to unwrap the nightmare to discover our associations with it and its symbolic meaning, as shown in the practices in chapter 2. Keeping a nightmare journal is also essential, because it helps us to identify recurring themes and pinpoint when a particular nightmare recurs, so that we can begin to connect the dots: "Aha! I get the haunted house nightmare whenever my mother-in-law visits!"

Nightmares are working for us, not against us. They create their gruesome creative theatre so that we can engage with our wounds for empowerment and greater happiness. When we work with a recurring nightmare, we will usually be able to identify not only the issue it refers to but also how we can take action in our lives to begin the healing process. In Kris's case, the dream was highlighting that there was something horrifying happening within her home life, and emphasised her awful feeling that "I will never be able to escape living here." In the end, by divorcing her husband, she took steps to "escape," and the nightmares ceased after that.

Sometimes nightmares do more than flag up something that we need to face: they reflect our process of empowerment as we move through a difficult situation, as seen in the following example.

Nasty Companions:
Nightmares That Personify Shame and Abuse

Nightmares change to reflect our inner changes, and when we keep a dream journal, it's easy to track recurring themes and observe ourselves reflected in a symbolic mirror. Sometimes we encounter dream figures who personify feelings of worthlessness or shame that we have internalised at a young age. Such nightmares may feel abusive themselves, but it's valuable to remember that all nightmares come to help and heal us, and the reason such nightmares occur is to flag up the fact that we have not yet liberated ourselves from this internalised shame. This is a call to action from our soul, and our opportunity to do some healing work.

Another woman who generously shared her nightmares with me and described how they fit with her brave life story is Delia, who hopes her experiences will help others. She had just left her ex and was in the process of disengaging from his cycles of abusive behaviour when she had a series of nightmares whose recurring theme was that of being pursued by killers. In her brave and resourceful reaction to the nasty man in the following nightmare, we see a shift from fear to empowerment. Though at the beginning the dreamer only pretends to appear strong, she actually becomes strong and speaks a powerful truth. Subsequent dreams continued this trend. Delia remarks, "More dreams around this period involve me successfully and adeptly outsmarting and evading these relentless killers or acting defiantly in response to malicious verbal attacks."

> Sitting with my ex at a café. A few tables away sits a hideously ugly, badly dressed, terribly out-of-shape man with a nasty and hateful attitude. He hurls insults and expletives at us. This man is mentally unstable and quite dangerous. He comes over and sits at our table; now my ex is gone and it's just him and me. Now that he's so close up, I can clearly see how revoltingly ugly and unkempt he is.
>
> With this closer view, disgust and repulsion begin to equal my fear of him. He continues talking in the most unnerving manner about having the power to kill, and I become even more afraid. Nonetheless, I offer responses in an effort to appear strong and unshaken, acting defiant and making it all up as I go along. Although I start out pretending, as I continue this act, I begin to actually find reason and truth in my words—I'm quite surprised at myself! One thing I say to him is, "Having the power to kill and choosing not to is far more powerful."

Delia felt that these nightmares in which she acted with power helped her to release long-held trauma stemming from childhood abuse. In particular, she was empowered to release the overwhelming sense of being unsafe and doomed that had been showing up for years in various guises in her nightmares as a relentless attacker who would inevitably track her down. She explains:

As I increasingly rejected the abuse, along with the long-standing internalised shame and sense of worthlessness, my dreams increasingly depicted these attackers as ugly and pitiful, inciting repulsion to snap me out of unwitting acceptance. Attackers in the dreams of this era usually heaped verbal abuse on me, as if I were facing a personified manifestation of internalised shame. Having the chance to see such an intangible aspect, one that thrives by lurking in the shadows, I saw it for what it was: this nasty companion that had been trailing me all along.

Dreams and nightmares act like emotional, psychological, and spiritual barometers, providing us with a reading of how we're coping and where we are in life. The nasty companions created by Delia's dreaming mind enabled her to see clearly what she needed to release in order to move into a more joyful life, and they enabled her to practise standing up for herself and refusing to accept abuse. Delia comments:

> The more I tried to rebuild my life, the more encouraging and reflective my dreams were of this. The more of these dreams I had, the more empowered and guided I felt to continue.

When we know how to use dreamwork tools, we can receive gifts of insight, healing, and action steps from our nightmares at a far earlier stage in the proceedings. Dreamwork can support us through the worst of life events and bring us healing gifts. Many years of teaching transformative dream workshops has taught me that when we work with nightmares in a self-induced waking trance, we open the gateway to our unconscious and can work with it to co-create something new. This might be a new perspective on our relationships, a new creative concept, or a new stream of healing imagery. Let's look at how three of my core Lucid Dreamplay techniques can help resolve recurring nightmares.

Resolve Recurring Bad Dreams with the Lucid Imaging Nightmare Solution (LINS)

Dreamwork can help us speed up the process of resolution and empowerment, because when we work actively with a nightmare, we enable profound transformation. A joyful woman I know, Cornelia from Austria, recounts how she resolved a recurring nightmare in one of my workshops. This is her nightmare:

> I had recurring nightmares about an extremely aggressive infant. It used to jump out of a lying position right into my face, like a kamikaze warrior, while I just stood there with staring eyes, not able to move.

Here is Cornelia's report of how she changed the nightmare story through the Lucid Imaging Nightmare Solution. The basic steps are feeling safe and secure, reentering the nightmare at or just before the tipping point when things get unpleasant, then interacting consciously and intuitively with the nightmare with an intent to heal or learn something.

> I visualise the zombie baby lying in a dark room on a glass table. It jumps towards me, but this time I'm ready to catch it like a fireball. "Let's switch roles," I say, and feel the baby's energy streaming into my body. This energy shift is accompanied by flashes and the arising of a green vortex spinning faster and faster around us. After the energy transfer, I feel strong and ready to fight, not against but *for* the baby. I'm in the role of a protective mother now, and at the same time I'm the baby, not aggressive anymore but peaceful and secure in the arms of a parent. We are a unity, a rearranged inner team. The dream scenery has changed as well: The room is lighter now due to several glass doors in front of us. I know exactly which door I want to open.

Notice how the entire dreamscape lightened in response to this integrative dreamwork. When we reenter our dreams with lucid awareness, we change the energy of the dream! We reclaim this powerful energy that we have somehow become separated from along the way, and when we empower ourselves in this way, we feel stronger, more resourceful, and joyful. Cornelia's face was luminous with delight as she shared her nightmare transformation with the group. She was shining like a star.

When we let our fear rule our dreams and rule our life, we become like cardboard cutouts, not daring to live fully, just going through the motions of being alive. It can be painful and difficult at first to embrace self-knowledge, but when we are brave and turn to look at the deepest part of ourselves through our dreams and nightmares, we become truly alive. We are able to tap into our own spiritual power and our deep healing potential. We find ourselves embracing life with joy!

Changing the Nightmare Story Through Lucid Writing

In a Transformative Lucidity workshop, Cornelia worked on another recurring nightmare with my Lucid Writing Technique for Nightmares (practice 24). If you're not someone who likes writing, exactly the same technique can be done in other ways, including drawing the nightmare or speaking your inner process into a recording device. Here is Cornelia's second nightmare:

> I dream repeatedly of a mountain. I want to climb up it, although it's far too late for a one-day hike. In all of these mountain dreams, I set off, but I never reach the top of the ominous mountain, which is very frustrating.

Here's Cornelia's report of how she changed the nightmare story through Lucid Writing:

> With my new, determined energy I gained from the first exercise of Clare's workshop, I write lucidly:

> It's five and there is this mountain, teasing me. I start climbing and suddenly a chairlift appears, glittering golden like the sun. The lift takes me upwards. The whole mountain is crossed by glittering threads. How could I have missed seeing this network before? I reach the mountaintop. What a peaceful and lovely place! And it only took me half an hour to get here. I notice a temple in the shade of a small garden where a few people are celebrating a party. It's getting dark and suddenly golden snow is falling onto us.

Cornelia explains:

> This dream image reminds me of a lucid dream I had some months before in which I asked for healing and found myself in a night garden in the middle of a golden snow flurry. Being connected again to my healing dream through the Lucid Writing exercise was a wonderful

experience. The golden chairlift was an important reminder that there are options for the mountains in life. It's not about starting from zero, but being aware of the resources we expand over time.

In her Lucid Writing, Cornelia spontaneously connected to a beautiful and soulful past dream. This often happens, or, alternatively, fresh healing imagery is generated. When we manage to shift from a recurring nightmare to positive imagery through dreamwork, this gives us a fantastic opportunity to go one step further and deepen the healing process by bringing this beneficial imagery into our bodies. Next, I share my practice for bringing soul dreams and healing images into the body.

practice 28
BRING SOUL DREAMS AND
HEALING IMAGERY INTO THE BODY

Please note that it's important to try this practice only with imagery that you find beautiful, positive, healing, and healthy. This is because when we consciously bring images into the body, their power and intention enters us, thrums through our blood, affects our mood, and speaks directly to our conscious and unconscious, becoming part of us in a very visceral way. Experienced dreamworkers may choose to bring nightmarish imagery into the body in order to work on clearing it, but if you're working alone without a therapist, I'd strongly advise you to stay with happy, healing images unless you really know what you're doing, as these can only be beneficial to your body, mind, and soul. This practice is geared towards the embodiment of vibrant, uplifting dream imagery and soul dreams.

A *soul dream* is a luminous dream that seems significant on a spiritual level and may feel profoundly beautiful, wise, or aware. Soul dreams often feature light in all of its forms, including glowing colours, people and animals in vibrant health, or powerful emotions such as joy and a sense of belonging. There may be incredible music in soul dreams, a sense of divine presence, or archetypal and symbolic imagery that speaks to us with great impact.

Soul dreams are not restricted to the dreams we have at night! They can appear in any state of consciousness, from active imagination to deep relaxation, and they can arise as the result of dreamwork. Any marvellous and numinous waking experience can also be used effectively for this practice: if, while walking the dog the other night, you saw a perfect full moon in a starry sky that made your heart leap with hope, you can bring this luminous vision and hopeful feeling into your body. There are no limitations. The same goes for healing imagery, which might range from the thrill of seeing a hawk flying close by while awake to finding a jewel during a nightmare reentry exercise.

1. Choose the soul dream or healing image you'd like to work with. Make sure this image carries highly positive and life-enhancing connotations and emotions for you, and therefore feels like something you would want to embody.

2. You can do this practice to music if you like, but it's not necessary. A dream of wild horses running may work well with shamanic drumming, while an image of a sparkling lake could gel with a chill-out soundtrack. I usually teach this practice in workshops with no music, and it's still very effective, so silence is good, too.

3. Stand up in the centre of a room where you have space to move around. If you have mobility issues, just sit or lie comfortably. Even the tiniest body movement, such as wiggling the fingers or shimmying the hips from side to side, can be enough to embody a dream.

4. Close your eyes and relax by breathing deeply a few times. Then summon your healing image or soul dream. Bring it into your mind's eye with vivid presence and feel its energy fill your whole head with warm light. Imagine this beautiful, alive image beginning to expand.

5. Breathe in, and allow each inward breath to pull your healing image deeper into your body, right down through your neck and into your chest, the heart space. Allow the energy of the image to gather in your heart before moving on down through your belly and sex organs and all the way down your legs to your feet. You may experience places in your body where the energy of the image flows less easily or feels blocked. Just notice this and carry on concentrating on breathing in your image. This stage of the practice can be as long or short as you need.

6. When you feel that your image is fully present in your body, it's time to start moving in any way that feels right. Walk like a leopard, wave your

arms like tree branches, spin and twirl like a butterfly … Do whatever it takes to embody your imagery. Combine your movement with sound: sing, use exclamations of wonder, hum, repeat words from the dream, smile and laugh, create an affirmation that goes with the imagery, or whatever you feel! Imagine yourself becoming the wise dream figure or the mighty stag. Become the glistening water or reexperience the sensation of fusing with golden light. If any ambiguous imagery arises, be present to it and remember that you are free to transform it. If you feel any blocks, resistance, or places in your body where it feels frozen or unyielding, dance and shake that part, or place your hands on it and send love and light.

7. Do your movements and sounds as long as you like, until you feel you have fully embodied your image. You may feel tingling sensations, emotions, and a flow of energy to particular parts of your body. You may feel empowered or liberated. When you are done, smile and thank the image for becoming part of you.

We can work with healing imagery and soul dreams at any moment by simply conjuring the image in our mind's eye and taking a deep, healing breath to embody it again. It is a super-quick act of empowerment and healing, and nobody else will know we are doing it. We can do this while waiting in line for a coffee or while having a difficult conversation with our child or our boss. It's a dream mindfulness practice that connects us with the higher part of ourselves, and it helps us to connect with the kind of energy we need more of in our life. The more we connect to soul energy, the more we will notice our lives reflecting this deep, harmonious energy—and our relationships with ourselves and others will change accordingly.

Cornelia reports on how it felt to bring her golden snowflakes from the Lucid Writing exercise into her body:

For the rest of the workshop, as we brought soul dreams into the body, I stayed with this dream image. I visualized myself investigating the glowing snow, letting the snowflakes touch my palms. The snowflakes were whirling vividly around me, covering my shoulders and my head and finally permeating the innermost layers of my being. The workshop exercises interlocked in a perfect way, and I was happy to regain a feeling/image from a former lucid dream. It brought the image back not only into my mind but also into my body. Clare encouraged me to bring the supportive dream image into my mind whenever I'm in a stressful situation. Doing so in my everyday life really helps me to cool down!

When we move from a troubling recurring nightmare to a level of transformative healing that helps us in our daily lives, we have truly mastered the ability to do effective dreamwork.

....

Traumatic Nightmares and PTSD

We lose vital energy and spiritual power when we are hampered by our past. When traumatic past events colour and define our present state of consciousness, we are bound to have a difficult time navigating life. When we listen to recurring nightmares, we allow our soul to speak to us and show us the wounds that need healing. The philosopher Rumi is often credited as saying, "The wound is the place where the Light enters you." This is true: the psychological, emotional, and spiritual wounds we incur as we go through life offer us enormous potential for growth and enlightenment. We just need to be brave and listen to what our dreams and nightmares tell us about the state of our soul. Then we can use the magical tools of dreamwork and storytelling to move through the portal of the wound into healing and light. If we can free ourselves from our past demons, we recuperate the parts of us that we lost along the way: the parts of us that remain frozen or lost or mired in terror, or the inner child who has been hiding in the wilderness for half a lifetime.

In the case of traumatic recurring nightmares, our dreaming mind is desperately shouting to us that healing or change is needed for us to become whole. It is unhealthy, both psychologically and physically, to ignore and suppress old pain and past traumas. But this doesn't mean we must relentlessly rake over the past and risk getting bogged down in old feelings of hopelessness or misery. Indeed, when we choose instead to work with the symbolic imagery of nightmares, we can effectuate healing change without directly revisiting painful experiences, as we are dealing with a metaphorical representation of that pain.

It is often easier for people to work with a traumatic *dream story* than come face-to-face with raw memories of their trauma. When we play around with the storyline and imagery of a nightmare, we feel as if we are at one remove from the characters and events, which makes us feel safer and frees us to engage with the story with greater perspective and empowerment. This enables unconscious changes that might be difficult to make when we remain on the surface and talk about past trauma while fully awake.

Transforming the nightmare story through working with our personal dream imagery is a very powerful process, because we are communicating with the deepest part of our mind in its own language: the symbolic language of dreams. In this section, we'll take a look at some effective practices for transforming the nightmare story and examples of how this has helped individuals to overcome varying degrees of trauma and alleviate post-traumatic stress disorder.

What Is PTSD?

Post-traumatic stress disorder can arise following experiences of trauma, such as suffering violence or sexual abuse, serving in combat zones, being in a car wreck, experiencing a humanitarian crisis and witnessing others suffer and die, being a slave or otherwise held captive, and other terrifying experiences where the victim is often helpless to change the course of events. The symptoms of PTSD can include flashbacks and intrusive, distressing memories of the event, high levels of anxiety and dread, emotional numbness or hopelessness, and nightmares.

Complex PTSD can arise from prolonged periods of trauma, such as sexual abuse lasting for months or years or ongoing domestic violence. Symptoms can be wide-ranging and may include feelings of hopelessness, suicidal wishes, dissociative symptoms, uncontrollable emotional outbursts, and flashbacks. Nightmares may be only a small part of complex PTSD symptoms. A single traumatic event such as a car crash can also trigger PTSD nightmares where the triggering event is relived or the emotions surrounding it reemerge.

Some PTSD nightmares are exact replicas of the traumatic event in every detail. This happens when a process called *dissociation* occurs: to protect the psyche, a traumatic memory is stored in a different part of the brain that is not usually used for this purpose, so that it is not accessible in the same way as other memories.[26] This suppressed traumatic memory can suddenly surge into consciousness in the form of a terrifying nightmare. Other PTSD nightmares mingle the original triggering event with metaphorical imagery, and still others retain the theme and emotions of the trauma but couch it in a completely different symbolic story.

An encouraging element at play in PTSD nightmares is that of *mastery*, when the dreamer becomes empowered within the nightmare, moving from the role of victim to someone who reacts by escaping the threat, facing it, acquiring magical powers or allies, or changing the course of action. Having read this far, you'll immediately understand how waking dreamwork could help with this aspect of nightmare empowerment.

Bob Hoss, director of the the DreamScience Foundation, reports on a Vietnam veteran who logged 130 post-combat nightmares into the University of California at Santa Cruz dreambank.net database over a 45-year period, and notes the pattern of mastery that emerged over time:

> During the initial three years following combat, 70% of his dreams appeared as partial replications of traumatic combat memories such as this one: *This time, it is not the popping of the tubes, but the whistling of the mortars themselves that alerts us. We run for the bunkers. … There is no roof, only a few pieces of lumber overhead; it is very, very open. The mortars begin to drop…* Throughout his 45 years of dream records, post-conflict attempts at "mastering" the threat varied from just a few of the nightmares initially to 60% over time … The mastery can involve magical powers: *Attacking soldiers find me. The first one shoots me point blank; his rifle misfires. The second aims and shoots just as the atmosphere begins to freeze. It forms a protective shield in front of me. The bullet punctures the ice, then falls to the floor.*[27]

One trauma therapy with an apparent link to dreaming was discovered in 1987, when clinical psychologist Dr. Francine Shapiro discovered an eye

26. Paul, "How Traumatic Memories Hide in the Brain, and How to Retrieve Them."
27. Hoss, in Pagel, *Parasomnia Dreaming*, 152.

movement technique called eye movement desensitization and reprocessing (EMDR). In this method, the patient is invited to recall a past trauma while engaging in specific left-right eye movements. This helps trauma sufferers process stressful memories and enables the brain to activate self-healing. Psychiatrist Bessel van der Kolk, author of *The Body Keeps the Score*, comments that "traumatized people are trapped in frozen associations: Anybody who wears a turban will try to kill me; any man who finds me attractive wants to rape me."[28] Dreaming sleep plays an important role in mood regulation and the integration of memories and experiences, and our eyes move rapidly to the left and right during REM sleep, so the EMDR method may mimic or stimulate the process of dreaming sleep.[29] Psychologist Robert Stickgold remarks, "There is now good evidence that EMDR should be able to take advantage of sleep-dependent processes, which may be blocked or ineffective in PTSD sufferers, to allow effective memory processing and trauma resolution."[30] EMDR is now one of the treatments for PTSD sanctioned by the Department of Veterans Affairs.

Another approach to PTSD nightmares is to engage with them directly while lucid dreaming.

How Lucid Dreaming Can Help with PTSD Nightmares

Visualisations and rewriting the nightmare story while awake can help with nightmares rooted in trauma. Studies show that lucid dreaming can also be effective at reducing recurring nightmares,[31] and there are some documented cases where lucid dreaming has kept PTSD nightmares at bay for long periods of time. One Vietnam veteran had suffered for thirty years from a recurring nightmare in which, while fighting the Viet Cong, his friend was killed. Clinical psychiatrist Dr. Timothy Green advised him to pick a place in the nightmare to prompt lucidity and visualise himself becoming lucid and changing the dream. The veteran soon became lucid in his nightmare. Knowing that he was free to create a new outcome, he told his fallen friend that the

---

28. Van der Kolk, *The Body Keeps the Score*, 261.

29. Greenwald, "EMDR: A New Kind of Dreamwork?"

30. Stickgold, "EMDR: A Putative Neurobiological Mechanism of Action."

31. Zadra and Pihl, "Lucid Dreaming as a Treatment for Recurring Nightmares."

war was over. His friend sat up and smiled, and together they walked off the battlefield. Over two years later, the nightmare still had not returned.[32]

The only time in my life that I've suffered from recurring trauma-induced nightmares was after finding my four-week-old baby blue-faced and stiff in her cot. She had probably suffocated on some regurgitated milk and was completely unresponsive; she seemed to be dead. Thank goodness, I managed to resuscitate her by breathing into her mouth and pumping her heart. At the hospital, my husband and I were told that after this type of incident, babies were at higher risk of it happening again. That worried me immensely. As a new mother, I was already sleep-deprived, and now whenever my baby was asleep (which was over fourteen hours a day!), I was anxious and kept checking the rise and fall of her belly in case she stopped breathing again.

I began to have traumatic nightmares of finding a baby dead in her cot and arriving too late to bring her back to life. I would scream in anguish and wake up in a panic.

I decided to recognise that I was dreaming the next time the nightmare happened. I became lucid while screaming in that nightmare. With my new, lucid gaze, I saw that the "baby" was in fact a shabby rubber doll that looked nothing like a real baby. It was like discovering that someone had played a really bad-taste joke on me. Suddenly I was furious. I grabbed the doll and shouted full force, "I refuse to have this sort of imagery in my dreams again! I am lucid, and I *know* my baby is alive!" Then I threw the doll onto the ground. It dissolved into the floorboards, and my anger and anguish dissolved along with it, to be replaced by a deep feeling of peace and radiance. I felt that I was heart to heart with my dreaming mind; I experienced a surge of love, and my whole body buzzed with rainbow yoga energy and light. It felt fantastic. I woke up with my body still buzzing.

The dead baby nightmares never returned. My anxiety levels around my baby dropped, and I felt as if shouting the words "my baby is alive!" in my dream was pure reality creation: as if, with those words, I voiced my intent and manifested her aliveness, her continued existence. Ten years on, Yasmin is a vibrant, energetic child who brings light and laughter into my life every

32. Green, "Lucid Dreaming in the Treatment of Veterans and Others with Post Traumatic Stress Disorder."

day. Becoming lucid in a trauma-induced nightmare can completely turn it around in astonishing ways and result in profound healing resolution.

Trauma can cause people to shut off from their dreams or experience terrible nightmares. Some people contact me to say they only ever seem to have terrifying dreams, never good ones. This may indicate a case where a root trauma has not yet found resolution and the unconscious is desperate to get the dreamer's attention so that it can be integrated and healed. However, nightmares are not always a part of PTSD, and dreams can provide a safe space for those healing from trauma. Trauma splits a person open, and it seems that for some, this can result in an open gateway to the world of lucid dreaming.

Bill is a PTSD sufferer and has been an incredibly frequent lucid dreamer since early childhood, so he has been lucid dreaming for over six decades. He told me he's never had a nightmare, as he is always conscious enough to know that he can change the plot, should it get too bullying, or simply wake himself up. Speaking of his rich and prolific lucid dream life, he remarks:

> I was subjected to early and intense childhood trauma, and I'm pretty sure that my dream life has long represented both an escape and a profound way of processing that trauma without reliving it directly. For me, this lucid dreamworld has literally been life-saving. And enriching beyond words. I have this unshakeable feeling trauma has actually been profoundly generative in my ability to lucid dream. PTSD often comes with surprising gifts that are so important to take into account on the road to healing. Given that PTSD so affects the spectrum of consciousness, the capacity for lucid dreaming just might be one of these gifts.

Let's look at how we can transform a post-traumatic nightmare so that instead of feeling fearful and attacked by it, we learn that we can be strong within the nightmare and engage with it in deeply healing and empowering ways.

practice 29

HOW TO TRANSFORM A POST-TRAUMATIC NIGHTMARE

The first step in this practice is incredibly important. You need to be sure that you feel completely supported, safe, and protected by your allies before reentering a traumatic nightmare. In particular, doing nightmare work when you have PTSD carries a risk of retraumatisation if it is not done with adequate care and respect. We are working here for profound healing, resolution, and insight, and preparation is needed to do this successfully. You can do this practice in the company of a trusted friend if you like, or with a therapist trained in dreamwork.

1. **Choose allies and protectors** until you feel safe about reentering this nightmare. These might include a shield or protective force field, divine light, a real-life friend, a fictional character such as Luke Skywalker, a historical figure like Boudicca the warrior queen, or a power animal, guardian angel, or religious figure. Choose an ally with the ferocity, serenity, or comic genius you feel you need to face this nightmare. Choose a magical object from mythology, fiction, or film, such as Excalibur or a Harry Potter wand. Invest yourself with a magical power such as invisibility or flight. Pick up as many of these allies and protective powers as you want. Move on to the next step only once you feel supported by and in touch with these protective energies.

2. **Set a goal.** Decide what you want to do once you enter the safe imaginal space of the dream reentry. Will you forgive your attacker? Talk to the shark who bit off your leg? Enter the locked room in the haunted house? Will you and your allies save your dream self from whatever is upsetting them in the nightmare and bring them into a space of light and freedom? Or is your goal to send love and healing energy throughout the very fabric of the nightmare and see what happens when you do this? It's your call, and there are so many options. See Practice 14: Creative Nightmare Responses for more possibilities for engaging with nightmares.

3. **Reenter the dream** using a technique such as Practice 8: Reenter the Nightmare. Be sure to feel safe and protected by your allies and magical objects, knowing that you can stop this process at any time by opening your eyes and taking a deep, steadying breath.

4. **Once in the nightmare, engage calmly with the imagery,** knowing you are completely safe and protected. You are totally free to change your initial plan of what you'd like to do in the nightmare; just go with your intuition. You might want to change the landscape of the nightmare or add light. You may feel inspired to send divine light to nasty or aggressive dream people or animals. You may ask questions and receive answers and wisdom. New symbols and new streams of imagery may arise.

5. **You might want to imagine a different, more positive outcome to your nightmare,** or this may happen spontaneously, with the imagery evolving naturally as you engage with it with calmness. If you need other help or resources beyond the allies that are already present, bring them in whenever you like, such as a firefighter to carry you from the burning building, or a golden eagle to guide you to a place of safety and nourishment. You are free to rehearse a happier or different ending to your nightmare as many times as you like, changing details if needed until this feels like a very realistic and satisfying dream.

6. **You are free to rehearse a happier or different ending to your nightmare** as many times as you like, changing details if needed until this feels like a very realistic and satisfying dream.

7. **Slowly open your eyes, breathe, and smile.** You have been on a healing journey and have taken important steps to transform your traumatic nightmare and move decisively towards health, happiness, and a peaceful night's sleep!

8. **Write down your new dream.** Make any additional changes you'd like as you write. The imagination is powerfully intuitive, and this can be an important part of the process.

9. **Decide on action to take in your waking life to honour this new dream** and empower yourself. For a nightmare where there were puddles of red blood that transformed during the dream reentry

into a carpet of yellow daffodils, the action could be wearing yellow or planting some daffodil bulbs. For a nightmare where you stood up to a past abuser with the help of a powerful elephant, you could buy a little figure of an elephant to put on your desk or a cushion cover embroidered with elephants. These small actions will remind you of the power you have to change your story and move forward into the wonderful life you deserve. Of course, the actions can also be much larger: you take the first step to moving house, or begin to hunt in earnest for a different job.

10. **Rehearse your new dream before you sleep** to embed this new, empowering story into your mind. Really focus on the visual clarity of the imagery and the positive emotions. This is an excellent way to communicate your message of healing to your dreaming mind.

11. **Keep a dream journal** and notice the changes reflected in your dream life. You may find the nightmares cease altogether, or that they become less frequent, or that their story changes so that healing elements and new imagery are incorporated into the plot. If you find that transformation seems slow, it may take more than one attempt at this nightmare reentry practice to reach the healing you need, and it can be fascinating to see what shifts during subsequent nightmare reentries. Keep a record of these changes and cheer yourself on as you continue along your path to healing.

....

The Power of Storytelling

We all have an innate story-making ability. We can open up a powerful path to healing when we reenter nightmares and respond spontaneously and intuitively to the imagery in a spirit of communication and curiosity. Practice 13: The Lucid Imaging Nightmare Solution (LINS) shows how this can be done in relaxed states of consciousness or while drifting between wake and sleep. One popular and widespread therapy for working with recurring traumatic nightmares is Imagery Rehearsal Therapy, where the nightmare story is changed, written down, and then reread and focused on every day to absorb it. Rewriting a nightmare to give it a new ending may sound simplistic, but it can be astonishingly effective. When we work directly with our personal unconscious imagery, reform it, and change its direction, it can be like changing the points so that a train is directed onto a different track: the new healing nightmare story replaces the old one.

The imagery in some nightmares is so gruesome or upsetting that it may at first seem impossible to change: "I'm cutting up a baby in a basin and trying to wash it away down the drain. It is more a foetus, really, but even when it's in bits the eyes stare at me with deadly accusation."[33] The woman who dreamed this had recently had an abortion. The dream narrative might be rewritten so that instead of cutting up the foetus, the woman holds and heals it, or asks for forgiveness, or watches in fast-forward as the baby grows up and thrives. Only the dreamer can hit on the best way to rewrite their own nightmare. The main thing is that the rewritten version should not be forced; it needs to intuitively feel right to be effective.

This rewriting is like a waking version of lucid dreaming, because you have the freedom to change your dream narrative if you want to. It's relatively easy to do this on paper, yet once it exists on the page, the changed narrative gains a certain reality and we may experience anything from relief to a profound sense of healing and completion. When we change the nightmare story, we create our own reality. This gives us power.

In the case of the foetus-in-the-basin dream, although on the conscious level the woman claimed to her therapist that she wasn't affected by having had an abortion, her nightmare suggests that on the *un*conscious level she saw herself as guilty of murder. Nightmares can flag up divisions in the psyche and signal the need to come to terms with specific events in our lives. As such, they can be useful indicators of the current state of our soul.

Incorporating the new, positive scenario into waking life by replaying it in the mind's eye can begin the process of improving our state of mind and self-image. Even nightmares without scary imagery—ones where there is simply an overriding feeling of spookiness or danger—can be remoulded by the imagination so that the unpleasant feelings are guided into new ones such as serenity or a sense of safety. When we do dreamwork, we attend to our psychological wellbeing. If we aren't paying attention to a particular area

33. Peters, *Living with Dreams*, 160.

of our life—our current relationship, our sense of dissatisfaction at work, our longing to travel—then our dreams and nightmares will reflect this lack of balance. When we work with our dreams, we gain insights into how we really feel and can address our needs as we go along.

Bad dreams can be changed spontaneously with strong effect. A participant in one of my Lucid Writing retreat sessions in Portugal was creatively blocked and having a hard time in his personal life. He worked on a recurring nightmare of a storm where he was standing on a clifftop watching helplessly as a fleet of beautiful galleons were swept in by the rough ocean and dashed to pieces on the rocks below him. As I guided the group into an exploration of their chosen dream with their eyes closed, I said, "The image might move and transform into something else, and you can let this happen." Later, the man told me that when I said this, in his mind's eye the ships rose from the water and sailed right over his head to safety. He felt that this was a huge breakthrough, both in the psychological impact of the nightmare and in its reflection of a situation in his life in which he felt helpless to act. "Things *can* change, even such terrible things!" he realised. When I saw him in another workshop six months later, he reported that his circumstances were happier, his creative block had disappeared, and his nightmare had not returned.

Today, neuroscience recognises that "the imagination can form the brain almost to the same degree as actual experience."[34] The imagination is a flexible tool of great power, and working with it in specific ways can rewire the brain, boosting our self-perception, kindling our creative thinking, and making both our dreaming and waking lives happier. Imagery Rehearsal Therapy is a wonderful nightmare therapy that sleep disorder specialist Dr. Barry Krakow developed with psychiatrist Joseph Neidhardt in the early nineties.[35] Dr. Krakow's studies with chronic nightmare sufferers have shown that rehearsing a different nightmare outcome decreases nightmare frequency.[36]

34. Klein, *The Science of Happiness*, 54.

35. Neidhardt, "The Beneficial Effects of One Treatment Session and Recording of Nightmares on Chronic Nightmare Sufferers."

36. Krakow et al., "Imagery Rehearsal Treatment for Chronic Nightmares."

practice 30

IMAGERY REHEARSAL THERAPY:
REWRITE A NIGHTMARE FOR HEALING RESOLUTION

PTSD sufferers should not attempt this practice without support in the form of a friend or therapist, as working with PTSD nightmares can cause flash-backs. This is a cognitive-behavioural imagery technique where we rewrite our nightmare in any way we wish, then spend time each day absorbing this new, altered imagery. It's like a waking version of lucid dreaming. It's also a great exercise for anyone with recurring nightmares, so even if you're not suffering from PTSD, you can benefit from this.

- If this is your first attempt, choose one of your less scary nightmares—start small and work up to the most terrifying ones.
- Change the nightmare in any way you wish. Think of this as a flexible *story* that you can change at will. There is no push to try to remove all of the distressing elements. What happens in the story is your choice. Some people choose to make up a new ending, some people want to change the entire nightmare, and others only want to change small details. It's your call. Changing the story might involve humour or fairy-tale elements and magic (the evil man changes into a harmless toad), or aggressive actions may be diffused through the transformative power of love and light. The new story might involve dialoguing with scary people or elements of the dream, or removing yourself from danger. Anything is possible—you are the creator of your new dream story! The overall goal is to gain a sense of control over the story.
- When you are happy with your new ending, mentally rehearse your new dream story every day to retrain the mind. Paint a vivid inner picture of the altered version, and link this to the confident feeling that this new version overrides any previous versions.
- Write down your dreams and pay attention to any changes.
- You can use this technique on any other recurring nightmares.

By fictionalising recurring nightmares, we gift ourselves with the ancient power of the storyteller. We might choose to rewrite our fearful dream selves into confident protagonists who can defend themselves and others, heal on all levels, and act with power. Once our new story exists on the page, it gains a certain reality. It can be surprisingly cathartic to do this simple storytelling work and feel the relief of steering our inner lives into a new, healthier direction. And what's more, we should soon experience positive changes in our dream life.

....

Changing the Nightmare While Lucid in a Dream

Lucid dreamers can change the story of a recurring nightmare while they are actually experiencing it. This can be deeply and instantly effective, because when we become lucid, we are in direct, conscious contact with the raw material of our nightmare, fully immersed in its three-dimensional, super-realistic imagery and sensations. One little girl who was bitten severely by a dog had recurring nightmares about the attack.[37] Her therapist told her about lucid dreaming and that she could change the dream. The next time the nightmare happened, she turned the aggressive dog into a hot dog...and ate it up! The nightmare never came back.

A recurring nightmare is an excellent lucidity trigger. One high school teacher I know has recurring dreams about finding himself in front of an irrepressibly unruly class. But instead of remaining in that difficult situation, these days he realises: "Hang on—I'm not as bad a teacher as this!" He then goes lucid and flies out of the window into happy adventures. For those who suffer from debilitating nightmares and rarely become lucid in their dreams, it may be possible for them to be referred to a sleep lab where dream lucidity can be triggered using transcranial stimulation[38] so that these nightmare sufferers can go ahead and change the story of the dream while lucid. Here's a practice to link lucidity to a recurring nightmare.

---

37. Green, "Lucid Dreaming in the Treatment of Veterans and Others with Post Traumatic Stress Disorder."

38. Voss et al., "Induction of Self Awareness in Dreams through Frontal Low Current Stimulation of Gamma Activity."

practice 31

LUCID DREAMING TO
TRANSFORM A RECURRING NIGHTMARE

Determination is a powerful force. If we feel truly determined to change our dream life for the better, reduce our nightmare frequency and intensity, and experience a restful night's sleep so that we wake up glowing with life, then we have a high chance of succeeding! This simple practice shows the steps to take.

1. **Focus your intention to become lucid** the next time you have this recurring nightmare. Feel determined about changing the story of your recurring nightmare.

2. **Visualise yourself successfully navigating the nightmare while lucid.** Pick the recurring nightmare you want to work with, and mentally reenter it, knowing you are safe and can stop this process at any time. Now imagine that you are in fact lucid in this nightmare! This comes with a feeling of relief and empowerment—you know that you can act with power in total safety to change the story of this dream in any way you wish. Vividly imagine changing the dream so it has the ending of your choice.

3. **Set a rock-solid intention to recognise that you are dreaming** the next time you have this nightmare. Remind yourself of this frequently, and feel the excitement of knowing that it will happen soon and that you will then be free of your recurring nightmare.

You can also return to Practice 4: Top Ten Tips for Getting Lucid in Your Dreams and Nightmares, and it's good to read up on this subject if you're keen to become an adept lucid dreamer. *The Art of Lucid Dreaming* has a lucidity quiz to fast-track you to the most effective lucid dream induction practices for you personally.

To close this chapter, let's look at the power of forgiveness and the importance of releasing heavy emotions and past traumas so that we can create a freer life for ourselves.

practice 32

FORGIVE AND RELEASE

In life, it's wise to release our heaviest emotional baggage as we go along, or we'll end up bogged down with it, hindering our every step. Have you ever dreamed of lugging around huge bags, rushing for a flight or a train, and trying to heave all your stuff with you? Such dreams can turn into nightmares where we have to make a choice: "If I keep dragging this baggage with me, I'll never make my flight! And my whole family is waiting for me on the plane! Should I just dump my baggage and go?" The answer is yes! Nothing material matters as much as human relationships, and although we're super attached to our baggage and don't want to lose it, just imagine the feeling of freedom when we get on that dream flight with our loved ones and soar into new adventures.

Baggage can be made of many things, including imagined slights, past hurts, or big, festering wounds. One of the heaviest bags is guilt. Another is resentment. Yet another is regret. Blame is a pretty hefty one to lug around, too. There are as many bags as we create. We don't know how cumbersome they've become until we release them and feel light again for the first time in years. The key to releasing these old emotions is forgiveness: forgiveness of others and, just as importantly, self-forgiveness. When we work closely with our nightmares, plenty of old emotions can come up. Dreamwork can be an excellent way of releasing them, but it's always good to throw in a little extra forgiveness, especially if we have been wronged or abused in the past. Here are two practices to ease some of your emotional baggage and regrets and open your heart to love.

- My forgive-love-release technique first appeared in my book *Dream Therapy*. Here is what you do. Close your eyes, relax, and picture the person you want to forgive. If this person triggers strong negative emotions in you, picture them as a child or baby instead. Say, "I forgive you, X, for causing me pain." Really mean it. Then say, "I send you love, X," and visualise warm golden light encompassing them. Then say, "I release my pain." Breathe out your pain and visualise it leaving your body in a dark mist. Then breathe in light. Do this several times. If at any point you feel resentment rise against the person you want to forgive, begin this practice from the start again. At the end, take a moment to say, "I forgive myself," and list all the things you forgive yourself for. Finally, say, "I love myself." Mean it from the bottom of your heart.

- You may have heard of the simple yet powerful Hawaiian forgiveness practice known as *Ho'opono'pono*. This practice comes from the idea that whatever is happening outside in the physical world also has its roots within individuals—we are all one consciousness, so we can change what's going on around us by changing ourselves from within. Forgiveness creates harmony within us, and this has a healing effect on the physical world. At the heart of Ho'opono'pono is a mantra to repeat over and over in a heartfelt way: "I'm sorry. Please forgive me. Thank you. I love you."

In this chapter, we have explored recurring nightmares: what they are, why they happen, what we can learn from them, and how to transform them. We've considered the importance of feeling safe when doing nightmare work, and how wonderful it is to be supported by allies and magical objects. We've investigated the power of storytelling in nightmare transformation, and looked at how to work with nightmares caused by post-traumatic stress disorder. We've seen how to use recurring nightmares as effective lucidity triggers, and change the nightmare story from within the dream.

When we illuminate nightmares with calm, conscious attention and feel empowered to work with them, we can liberate ourselves from fear and achieve true transformation. The next chapter looks at the art of transforming fear in what can be a deeply troubling state: that of sleep paralysis.

CHAPTER 7

sleep paralysis and the Art of transforming fear

Sleep paralysis is the sensation of being fully aware but unable to move. It is often accompanied by frightening imagery and bizarre sensory impressions, and tends to occur during sleep transitions, such as falling asleep or waking up. Some people get a choking sensation or feel they are suffocating. Some feel weightless, while others feel pinned down and stuck. Some only experience partial paralysis while scary imagery continues—this leads to that sluggish feeling of running through quicksand, fuelled by terror but unable to flee a dream attacker because your legs won't react. Still others experience a sense of presence, as if there is a malevolent supernatural being in their bedroom or even crouching on their chest. Myths and assumptions about sleep paralysis abound. In the past, it was widely assumed that dreamers were experiencing supernatural attacks.

The common sleep paralysis experience of weight on the chest and accompanying visions of monkeylike beings led to ideas of visitations by an *incubus*: a male demon who has sex with women while they sleep. The female counterpart is a *succubus*. You may be familiar with the famous painting of Henry Fuseli, *The Nightmare*, which depicts an incubus squatting on the chest of a sleeping woman. The term *Hag* has also been commonly used in relation to sleep paralysis. The journal *Sleep Medicine* reported a study of 185 people with sleep paralysis, where over 57 percent of them sensed a presence in their bedroom during an episode. More than 21 percent actually saw a figure in their room.[39] The following sleep paralysis account was shared with me by Kris, and reading it helps to understand why people often attribute such horrifying experiences to demons.

> I'm lying in bed. I feel like I am wide awake but I am totally paralyzed from head to toe. I am quite alarmed to see a hideous creature sitting right on top of my chest looking into my face. It is smallish and brown and evil looking. Not human, but its body resembles a human body. It's all withered and wrinkly. It sort of resembles that creature in the movie about the coveted magical ring that everyone wanted to possess. I'm quite alarmed that I cannot move a muscle, so much so that I break out into a sweat. I am sure that this presence is quite evil. Up to this point in my life, I did not believe in demons but surely there is a demon sitting on me right this moment! I feel sure of that!

Imagine waking up from this experience and having everyone you tell shake their heads in dismay and say, "Oh, yes—you're definitely being attacked by demons." This supernatural explanation would exacerbate the situation by causing the dreamer to feel badly frightened of falling asleep. Often, the more sleep-deprived we are, the easier it is to enter sleep paralysis. It would therefore be unsurprising to learn that the frequency and fear factor of sleep paralysis would increase after telling someone they are being hounded by actual supernatural, demonic forces. Seems to me a great way to turn someone into a nervous wreck!

My colleague from the International Association for the Study of Dreams, Dr. Michelle Carr, has conducted research at the Dream and Nightmare Laboratory in Montreal. I asked her for her view on the physical and psychological factors that can influence what we feel and see during sleep paralysis. This was her response:

> The physical factors are real sensory experiences: the feeling of paralysis or pressure is caused by the muscle atonia of REM sleep, but there are psychological factors that can affect one's interpretation of sleep

---

39. Sharpless and Klikova, "Clinical Features of Isolated Sleep Paralysis."

paralysis. For instance, cultural and religious beliefs can shape the hallucinations that form in sleep paralysis. Someone with a Christian background might perceive the devil or demons threatening them; someone with a more occult background might hallucinate witches. So the hallucination is taking a form based on our beliefs. Our mind is trying to make sense of the physical experience: What could be holding me down, keeping me from moving my body or waking up? And our psychological beliefs project the answer: the devil, a witch, an alien.

Historically, people risked being denounced as a witch if they dared speak of their bizarre sleep paralysis encounters or out-of-body experiences. As someone who has had thousands of lucid dream adventures and many hundreds of out-of-body experiences and sleep paralysis episodes, I would have probably been dragged off and drowned or burned at the stake (if they had managed to catch me—I'm pretty fast on a broomstick!). I look back at that dark and ignorant time in history and shudder to think of all the innocent women and men who were slaughtered for having a conscious dream life. The worrying thing is that even today there is still a massive and widespread lack of understanding about what sleep paralysis is, why it occurs, and how to handle it. Just recently, a young French woman asked for mentoring sessions with me to help transform her terrifying nighttime experiences. When I heard about her route through the medical and religious communities, I was shocked and disheartened.

She told me that she had discussed her debilitating and extremely frightening sleep experiences with various medical doctors in France, none of whom gave her a correct diagnosis. Instead, she was plied with antidepressants. She even had a session with a neuropsychologist who told her she was suffering from anxiety attacks and prescribed anti-anxiety medicine. The medications would suppress her scary sleep episodes for a few weeks, but then they would return with a vengeance and rock her world again. Since the young woman's family was religious, she spoke to an elder about her experiences, and he told her she was possessed by an evil spirit. He then recommended an exorcist. She duly paid to free herself of this "evil spirit," but this did not have any effect. After *years* of misdiagnoses, the young woman finally worked out with the help of a search engine and online forums that she was in fact suffering from severe sleep paralysis!

I wonder how hard it can be to alert doctors all around the world to these fairly common nocturnal experiences? After all, millions of people suffer from sleep paralysis and other sleep disturbances.[40] A 2011 review of sleep paralysis revealed that 7.6 percent of the general population and over 28 percent of students will experience it at least once, with higher levels among people with post-traumatic or panic disorder, and psychiatric patients.[41] Sleep paralysis is also a common symptom of narcolepsy, a condition where people experience excessive sleepiness and may involuntarily fall asleep several times a day.

The other issue is the lack of widespread, effective treatments for sleep paralysis. The link between sleep paralysis and the paranormal, ghosts, demons, and general spookiness undoubtedly delayed the availability of literature that would actually offer helpful practical solutions to sleep paralysis sufferers. In this chapter, I hope to redress the balance in my own small way by offering my best practical techniques for moving from fear to empowerment during scary sleep experiences, creating a new sleep paralysis story, as well as tips on everything from insomnia (sleeplessness) to hypnopompia (imagery that arises as we awaken and may linger in the bedroom even after we open our eyes). First, let's look at the physiology of sleep paralysis and why it occurs.

Why Does Sleep Paralysis Occur?

We all go through sleep paralysis every night. You might be thinking, "What? I've never had it!" But the fact is, as we fall asleep, our body relaxes and is less responsive to physical signals sent by our brain, and we all enter a state of muscle paralysis during rapid eye movement sleep. It's just that most of us simply lose awareness early on in this process and remain largely unaware throughout the night, so we don't notice that we can't move our muscles. An

---

40. Schenck, *Paradox Lost: Midnight in the Battleground of Sleep and Dreams.*
41. Sharpless and Barber, "Lifetime Prevalence Rates of Sleep Paralysis."

experience of sleep paralysis occurs simply *because we remain consciously aware* in a state in which we are normally unconscious.

Every night, we transition multiple times from our physical body into our dream body and back again, because we experience mini-awakenings during our night of sleep. Usually we are unaware of this process, but in sleep paralysis, we feel it. It's a weird feeling: we have separated from the physical body in the sense of not having the bodily control we have when fully awake, and we often experience dreamlike imagery, but we haven't yet entered our light, flexible dream body. We are in a sort of transitional limbo, and trying to force ourselves fully into the physical body so we can move again can be super hard, especially if we're panicking.

Muscle paralysis is a necessary protection for dreamers so that when we're playing a game of football in a dream, we don't kick our bed partner to pieces or flail and shriek when a sea monster attacks us. Yes, some nightmares do involve flailing and screaming when we are in such a panic that we rise closer to the waking state and bust through the protective muscle paralysis, but for the most part, we remain relatively still.

Terrible things can happen if the muscle paralysis is completely lifted during sleep, as is the case with REM sleep behaviour disorder, where sufferers physically enact a dream and end up hurting themselves or others. They might dream they have to escape from a fire and then actually leap out of their own bedroom window while asleep, only to wake up to incredible pain, broken bones, or worse. Others have dreamed of attacking an intruder, then woken up to discover to their horror that they have actually attacked their wife or child. People have killed others during REM sleep behaviour disorder episodes.

So we can feel thankful for our muscle paralysis! Even when we're stuck in sleep paralysis, it's nice to remember how clever our body is for creating this safety lock on our limbs so that we don't get hurt or harm others. That way, instead of seeing the paralysis as the enemy and struggling against it (which rarely has the desired effect of freeing us instantly from its grip), we appreciate it and understand its purpose. This alone can help us release excess fear. It's also helpful to be aware of the different sleep stages and what happens in each one. The more information we gather about sleep paralysis and the nature of sleep, the more able we become to keep an open, curious mind when experiencing strangeness in the night.

We pass through four stages of sleep every night in a series of recurring cycles that take around ninety minutes each. In stage one, which lasts around 5–10 minutes, we are in a drowsy state with alpha brain waves. This stage is easily interrupted and we may suddenly jerk awake (the hypnic jerk) as our bodies transition from wake to sleep. Hypnagogic imagery (which can include auditory hallucinations and other sensations) is present in this stage. Stage two is slightly deeper, a non-REM stage from which it is harder to awaken, with an overall theta rhythm of brain waves. In stage three, we enter deep, restorative non-REM sleep. It's hard to rouse someone from this third stage of sleep, and slow delta brain waves are present. Sleep terrors and sleep-walking can occur.

In stage four, we experience rapid eye movement (REM) sleep. Our bodies go into muscle paralysis to keep us from physically acting out our dreams, and this safety net of physical paralysis is what we experience when we feel pinned down and unable to move during sleep paralysis. In this sleep stage, there is increased heart rate, rapid eye movements (hence the name), genital arousal, and highly active brain waves similar to those observed when awake. Vivid and bizarre dreams are very common in this stage. Over the course of a night, the deeper sleep stages grow shorter, while the REM cycles grow longer, so we tend to have a long burst of vivid dreams right before we wake up in the morning.

The other thing to know is that whenever we awaken from sleep, we may experience hypnopompic imagery. This is similar to the surreal imagery we see in the pre-sleep hypnagogic state, only sometimes it has a curious tendency to hang around in midair even once we feel fully awake and have opened our eyes! People have reported seeing the strangest things present in their bedroom, from animals to shadowy strangers, and this can also be linked to sleep paralysis experiences. Anne, a lady from England, reports:

> One night I awoke to find a very bright lime green rugby ball–shaped toy puppet with a pointy head and little black eyes, which was moving up and down, up and down, at the side of the bed. Another night,

turning over in bed, I found a man kneeling in the middle of the bed staring down at me. In the past, I have awoken to hear curtains being drawn or the doorbell ringing. I have seen posies of flowers floating in the air many times. Everything I have told you here is perfectly true, without exaggeration. However, reading all this, I hope you won't think me a nutcase who needs certifying!

Both hypnagogia and hypnopompia can include sounds and sensations as well as visuals. It's good to be aware of all of the many weird things that can happen during a night of sleep so that we don't feel quite so odd when it happens to us, and also because when we know about the possibilities, we may not feel so terrified if we experience them in sleep paralysis.

As I mentioned earlier, in sleep paralysis there seems to be an overlap between some features of REM sleep and the waking state. Instead of our brain and our body falling asleep (and waking up) simultaneously, so that we don't even notice the transition into and out of sleep, our brain remains awake and aware. We are therefore conscious during a process in which we normally lose conscious awareness. We experience the strange sensory transitions of falling asleep (or waking up) along with the muscle paralysis and bizarre imagery associated with REM sleep.

This awareness is actually a gift!

Yes, you get to experience a lot of weird and sometimes frightening stuff in this state, but you are effortlessly lucid. Think of all the lucid wannabees who spend hours reading books and watching videos on how to become lucid in their dreams. They even ask around for the secret to inducing sleep paralysis, as they've heard it's a gateway to lucidity, yet to their dismay, they fall deeply and unconsciously asleep every night. And then look at all the people on the other side of the spectrum who are naturally lucid in sleep paralysis … and both sides lament their situation! I am often struck by the irony of these polar opposites, because I get people from the extreme ends of each spectrum writing to me for help. It would be fantastic to be able to give the would-be lucid dreamers a pinch of the bright, stable lucidity that people with recurring sleep paralysis have!

My firm belief is that lucidity is a wonderful gift, so when it falls into our lap in the (admittedly sometimes unpleasant) form of sleep paralysis, the best thing we can do is embrace it, leap on its back, and let it carry us into marvellous lucid dreams or out-of-body experiences. Practice 35 later in this chapter shows how to use sleep paralysis as a magical gateway into lucid dreaming. First, let's look at the all-important issue of fear: how it can escalate in dream states and how to release it in sleep paralysis episodes.

How Fear Escalates in Thought-Responsive Environments

A first step to transforming sleep paralysis is understanding the nature of dream spaces, which respond naturally and instantaneously to our thoughts, emotions, and fears. Imagine a situation where you are left in a straitjacket in a pitch-black room, with your mouth gagged. The door closes and you have no idea when you will be released. What would you do? Would you panic, try to thrash your limbs free, and try to scream through the gag, and when you find that you can't get free, would you enter a state of blind panic?

Well—that would be one choice.

Another choice would be to consciously calm yourself down, focusing on your breath and allowing this inner focus to take you into a deep, calm space.

Which of these choices is likely to lead to extreme mental and psychological stress, and which one will leave the prisoner relatively unscathed?

I know it's easier said than done to calm down when faced with a frightening situation, and some sleep paralysis experiences are truly awful, such as those where the sufferer feels they are being raped or sexually assaulted. Still, I always like to look at the response of the sleep paralysis sufferer (and indeed any nightmare sufferer) to *fear*. Looking at the nature and root of the fearful reaction often reveals a healing direction: we can educate ourselves, work on healing any root trauma, and train ourselves to change our fear response. On Stase Michaels's website interpretadream.com, I found this very clear example of the thought-responsive nature of dreams and how fear amplifies the terrifying aspects of the imagery:

> I'm in an empty white room. It is bright as if the sun is shining but there are no windows. There is a small ball in the corner, a pulsing black ball, densely packed with needles that give off static electric-

ity. I start to become afraid of it. As my fear increases, the ball grows and pulses faster. I try running but get trapped in the corner. The ball becomes huge and almost fills up the room and pulses at an incredible speed. At that moment, I realize the ball is pulsing at the same rate as my heartbeat. I start to breathe slower and as I do, the ball shrinks and makes its way back to the corner. I wake up at that point, in a cold sweat.[42]

Note how the ball grows bigger and appears menacing only when the dreamer starts to become afraid of it. And as soon as the terrified dreamer consciously regulates her breathing, the ball of fear shrinks and retreats. The way we react to situations really is a choice. It may not seem like one at first, but in fact, we do have the choice whether or not to enter a state of full-blown panic. We can train our brains to switch into "emergency calm" mode, where we swiftly put our entire mental energy into calming down in the face of frightening events.

In order for this mode to be effective, we need to practise calming techniques regularly while awake so that it becomes second nature to swing into this mode as soon as we notice that we've entered sleep paralysis again. Here are some excellent calming techniques that many people find helpful. Take your pick or invent your own, bearing in mind that what you need in sleep paralysis are visualisations or breathing techniques that require no actual physical movements beyond inflating your lungs with air, and they need to have an instant calming and protective effect on you.

practice 33

HOW TO RELEASE FEAR IN SLEEP PARALYSIS

1. **Take a deep breath.** This is the first thing to do to save your state of mind when things become scary in any state of consciousness. In sleep paralysis, you can still control your breathing apparatus and your eye movements, so this is not complete paralysis by any means. Use your freedom to breathe and relax.

---

42. https://www.interpretadream.com/liibrary-of-dreams/blank-31/.

2. **Stop struggling.** This generally only makes things worse, as it propels you into panic, and you are in a thought-responsive environment, so that will only exacerbate any fearful elements that are present. Relax! It's far easier to stay asleep than to wake up: you would have to battle through numb limbs, odd sensations, and pins and needles that can arise as you wake up.

3. **Make a conscious choice to calm down.** Remember, you can choose how to react—you can choose your attitude. This is key to moving through sleep paralysis without panicking. Feel grateful for protective muscle paralysis: at least you aren't leaping out of bed attacking furniture and endangering your relatives. Be grateful for small mercies. This really isn't the end of the world, being here in this spooky, black space, because you can transform it into anything you want! Try to view it as a space of infinite potential. Plus, you are effortlessly lucid! Many people seek lucidity—you are one of the lucky few who gets it handed to them on a plate. And remember, your body is lying safely in bed, and you don't *need* your physical body anyway—why would you, when you're asleep? All that's happening is that you are transitioning from your physical body into your dream body and got a bit stuck along the way. Just think calmly, "Aha! I'm experiencing the transition from my physical body into my dream body. How cool is that?"

4. **Bring protection into your space.** Practice 23: The Egg of Light and Other Nightmare Protections goes into detail about this. You may bring any person, god or goddess, higher power, magical object, music, shield, or force with you into sleep paralysis. Bring whatever it takes to make you feel safe simply by imagining it with you and believing in its power to protect you. And never forget that no matter how weird or frightening things can get in this state of consciousness, you will wake up safely in your bed after the experience. It's beneficial to pursue an attitude of curiosity and observation, and keep the fear at bay by imagining yourself whistling a jaunty tune or by communing with the god of your choice.

5. **Practise the Lucid Imaging Nightmare Solution.** There's no time like the present, so if you are experiencing scary imagery, think back to

the moment when you became fearful (the tipping point) and work to restore the balance. If there's a demon on your chest, have a little chat with it or blast it with healing light. Be creative—you are, in fact, in a state of infinite creativity. Practice 14: Creative Nightmare Responses reminds you of the different nightmare solutions available to you.

6. **Meditate, create, or travel into a lucid dream.** Once you feel calm and protected, you could try meditating. It's amazing to try this when you manage to stop focusing on your body and the feelings of paralysis and simply experience being bodiless. Alternatively, you could create some wonderful imagery in the space around you by vividly imagining it, or you could allow yourself to drift into a lucid dream using the techniques in Practice 35: Sleep Paralysis as a Springboard for Lucid Dreaming later in this chapter.

7. **If you want to wake up,** then once you are fully calm and still, just focus on trying to wiggle a toe or finger in a relaxed way. You can also move your eyes intentionally from left to right while deciding serenely that you will now wake up. Sometimes these small, calm movements will easily lead you back to the waking state. You can also try holding your breath to shock your body into waking.

....

There are things you can do to discourage episodes of sleep paralysis, and this may involve trial and error. The next practice looks at some things to consider so that you can modify your sleep routine.

practice 34

HOW TO DISCOURAGE SLEEP PARALYSIS EPISODES

- **Get enough sleep.** Keeping regular hours really helps your body adapt to a healthy sleep schedule.

- **Avoid alcohol and other stimulants before bed.** Eating big meals, taking drugs, or boozing before bed are triggers for sleep paralysis in some people. It's better to stop these activities around three hours before you go to sleep, and caffeine may need to be stopped much earlier or even avoided completely. Experiment to see what works best for you.

- **Avoid reading on electronic devices before bed.** Reading on lit screens stimulates the brain and can make it harder for us to switch off mentally and slide easily into sleep.
- **Meditate before bed.** Calm your mind. Free yourself from your worries and troubles, and let your to-do list evaporate. Take this time to ground yourself and create a feeling of peace to carry with you into sleep. Try Practice 6: Pre-Bed Meditation to Calm the Mind. You could also explore the healing ancient meditation practice of yoga nidra; see Practice 41: Yoga Nidra: Balance Between the Worlds. I have created a Yoga Nidra for Lucid Dreaming and Blissful Sleep video course with audio recordings of different yoga nidra journeys, some of which are specifically geared to helping sleep paralysis sufferers to release fear and summon beautiful imagery in order to enter a lucid dream.
- **Avoid sleeping on your back.** Although it's not the case for everyone, many people find that they are far more likely to experience sleep paralysis when they fall asleep on their back.
- **Signal for help during an episode.** If you have a bed partner, make sure they know about your sleep paralysis, and let them know to wake you up if they hear you groaning in the night. It's often possible to make sounds while in sleep paralysis, and some people even manage slight movements. A prolific lucid dreamer I know, Natalie from the UK, shares how she eliminated her sleep paralysis episodes for good:

> I was aware of everything but could not move my body at all. I was pinned and saw terrible visions. I would try and scream out to my boyfriend. I would try and will myself to move. After this happened many times, I managed (no idea how) to move my hand and tap my boyfriend, who was aware of my experiences. He was able to shake me and wake me up, but it took a while. I never had this again afterwards.

I'm aware that many people, especially those who wish to increase the frequency of their lucid dreams, would love to experience sleep paralysis, as they have heard that it can be a gateway to lucid dreaming. If you fall into this category, you could invert one or two elements of this practice. For example, you could stimulate your brain and body before taking a nap lying on your back, or listen to a yoga nidra visualisation to help you balance between waking and sleeping and consciously induce a sleep paralysis experience so you can use it as a tool for consciousness exploration or a springboard into lucid dreaming.

It seems noteworthy that students report a much higher level of sleep paralysis than the general population. When I was a student, I partied hard, slept erratically, didn't eat proper food, and took plenty of naps. Over a period of about one year, I had sleep paralysis pretty much every time I fell asleep! I'm certainly not recommending this unhealthy lifestyle, as a good night's sleep is immensely beneficial. I'm just pointing out that lifestyle changes can have a strong effect on our sleep and dream life, and it works both ways.

practice 35

SLEEP PARALYSIS AS A SPRINGBOARD
FOR LUCID DREAMING

Sleep paralysis can be thought of as a stable lucid state: a gift that many people hanker after. Here are some ideas of what to do during sleep paralysis to use it as a springboard into a lucid dream.

- Yoga nidra is the wonderfully relaxing practice of balancing on the cusp of sleep and observing any thoughts, imagery, or light. In sleep paralysis, your advantage is that you can float effortlessly in your dream body once you stop trying to stay in your physical body. So release your attachment to your body and the feelings of paralysis: your body is lying safely in bed and you can return to it later. Simply focus on feeling relaxed and peaceful, and observe with clarity everything that is happening. Practice 41: Yoga Nidra: Balance Between the Worlds in the next chapter gives more tips. You may experience sensations of falling, spinning, floating, or flying. There may be auditory hallucinations or vivid visions. The art of staying calm, focused, and fearless is vital if you are hoping to transform sleep paralysis into a beautiful lucid dream.

- Your physical body may be paralysed, but your dream body isn't. Try moving your light, flexible dream body. This can be a very beautiful experience. Why not do a somersault or twist through the air like a dolphin?

- Imagine your lucidity as a powerful tiger (or any other animal of your choice). Leap onto the back of your tiger and let it carry you into an amazing dream adventure. Once, while floating on the cusp of sleep, I saw a fire, and out of the flickering flames emerged a phoenix. It was easy to merge with the phoenix and fly straight up into a lucid dream with it.

- Using your imagination, create a portal to conscious dreaming: strongly visualise a blue lake, a shining mirror, or a window, then dive through it with the intention of arriving in a lucid dream.

- Create a lucid dream by visualising a fantastic, welcoming scene. Build it up element by element, and allow your creative imagination to invent anything it wants. You are in a state of consciousness where everything is possible, and your mind is a natural creator, so give it free rein. If your fantasy scene is a Caribbean island, then turn into a mermaid and swim to it, or parachute down to it, and as you arrive, you'll realise that you have managed to enter a lucid dream. Rolling into a fantasy scene in your dream body also works well, as does allowing a scene to build around you three-dimensionally.

There's a quote commonly attributed to the thirteenth-century Sufi mystic and poet Jalal ad-Din Rumi that I love: "Wherever you stand, be the soul of that place." This is what lucidity teaches us: to be fully present at every moment and to step into our spiritual power and expand our compassion for other people, animals, plants, ourselves, and our planet. When we manage to carry this soulful presence with us into a nightmare or a frightening sleep paralysis episode, we transform our experience and enable deep and lasting change.

....

Acting to Protect Ourselves in Sleep Paralysis

Women sometimes contact me to share horrifying sexual attacks or unwelcome sexual encounters they experience during sleep paralysis. These may happen regularly or be one-offs. I advise them on reducing fear and panic levels and remind them of the possible ways of asserting themselves within that state. I also give them tips on how to wake themselves up (such as holding the breath to shock the body into waking, making strong eye movements, or calmly trying to wriggle the fingers and toes). I also emphasise the value of bringing a sense of safety and protection into sleep paralysis. Let's look at the story of one woman who managed to stop recurring sexual attacks and turn the sleep paralysis experience to her own advantage.

> This was always a very frightening experience and very much a sexual thing. I could feel the weight of this entity sitting on my bed and moving around under the covers and engaging in sexual activities with me. I would lay there unable to move or react. I would desperately try to wake up, but would only partially wake, and fall straight back into the same deep scenario. It was always a large, athletic, faceless male figure. Very sensual but frightening at the same time. I decided I would fight these dreams away ... I started to yell at the entity when it appeared. I'd yell, "Get out! You are not real. Get out now!" Suddenly it would vanish. I was in control. I would manage to wake myself very violently.
>
> After doing this only a few times, this experience stopped. Since taking control of this frightening sleep paralysis, I have learned to take control of other dreams such as my flying dreams. It's truly amazing. I have actually started to take even more control of my sleep paralysis dreaming, and it is wonderful.

This lady then went on to explain that she is married but shares a mutual attraction with another man. Since she doesn't wish to be unfaithful to her husband in waking life, she instead summons this other man into her sleep paralysis: "It all feels so very real. I can see him, feel him, hear him, and converse with him. It's magical."

This shows how a recurring, terrifying sexual sleep paralysis experience can be completely transformed: first the dreamer asserts their own power within that state, then they become more adept at guiding dreams, until they reach a point where they can create their own super-real, satisfying erotic experiences within sleep paralysis.

You can invoke any protective powers you like during sleep paralysis, such as magical objects, a protective egg of light, or a powerful superhero. Some people find it helpful to invoke the name of a god or goddess. Kris, who encountered the unpleasant brown demon at the start of this chapter, explains how she got it to go away:

> The only thing I can think to do is to say the name "Jesus." I try hard, but nothing will come out of my mouth. My vocal cords are paralyzed. So I think the name really hard in my mind. It seems like I may have pushed out a little bit of weak sound from my mouth? Suddenly the thing vanishes off me. It takes a couple of very long moments for me to come out of the paralysis. I am finally able to move slowly and then fully, feeling convinced that I just had an experience with a demon, not yet understanding that this was sleep paralysis, and not a demon at all.

The next practice looks at how to feel safe and protected during frightening sleep experiences.

practice 36

INVOKE PROTECTIVE POWERS: BALL OF LIGHT

This practice first appeared in *Llewellyn's Complete Book of Lucid Dreaming*. It's based on one of my favourite energy work exercises of creating a healing energy ball, and I've adapted it so you can use it as a visualisation during sleep paralysis. It can be modified as you wish to invoke your preferred protective powers. It is specifically designed to help you in any unpleasant lucid situation, such as being "trapped" in sleep paralysis or faced with a lucid nightmare. The more often you practise creating a ball of light (this whole visualisation need take no longer than two minutes), the easier it will be to recreate it in scary liminal spaces in the sleep state. The basic practice of breathing in peace and safety can be done at any moment in your day. Once this practice becomes an automatic response, you will be much better equipped to deal with sleep paralysis experiences and stressful daytime situations too.

- Sit or lie in a comfortable position that allows your breath to flow freely. Close your eyes. Inhale deeply while mentally saying, "Peace." Exhale slowly while affirming, "I am safe." Be aware of your belly rising and falling in rhythm with your breathing. As you settle into these deep, steady breaths, continue to repeat those same words: "peace" on the inhale, "I am safe" on the exhale (or substitute with your own preferred calming words). Feel yourself growing calm and relaxed.

- Now imagine you feel something warm tingling in the palm of your hand. Looking down, you see it is a sphere of light the size of a marble. It radiates warmth, and as you focus on it, it grows larger, filling your palm so that you are holding a ball of this radiant light. As the ball continues to grow, any unpleasant emotions you may be holding, such as fear or anger, dissolve.

- Imagine holding the ball in your two hands now. Feel it expanding effortlessly. Nothing can hurt you when you are holding this ball of light. You understand that anything fearful you see or experience is directly linked to your own thoughts and expectations. You are perfectly safe. Your heart grows calm and you feel a powerful sense of love and safety as the warm energy of this ball of light moves through your body, illuminating you and everything around you.

- Everything the light touches, it heals. Notice how any imagery or sensations transform when touched by the light. Fully expect to see or feel powerful positive changes. There is so much beauty now in this space, such a feeling of wellbeing. Keep your attention on your breath as your environment responds to your calmness by creating harmonious sensations and colours. Remind yourself, "I am lucid and all is well." Creating a ball of light during sleep paralysis can also be a wonderful bridge into a lucid dream.

- It can also be beneficial to do this practice in the mornings to bring a sense of protection into your daily life. You could either do it as a visualisation while lying in bed or stand up and enact it with physical movements and gestures, with closed eyes.

- It's good to have a deep understanding of your personal experience of sleep, dreams, and sleep paralysis. The next practice is like a mini quiz, its aim being to inspire you to work out the kind of sleep paralysis story you currently have, so you can take steps to change it.

....

practice 37

CHANGE YOUR SLEEP PARALYSIS STORY

This is primarily a writing exercise, but if you don't like writing, feel free to speak your answers into a recording device. It's important to gently unwrap the story of a person with sleep paralysis to discover: Might this experience be rooted in trauma? Is it linked to stress? Is it affected by the ingestion of substances such as caffeine or marijuana? What is the habitual response of the sleep paralysis sufferer, and what are the fear levels we're looking at here? Once we have a full picture of the sleep paralysis experience, and a habitual "story" of how things usually go during an episode, we can move into a place of ownership and take action to change our sleep paralysis story in empowering ways.

- Describe your usual sleep paralysis experience: How does it normally go? How does it usually end? Write it down in as much detail as you wish.
- When did the sleep paralysis first appear, and what else was happening in your life at that time? It can be helpful to identify a triggering event. Some people find their sleep paralysis began when they got divorced or when someone they loved died. In such cases, it can really help to work therapeutically with the triggering issue to resolve the sleep paralysis.
- When does the sleep paralysis occur? Every night or multiple times a night? Or does it arise in response to a particular kind of emotional or psychological stress in your life? Does it come when you're overtired or overworked? Is it linked to periods of insomnia? Play the detective and discover your personal triggers.
- Have you ever experienced being physically or psychically attacked, sexually assaulted, or raped during sleep paralysis? Write down the worst thing that ever happened to you in this state—it can be just a sentence;

write as much as feels right. Studies show that writing down traumatic experiences can be cathartic as we liberate ourselves onto the page, a bit like sharing our troubles with a friend or therapist.[43]

- Do you drink alcohol or caffeine close to bedtime, take prescription drugs that may affect your sleep, or smoke marijuana? Jot down your pre-sleep habits and take note of any that may provoke sleep paralysis.

- Do you keep to a regular sleep cycle?

- What is your level of fear in sleep paralysis from 1–10, with 1 being perfect serenity and 10 being total terror?

- How do you normally react in sleep paralysis? (a) Relax and trust that all will be well, (b) try to will myself awake, (c) struggle, or (d) panic and enter a state of terror.

- To what extent does your sleep paralysis affect your quality of life? (a) barely at all; (b) it bothers me occasionally; (c) I regularly wake up feeling exhausted by my sleep paralysis experiences; (d) I am reluctant to go to sleep in case it happens; (e) I self-medicate with alcohol and marijuana in an attempt to avoid sleep paralysis; (f) I am terrified to sleep; or (g) sleep paralysis is currently one of the biggest problems in my life.

- If you could take any magical tool or any protective person, ability, or feeling into sleep paralysis, what would you take? What would you need to feel safe in sleep paralysis?

- Now comes the exciting, creative part: it's time to change your sleep paralysis story! Write down your ideal way of reacting in sleep paralysis. Anything is possible—you might imagine floating in a state of deep peace, entering a fabulous lucid dream, turning into a radiant ball of light, waking up quickly and calmly, or anything else. Bring in allies, magical objects, shields, or anything you like. For more ideas, see Practice 29: How to Transform a Post-Traumatic Nightmare. Writing down your ideal reaction is helpful, as you can then reread and absorb this new possibility and mentally rehearse it while awake so it comes naturally when you next find yourself in sleep paralysis.

---

43. Pennebaker, *Opening Up: The Healing Power of Expressing Emotions.*

- If you're a visual person, draw or paint your ideal sleep paralysis experience. Know that it is yours for the taking!

....

If your sleep paralysis causes you psychological stress, you may well be fearful of falling asleep. Let's take a look at another sleep disturbance that can be linked to sleep paralysis or occur independently of it: insomnia.

Insomnia

Insomnia is sleeplessness: difficulty falling asleep or the experience of long periods of wakefulness during the night. If it gets extreme, we can become permanently sleep-deprived, which can cause a decline in physical and mental health, slower reactions, and a rise in depression or anxiety levels.

Insomnia is a common problem in our fast, hardworking lives. We race around all day and somehow don't manage to switch off enough to get a restful night's sleep. Our schedule demands that we get up at a certain time, so we can't sleep when we're tired. We start to feel exhausted, and when a period of insomnia arrives in the night, it stresses us out even more because we know we need to sleep. Yet when we think about the nature of insomnia—an over-alert mind wakes in the night and can't fall back to sleep, often because of worries, relentless inner movies, or churning thoughts—it seems to me that this mindset could go very well with lucid dreaming.

In fact, I believe that lucid dreaming could become the world's most innovative and creative approach to insomnia.

After all, the insomniac has a tired body, an active mind, and plenty of time to try out lucid dream–induction techniques! During periods of insomnia, we are also close to the liminal state of sleep paralysis, which is itself a platform of stable lucidity from which we can launch ourselves into a lucid dream. Lucid dreaming doesn't have to be all about action: it can be deeply restful and refreshing to float gently on a sparkling lake or meditate on a mountaintop while lucid, and our body can sleep peacefully in bed while we do this. The trick is letting go of our busy thoughts and directing our energy into visualising gorgeous dream scenes so that we can drift gently into a lucid dream.

There are other things we can do to help insomnia, like a pre-sleep meditation to clear our thoughts (practice 6), soft lighting for a while before bed, no screens in the bedroom, no ticking clocks, and no lights of any kind on while we sleep, from glowing electrical plugs to charging phones.

A Belgian man, Carl, attended one of my lucid dreaming ocean retreats. He suffers from regular insomnia, and when I asked him what he does during his wakeful periods in the night, he said he has a fun gadget—a digital clock that projects onto his ceiling! So he lies there watching it … I couldn't help chuckling to hear this, because it strikes me as the worst thing to do if you're lying sleepless in bed! I told him this and made some suggestions. Soon afterwards, Carl wrote: "Since your retreat, I have shut off the ceiling clock, the alarm digital clock, and my cell phone. I now sleep much better, normal nights. Every dream at night is immediately recorded on my cell phone, in darkness, and my dream journal is productive again!!"

I've created a technique to resolve insomnia that I enjoy using myself if I wake up for too long in the night, which happens if I'm going through an intense stage of writing a book. It often leads me straight into a lucid dream, but even if it doesn't, I fall back to sleep relaxed and happy because I've spent my awake time focusing on beautiful things. Here it is.

practice 38

THE INSOMNIA FREEDOM TECHNIQUE

When we're lying awake at night, it's best not to look at a clock or watch at all, because this starts us off obsessing about how long we've been awake and calculating how many hours we have left until we have to get up for work, school, etc. It really amplifies the insomnia. So try to do this technique from start to finish without glancing at the time, without checking your phone, and without turning on any lights.

1. When you realise you have entered a period of insomnia, sit up in your bed in darkness and meditate. Focus fully on taking 21 deep, conscious breaths: one complete breath counts as a full inhalation followed by a full exhalation. If you lose count, start again. This 21 breaths technique

provides a simple route into meditation, even if you are not an experienced meditator.

2. If you find yourself distracted by trivial thoughts, return to breath number one and start again. Be strict about this rule!

3. After the 21 conscious breaths, continue to breathe slowly without counting, and allow imagery to flood into your mind. Give your unconscious free rein; enjoy floating between the worlds of wake and sleep. Relax more and more; let your shoulders slump if they want to. Watch every flicker of light or imagery your brain produces. Every time your mind goes to a particular problem or starts to prowl around a waking situation, framing and reframing it obsessively, take a mental step back and look casually around for imagery. Any imagery will do! You can play with this imagery, watching the way your thoughts change and shape it.

4. After a while, this practice becomes a sitting version of yoga nidra. Let there be no pressure about sleeping, no worries about your posture (it's truly fine to slump!), no concerns about whether or not you're "doing it right," and no sense of time passing. Just surf your inner imagery and relax.

5. The beautiful part comes last: when you feel truly relaxed and tired, simply let yourself sink slowly back into bed, still holding those threads of imagery. It is the most wonderful feeling to consciously let go of your body at this stage and float off into a liminal state where you are supremely relaxed. Often this leads to a wake-induced lucid dream or directly into restful sleep—but the trick is not to get anxious if it doesn't! Retaining that relaxed liminal state is so beneficial; just rest in that space. You might also choose to reenter one of your recent dreams by focusing lightly on the imagery and emotions of that dream and allowing yourself to drift into it consciously.

Carl tried the Insomnia Freedom Technique during a period of wakefulness following a dream in which his ex was asking him harshly to put his bedroom in order. He reports:

A breathtaking night this time, thanks to your advice. It was around 4 a.m., and so I tried the 21-breath technique and noticed that I could barely reach 5–6 breaths before parasitic thoughts came back. I was lying on my back, my worst position, but started seeing lights in the blackness of my closed eyes, even a vague light-face, like a guide trying to help. The light was dissipating, then coming back; however, I felt very relaxed, though uncomfortable on my back.

After a while, I decided to break the charm and move toward a position I know is good for me: left side, foetal position, and crossed arms. After strong or lucid dreams, I always awake in this position. So here, I stated mentally my intent to reenter the last dream, and started focusing on my breathing, and counting. And reenter the dream I did, in a long and enlightening lucid dream, where I said to my ex that I understood her point and agreed that the upstairs bedroom represented my thoughts, which I indeed have to make more orderly, eliminating the parasitic thoughts that create disorder at night. All in all, a beautiful lucid dream and very helpful—I am so glad!

With any technique, it's great to be flexible and adapt it to your own preferences. Here, when Carl changed positions, he entered the flow and was able to turn his insomnia into a wonderful lucid dream—and that has to be a lot more fun than staring at a ceiling clock for hours on end!

Sleep Paralysis as Spiritual Initiation and Sexual Transcendence

When I was a university student, there was one year when I experienced sleep paralysis episodes most nights, and often multiple times a night. I was highly lucid in my dreams and loving my extensive explorations of the imagery-rich lucid dreamworld, but I was flummoxed by these weird sleep paralysis experiences. I had no name for them, and nobody I spoke to seemed to know what they were. I had no books or practical advice to work with. I would repeatedly find myself unable to move my physical body, in blackness, with weird presences around me. These invisible presences would jolt me, spin me around in circles, shove me here and there. It was super annoying and also scary. At first, frightened, I would shove them away to no effect, struggle and squirm and try to shout at them to go away. Then I changed tactics. Instead of struggling and panicking, I tried defiantly ignoring them, sending out a force field of willpower around me to keep them at bay. That worked marginally better.

But it was only when I changed my attitude from one of fear and irritation to one of serenity that things really changed. While trapped in these nightly liminal spaces, I experimented with breathing deep into my belly, then releasing the breath very slowly while focusing on feeling more and more relaxed in mind and body. A couple of years later, when I travelled to India at age twenty-one and discovered yoga, I realised I had been doing a kind of yoga nidra to take me from fearful dream spaces into brightly lucid ones.

As soon as I began with the serene breathing and mind-calming technique, my sleep paralysis experiences transformed. The taunting presences vanished, the darkness lifted, and I would float in luminous spaces, experiencing blissful feelings of oneness and connection (more on this in chapter 9). Or I would zoom through infinite spaces as a speck of conscious awareness. Or I would travel directly into a glorious lucid dream. Over the course of many months, I turned from a small, struggling, helpless being into a vast, serene, light-filled being with no limits and the power of flight and transcendence. This whole process can happen a whole lot faster when we understand what sleep paralysis is and have practical techniques to draw on.

Sexual energy has always been a portal to transcendent mystical experiences. Some religions choose celibacy in order to sublimate orgasmic energy into mystical awakening, while others celebrate sexual ecstasy through sculpture, art, and conscious attempts to awaken the sexual and spiritual energy of the kundalini. Sexual energy is often present in dreams, as during REM sleep the genitals are naturally aroused. Clinical psychologist Dr. Patricia Garfield has written a wonderful book on her sexual lucid dreams called *Pathway to Ecstasy*. She describes her full-body lucid orgasms and how they become intense experiences of spiritual bliss:

> The pleasure that shudders through my body is not limited to the genital area. Like a pebble dropped into a pond, the ripples start from that spot and spread outward in great waves of bliss. During the most intense of these nocturnal orgasms, even my vision is involved. What-

ever scene is before my sleeping eyes, its color and pattern will break into parts, flash, and spin. This kind of "visual orgasm" is indicative of the totality of the response.[44]

I'd recommend Dr. Garfield's book for anyone interested in the mystical potential of sexual energy in dreams. Yet some sexual sleep paralysis experiences can feel highly traumatic. Some people report terrifying experiences of being raped by hideous beings during sleep paralysis. I occasionally receive messages from women asking me what to do about persistent dream lovers who keep returning to have sex with them in sleep paralysis states. Sometimes these experiences are pleasurable and the woman orgasms, but even then, there is often an accompanying sense of shame, coercion, or guilt. Other times, women report being physically touched by faceless or invisible beings despite their efforts to escape, or being raped by a terrifying presence. Men also report these intrusive and unpleasant sleep paralysis events. If you have such experiences, there are several ways of dealing with them.

1. If the attacks are frequent or distressing, see a therapist (preferably one who works with dreams) with whom you can talk about the themes of your regular dreams, your sleep cycle, what was going on in your life when you had your first experience of sleep paralysis rape, your past and current sex life and relationships, and your fears.

2. Sleep paralysis is a thought-responsive environment, just as dreams are, but when fear overwhelms us, we experience a lack of control, and as our terror escalates, the sensations and imagery become more and more threatening. It is good to consciously release fear in scary dream states, as this often has a calming effect on what we are experiencing. Try all of the practices in this chapter to reduce the frequency of these episodes, release fear, and feel protected while they are happening. Rewrite the story of your sleep paralysis nightmares and arm yourself with allies and resources to empower you. You can change your dream life!

---

44. Garfield, *Pathway to Ecstasy*, 136–137.

3. Consider the presence of sexual energy in your life. How do you respond to it? What outlet do you give it? Are you open to channeling this energy into creative or spiritual energy or harnessing it in some other way? There is nothing shameful about sexual energy; it is a natural life force, but it is powerful and needs expression.

Sexual sleep paralysis attacks can also lead to ecstatic transcendent spiritual experiences. Sometimes the scariest events can transform into powerful spiritual initiations led by the very guide who has just frightened us half to death, as shown in this example from Robert Moss, who is the author of many wonderful books, including *Active Dreaming*. He shares a sleep paralysis experience he had when he was just fourteen years old and had never been kissed:

> She is a hideous, black-skinned hag, with multiple arms. Jouncing against her withered dugs is a necklace composed of rotting human heads. I want to flee from this apparition, but I can't move. My body is completely paralyzed, except for my eyes, which are taking in everything… The black hag is on my bed, stamping on my chest. She lowers herself on her haunches. Despite my disgust, I am aroused and now she is riding me. Her teeth are like daggers. My chest is spattered by blood and foulness from the rotting heads. There is nothing for me to do but stay with this. I tell myself I will survive. At last, the act is done.
>
> Satisfied, the nightmare hag transforms into a beautiful young woman. She smells like jasmine, like sandalwood. She takes me by the hand to a forest shrine. I forget about the body I have left frozen in the bed. She tells me, "I am Time, and I give you power to step in and out of time. You can call me Kali Ma." When I return, I am different.[45]

Robert adds: "If we are willing to face our night terrors, we may find that the alien in the room is what is truly most alien to us, our own greater power. If we can endure the night hag, we may earn an encounter with the Goddess."[46] When we release fear, we become much more open to the spiritual

---

45. Moss, "Liminal Complaints: Demons, Night Hags and Sleep Paralysis."
46. Ibid.

potential of liminal states such as sleep paralysis, and able to accept their gifts.

In this chapter, we've explored the nature of sleep paralysis, how to overcome fear in this state, and how to move from sleep paralysis into a lucid dream. I've shared practices to help you change your sleep paralysis story, reduce the frequency of episodes, and invoke protective powers. We've seen how to benefit from the gifts of sleep paralysis by being open to spiritual experiences. The spiritual encounters we've just looked at carry us neatly into the final two chapters of the book, which explore the spiritual and multidimensional elements of nightmares, out-of-body experiences, dreams of the future, luminous dream spaces, and more.

PART FOUR

spiritual nightmares & transcendence

CHAPTER 8

Nightmares that Transcend Time, Space, and Death

Have you ever had a nightmare that came true? Have you ever received a communication from a person or animal in a dream, and woken up to discover that the information you received is correct? Have you ever been frightened by the sensation of shooting or floating out of your physical body? Did a deceased loved one ever show up in a dream to warn you of imminent danger? Perhaps a small percentage of you have even had a near-death experience, where you physically died (or nearly died) and experienced visions such as a tunnel of light or a life review, but then you came back to life again?

This chapter may bend your mind a little. For the most part, we still lack an effective scientific method for verifying the types of experiences that we'll touch on here. It's also hard to know how many people actually experience these things, as there are few statistics available for most of them. All I know is that I hear from plenty of people in my workshops and retreats and through my website who report "psi" dreams that appear to predict the future or involve telepathic communication, visitation dreams from people who have died, out-of-body experiences (OBEs), and near-death experiences (NDEs). So I figured this book needs a chapter that addresses the scary side of these experiences. We'll also look at suicide nightmares.

Dreams and nightmares that seem to involve extrasensory perception, where the mind appears to extend beyond its perceived boundaries to pick up information about the future or receive communications about simultaneously occurring events via telepathy, may be more common than we think. Certainly, there is a large number of anecdotal reports about these kinds of phenomena and some interesting literature on the subject, as well as some studies that test the existence of psi dreams, including the work of Stanley Krippner, PhD, and Montague Ullman, MD.[47]

Dream telepathy, precognitive dreams, near-death experiences, and the like may appear threatening to those who believe they know for a fact that time is linear, consciousness ends at the moment of death, brains are the generators of consciousness, and people's minds are separate from each other and entirely nonporous. What do you think? Do you think that when we die, we cease to exist, or do you feel that consciousness continues after death? Do you believe that we are separate from other people, or that our minds are intimately interconnected to one another? How do your basic beliefs impact the way you interact in the world and the way you lead your life?

We need to continue studying every area of conscious experience with an open mind in order to gain a deep understanding of the big questions: What is consciousness? What happens when we die? Why are we here? Here's hoping there will be many more scientific studies focusing on all of the types of experiences detailed in this chapter. The scientific method of enquiry is a wonderful way of exploring the world, and scientists tend to have bright and curious minds. It's worth remembering that the scientific worldview (as with any worldview) is also a belief system. We have to be careful not to swallow any belief whole. Practice 39: Question Your Beliefs, Assumptions, and Expectations later in this chapter encourages you to take a moment to consider your cherished beliefs about the nature of reality.

It's good to take a close and objective look at our beliefs and be willing to change our mind according to the weight of the evidence. This works both ways—before we accept the existence of telepathic dreams, for example, it's wise to inform ourselves about all of the possibilities, as well as experiment for ourselves. In terms of a scientific worldview, scepticism is important, but if we allow it to prevent further enquiry for fear of shaking the bedrock of

---

47. Ullman and Krippner, *Dream Telepathy*.

our prior conclusions about the world, we may unwittingly skate over the mystery that lies at the heart of consciousness.

It's beyond the scope of this book to go deeply into the heart of precognitive and telepathic nightmares and the other experiences that appear in this chapter, but the resources section and bibliography contain books that explore in detail psi dreams, OBEs, NDEs, and other topics touched on here.

Since this is a nightmare book designed to examine scary nocturnal experiences and offer relief through practical techniques, I'll focus here on the most fearful scenarios and how to handle them. However, let's keep at the forefront of our minds that many of the types of experiences covered in this chapter can quite simply be amazing, life-enhancing, and joyous events! They can extend and sharpen our consciousness and may increase our understanding of the malleable and nonlinear nature of time and space. Out-of-body experiences can be as delightful, soulful, and liberating as our most treasured dreams.[48] The majority of near-death experiences are also characterised as overwhelmingly positive events that lead to a renewed love of life, freedom from the fear of death, and a certitude of one's purpose in life.[49]

We'll see in this chapter that even an apparently worrying nightmare about suicide can become an inspiration and a true gift. It's good to bear in mind from the outset that telepathic dreams do not always transmit dire tidings; they may also convey reassuring information, such as the return to health of a sick person. Precognitive dreams of the future are not always portents of doom and grief, but can be glorious with promise—what about that dream of acing your exam results that came true?

Nightmares That Predict the Future

Have you ever had a scary dream that came true? What is that? Coincidence? A fluke? Intuition? Or the mind reaching out through time and space to show you a possible future? Dreams that show us glimpses of events that then actually manifest in waking life are known as precognitive dreams. Such dreams can be very trivial. For several years, I wore a silver star nose stud without incident, then one night I dreamed I lost it down the plughole of

---

48. Johnson, *Llewellyn's Complete Book of Lucid Dreaming*.
49. Sartori, *The Wisdom of Near-Death Experiences*.

the bathroom sink while washing my face. In the dream, it skittered away from me too fast for me to catch it. Infuriatingly, I then did lose it down the plughole while washing my face that morning, despite recalling that dream!

People with high dream recall often report a high frequency of low-significance precognitive dreams, such as dreaming that a letter arrives with the address handwritten in green ink…and finding such a letter in their mailbox later that morning, as once happened to me. I wasn't expecting a letter and didn't know the sender. It makes dream journaling even more fun when we spot these little synchronicities and occasional glimpses into the future, and it can bring us a deeper feeling of connection with the world when we sense the way our mind expands into the past, present, and future in our dreams.

Dreams of the future can also be deeply significant and rich with promise, such as the story Linda Davison tells in *Chicken Soup for the Soul: Dreams and Premonitions*. She tried for a baby for five years, lost hope, then dreamed she saw an eagle's nest with four eggs that hatched as she watched. The mother eagle spread its wings protectively over the babies and gazed right into the dreamer's eyes. Linda knew this was not just a dream, but a promise, and awoke feeling awed and grateful, knowing that she would have four children. Within a month, she was pregnant, and she had four babies over the next four years.[50]

However, precognitive dreams can also be terrifying, appearing to announce forthcoming calamities, accidents, losses, natural disasters, or acts of terrorism. It's important to work with these nightmares on the personal level before assuming they will come true on the world stage. The practices in chapter 2 are a good place to start. An interesting thing to remember when working with precognitive dreams is that they may seem to reveal *possible* future events or warn us of events that we can change to avoid an accident; that is to say, nothing seems absolutely set in stone. Here are three striking examples of precognitive nightmares that warned the dreamers to take action in order to avoid an undesirable outcome. Each example is from a wonderful

---

50. Newmark and Sullivan Walden, *Chicken Soup for the Soul: Dreams and Premonitions*, 340.

book of the International Association for the Study of Dreams, *Dreams That Change Our Lives.*[51]

Psychologist and academic Marcia Emery dreamed she had a car accident when her brakes failed. A week later, her brakes did fail, and although luckily she was unharmed, her car was totaled. And now for the part where it gets super weird: a week later, and now in possession of a new car, Marcia had another driving dream:

I put my foot on the brake, and it goes right down to the floor. I hear a ping noise. I see a policeman coming towards me and notice a no parking sign.

Marcia laughed this dream off, sure that her new car wouldn't have brake trouble. A few days later, driving along in her new car, she braked, her foot went right to the floor, there was a ping … and she saw a policeman approaching and also noticed a no parking sign. She observes: "I remembered the dream and guided the car to the curb. How could real life imitate the dream? I later found out that the brake cable had snapped in my brand-new car."

So the moral of that tale is: if you dream your brakes fail, get them checked! Although this type of dream is often a metaphor for rushing too much through life and not taking time to slow down or driving ourselves so hard that we can't stop, or a reference to failing physical health, dreams can sometimes be extremely literal. Marcia's dream is striking because very specific details, such as the pinging noise, the policeman, and the no parking sign, were all reproduced at the time of the brake failure. Have you ever experienced *déjà vu*, when you feel strongly that you have lived a particular moment before in perfect detail and are now reliving it? This feeling may well be linked to having previously dreamed that moment.

Another precognitive nightmare that contains startling and surprising details that then come true was shared by David Cielak, who dreamed he was running along a peaceful road when suddenly …

I see a horned black bull and a herd of five cows in a field. As I approach they break the fence and come charging down the road at me!

---

51. Hoss and Gongloff, *Dreams That Change Our Lives.* Quotes taken from pages 282, 288, and 286.

In the dream, the bull runs straight at the dreamer and tosses him on his horns. Later that afternoon, while running, David saw cows and a horned black bull, and recalled his dream.

> As I ran, the black horned bull broke through the barbed wire fence and, followed by the herd of cows, was running straight at me! I was shocked to see this! Just as in the dream! I thought, "I'm a goner."

Luckily, a car came along and David hid behind it as the bull and cows thundered past him before crashing through a fence into another field.

Sometimes other people have precognitive nightmares that feature us, and although it can be difficult to tell which dreams point to a possible future event and which are focused on our individual psychology, sometimes this kind of nightmare can even save lives.

Janice Baylis received a phone call from her carpool partner, telling Janice to meet her around the corner from their usual meeting place. While they were meeting around the corner, a small airplane crashed right in the spot where they normally would have met at that time. As they drove past the wreck, Janice asked her friend how on earth she had known to switch the meeting place. The friend told her she'd had the following dream, but hadn't wanted to mention it in case Janice thought her silly:

> I dream an airplane will crash at the place and time we are to meet, and we will be under it when it crashes.

These examples show how accurate dreams can be about future events, and that we can change the "possible futures" they feature. But let's not forget that it can be hard to distinguish a precognitive dream from a regular one, and even if the nightmare is super vivid and accompanied by feelings of urgency, this is certainly not always a reliable indicator that it will "come true." There must surely be a great number of dreams initially thought to be precognitive that then did *not* manifest in waking life, only these don't get reported. The more familiar we become with our own dreaming style and the more diligently we journal our dreams, the more likely it is that we will be able to distinguish precognitive nightmares from purely personal ones. Let's take a look now at another fascinating area of dreaming: telepathic nightmares.

Telepathic Nightmares

People write to me sharing their telepathic experiences in this area, and of course I hear the most disturbing cases, because it is traumatising to have a nightmare that your loved one is in a bad car crash and then later receive a phone call telling you that this actually happened. People ask how it can be possible that they "knew" this before even hearing about it. "How did the dream know?" they ask. Or they ask, "Am I going mad?" Such an experience can shake up our worldview.

A very proficient lucid dreamer, Natalie, went out with friends one evening and later had a lucid dream in which she saw one of those friends:

> I saw F in a coffin. She told me she was dead. I told her she couldn't be, as I had seen her only hours ago. She said she was sorry but that she was dead. I woke from this in shock and I knew it was real. I ran to my housemate and told him. I found out the next day that F had committed suicide the night I'd had the lucid dream. Her poor mother had found her dead.

This is a tragic worst-case scenario and understandably a horrifying and very sad experience for everyone affected. We must always consider that in many cases, such nightmares are not announcing or predicting the actual death of someone. Death dreams may simply mean that we need to face our own future death and the mortality of those around us. Death in dreams can be a wake-up call to say goodbye to old behaviours and seize life by the horns, or it can herald major change. As we've seen in this book, death in dreams is usually symbolic rather than literal, so before we spread panic by calling people up to warn them that they died a terrible death in our dream, it's wise to consider personal associations with the dream and work to unwrap it using techniques such as those in chapter 2.

Do you think that minds can become more porous during dreams and thus more able to communicate with other minds? I never seriously entertained this possibility until, out of curiosity, I entered a dream telepathy contest at an IASD conference in Copenhagen in 2004.[52] Contestants try to tune into the telepathy

---

52. The full version of the telepathy contest experience is shared in chapter 19 of *Llewellyn's Complete Book of Lucid Dreaming*.

target image via their dreams. That night, sceptical but curious, I focused on the telepathic sender, Dr. Beverly D'Urso, and had the following lucid dream.

> In a spacious park full of big, old trees, I hear a woman's voice shouting, "Tree! Tree!" as if she has discovered the answer to some fundamental question.
>
> Then I'm at the dream conference, discussing the telepathy contest. I see Beverly and figure she must be having a sleepless night trying to transmit the image.
>
> "How are you feeling?" I ask her.
>
> She flings out her arms and says, "I've just been shouting the word inside my head!"
>
> "That's funny," I say, "because in my last dream, people were shouting about trees."
>
> I want to ask Beverly if tree is the image she's projecting—but, get this—I think this might be cheating! So I don't ask her. Instead, we talk about the qualities of the colour green. Then I'm standing before a huge, leafy tree. I focus on it intently and slowly wake up.

The next morning, I entered the contest but had to fly home that day, so I missed the awards ceremony. As it turned out, the target image was indeed a tree. The judges informed me that I had won first prize in the contest, with the most direct hit they'd ever had. The image looked exactly like the tree I'd seen in my lucid dream. My dream had also accurately reflected the ways the sender had tried to transmit the image: she had flung out her arms like tree boughs, pictured parks in her mind, focused on the colour green … and shouted the word *tree* inside her head.

It's a very odd feeling when something like this happens, because it seems to go beyond what we can comfortably brush off as a coincidence, a fluke, a setup, or wishful thinking. It's easy enough to dismiss other people's "telepathic" experiences, but your own? Although I was in an academic mindset at that time, I began to wonder whether dreams were more than purely subjective phenomena. How had I heard Beverly shouting the word *tree* inside her head? How had I seen the target photograph in my lucid dream? Had our minds connected and exchanged information in some way? It seemed so. I was already highly interested in consciousness and the big questions of life, and after this experience I questioned everything more intensively. Practice 39: Question Your Beliefs, Assumptions, and Expectations is great if you are a deep thinker (or hope to become one!) and wish to uncover more of life's beautiful mysteries.

Another interesting thing to do is to notice more when we experience moments of intuitive knowing, or when we experience synchronicities, such as starting to hum a particular song at the exact same moment our friend does. When we travel with someone or spend a lot of time with them, we often "tune into" each other and come out with the same thought simultaneously. This seems very natural and common, but it's good to heighten our awareness of it if we're interested in lowering the barriers between our mind and others'. It seems that in some cases, the barriers between individual minds can become more porous, especially in cases where danger is present. Nightmares are a perfect conduit for this porous information exchange, because our critical mind is mostly dormant during dreaming. Let's look at one such account.

Telepathic nightmares may occur when a loved one is in pain or danger, suffering severe emotional distress, or close to death. In *Chicken Soup for the Soul: Dreams and Premonitions*, D. L Teamor shares a nightmare where she tuned into her tiny son's health predicament.[53] Born after only five months in the womb, her little boy wasn't expected to live at first. But he survived and was into his second month in an incubator when his mother dreamed that she was searching everywhere for her baby, saying, "I have to find him, he can't breathe." In the dream, she ran through an abandoned school building until she found his incubator in a classroom. He was breathing again, but she noticed that it was extremely cold in the classroom.

As soon as she woke up, she called the hospital and was told that her baby's lung had ripped when a doctor decided to see if he could breathe unaided. Once at the hospital, she found her baby terribly weak but breathing through a tube. However, she then noticed his body temperature was very low, and when she inspected the incubator, she found the rear window had been left open, so the temperature within was frigid. Her dream had been correct about two key details—respiratory distress and the coldness—and

---

53. Newmark and Sullivan Walden, *Chicken Soup for the Soul: Dreams and Premonitions*, 142–143.

coincided with the time of these events. Fortunately, her tiny boy survived and thrived! He grew into adulthood with healthy lungs.

Let's take a look now at nightmares in which deceased loved ones come to warn us about hidden disease or danger.

Warnings from the Dead

There are many accounts of people receiving messages from deceased loved ones during dreams. These include information about the future, health advice, or warnings of mortal danger. Vehement, super-real nightmares leave such a strong impression on the dreamer that they often prompt a radical change in behaviour, actions, and thought processes. It is natural for the dreamer to feel that this was an actual visitation from a deceased loved one who has their best interests at heart.

Some warning dreams are impossible to ignore. Wanda Burch is the author of *She Who Dreams: A Journey into Healing through Dreamwork*. Her dead father shouted at her in a dream, "You have breast cancer!" He was panicked in the dream because she wasn't "getting it," and it was time for her to react. She then had a follow-up dream about exactly where the cancer was. She went to the doctor and he couldn't find any cancer. But then Wanda put a dot over the exact spot she had seen in her dream, far below her breast, to show him where to put the biopsy needle. He found a lump. The biopsy showed that Wanda had a particularly aggressive and fast-moving cancer. The cancer cells were not amassing in such a way as to be visible on a regular mammogram. If Wanda hadn't paid attention to her dreams, she might not have discovered the cancer in time. As it was, they were able to respond quickly to intervene with the cancer's progress.

Dreams effortlessly transcend time and space and provide us with a world where our thoughts and feelings co-create events and telepathy is commonplace. (We often "just know" things while dreaming, and when we pay attention, dream people can often be observed "speaking" without visibly moving their lips.) We are naturally endowed with superpowers in the dreamworld, such as flying and the ability to turn invisible or shapeshift into an animal. Our psychic powers are naturally sky-high in dreamland. I have dreamed many times of levitating objects with the power of the mind, and of being able to skip ahead in time and see the future unfolding in a series of vivid images, like photographs. I have met wise beings and dissolved into blissful white light.

We can do such things in the flexible dreamworld, where the laws of physics exist as firm constructs only in our mind and can easily be transcended. Might it also be possible to receive communications via dreams from people who have transitioned into the death state? There is so much we still don't know about death and what happens beyond that veil. Studies into near-death experiences where people have been pronounced clinically dead yet somehow come back to life show that death does not happen from one second to the next: it can be a lengthier process than we assume, and sometimes it can be reversed.[54] Fear of the unknown often blocks us from keeping an open mind. I find it healthier to admit that we don't know everything and science cannot explain everything. It seems more "scientific" to observe and discover with an open mind as we go through life.

A man I know who has been a psychiatric nurse for over thirty years sent me the following two warning nightmares with the permission of his patients. Personal data has been changed to protect the dreamers.

A twenty-five-year-old man had suffered severely at the hands of his violent parents. He was beaten, verbally and physically attacked, and put under pressure. For a time, he was violent himself, but then he stopped of his own accord. His uncle was murdered by his partner by poisoning when the patient was six years old, and his cousin died in strange, unclear circumstances when the patient was seventeen years old. On the night of the death of his cousin, the patient had the following dream:

> My cousin, who died that night, sits upright in his grave and is buried only up to his stomach; his torso and head and arms are alive, and he tells me vehemently, "Disappear from here. Get out of this family. You are in great danger."

This dream was very shocking for the dreamer, and he took the warning very seriously. He soon moved from his parents' home to another region and was able to build a new, nonviolent life.

---

54. Parnia et al., "AWARE—AWAreness during REsuscitation."

A thirty-five-year-old married man had this dream shortly after the suicide of his wife, who had suffered from depression for a long time:

> My recently deceased wife appears to me in a dream, marked by the traces that the suicide left on her body. She tells me with great urgency, "Don't do it. Don't commit suicide. You will regret it, as I deeply regret it. I have not solved any of my problems through suicide; I have taken them all with me. What's more, I cannot return to my previous life and rectify the mistake of committing suicide. Don't do it!"

The patient himself suffered from depression and, after his wife's suicide, had played with the idea of taking his own life "to be with her again in the afterlife." The dream greatly helped to dissuade him from this idea, and for years now he hasn't had any plans to die by suicide.

Let's now consider nightmares where people in the dream actually kill themselves or dream of their own death.

Suicide Nightmares

There are two main types of suicide nightmares: those of people who are actually suicidal, and those of being dead or killing oneself that are purely symbolic and usually refer to the need for major change in the dreamer's life. Robert Litman, MD, discusses the nightmares of suicidal people in the chapter "The Dream in the Suicidal Situation" in the book *The Dream in Clinical Practice*. One symbolic example he cites is that of a woman who dreamed she was dead in a coffin, but when the dream was worked with, it turned out to be symbolic of the "death" of sexuality in her marriage rather than a reflection of a suicide wish.[55]

Litman describes suicide wishes as the desire to escape from intolerable pain, and points out that suicide is often rehearsed in fantasy before an actual attempt is made. This rehearsal can emerge in very anxious and depressive dreams and nightmares that often have themes of destruction, being killed, or killing oneself or others. However, when a person is close to making an actual suicide attempt, their dreams may change to reflect an attitude of sur-

---

55. Litman, "The Dream in the Suicidal Situation," in *The Dream in Clinical Practice*, edited by J. Natterson, 293.

render or giving up, or they may dream of peacefully departing from life. For example, one month before a woman took a fatal overdose, she reported, "I dreamed something wonderful: war had broken out, I was to go into the field. I said goodbye to everyone with the joyous expectation that I was soon to die." [56]

Occasionally, people write to me saying their nightmares are so relentless that they are contemplating suicide. Psychologist and professor of psychiatry Dr. Tore Nielsen, who directs the Dream and Nightmare Laboratory in Montreal, shared with me his advice for those in this extreme situation.

> Seek professional help right away, preferably a psychologist open to working with dreams. Research shows that having nightmares is a predictor of suicidal thoughts and attempts, so acting early on such symptoms could help prevent their thoughts from getting worse. As we learn more about the links between nightmares and suicide, the content of the nightmares might provide clues to the nature of the suffering and could be used as entry points for therapy; I would look closely at the nature of the interpersonal relationships in the nightmares.

Dreams and nightmares are emotional barometers; when we pay attention to them, they can reveal our state of mind. In this sense, listening to the dreams and nightmares of people in our lives who are suicidally depressed can help us to react quickly by getting medical help or calling a suicide hotline if it seems a dream is indicating an imminent suicide attempt. Practice 7: The Nightmare Reflection Technique shows how to listen when someone shares a nightmare and how to help them gently unpack its meaning. Practice 2: Keep a Nightmare Journal helps us to spot any worrying patterns in the nightmare content and identify recurring themes that may help us understand the larger picture behind the suicidal thoughts of ourselves or others. If you feel suicidal, or if your friend or loved one does, please do not hesitate to reach out immediately for professional help by seeing a doctor and calling a suicide hotline.

In his 2020 presentation for the 37th annual dream conference of the International Association for the Study of Dreams, nightmare researcher

---

56. Ibid., 295.

and clinical psychologist Dr. Michael Nadorff explained that in nightmare sufferers, the main factor for suicide is not the intensity of nightmares, but their frequency. If someone is having a high frequency of nightmares (several times a week or nightly), seek help. In a study involving placebos, Dr. Nadorff said that the placebo worked better with nightmare sufferers than a drug, which shows that simply feeling less hopeless about nightmares is very powerful: the belief in relief can already help a nightmare sufferer.[57]

Let's look now at the symbolic type of suicide dreams. Kim, an artist, shared that at a time when she felt traumatised by the death of her father and had numerous rejections as an artist, she experienced a nightmare that weighed on her, as it seemed to be a very clear suicide dream:

> I am standing in the library on the ledge that has no railing and am looking to my left at my mom. I am wearing a purple winter coat my mom had made me as a child. My arms are outstretched to each side, and I have many plastic shopping bags hanging from each arm. I step off the ledge to my certain death.

Kim then attended a conference of the International Association for the Study of Dreams, and in a morning dream circle, author Jeremy Taylor asked if anyone had a dream to work on. Kim recounts what happened:

> My hand shot up with my suicide dream. I thought he was crazy to pick my dream, but hey, what did I know? His first question, once we got started, was "Were the bags full?" Well, actually, no, they were empty. I was sure of that, because as I fell, I had heard the sound of empty shopping bags flapping in the wind. All I can remember from that day (now well over ten years ago) is the idea that if the bags were empty, then they were not weighing me down, but rather were *full of potential*. That blew my mind. I have learned that suicide dreams do not mean we are about to actually play out in real life the drama of our dreams, but rather that suicide means that a part of me had to die for me to move forward. That if I could truly let go, then I could use my wings and fly. … Wow, this was groundbreaking for me!

---

57. Nadorff, "Bad Dreams and Nightmares."

This dream I had thought to be a trauma or acting out of a very negative time of my life—rejection as an artist, death of my dad and other family members—was actually a gift I was giving myself. Understanding this dream on that day changed my life's direction, and I have not looked back. My arms are spread wide and I leap at all kinds of opportunities and possibilities that I may not have in the past. This dream is a gift I will treasure for my lifetime, of that I am sure.

Death in dreams and nightmares is often a powerful metaphor for change: we must die in order to be reborn. This is why we need to be super careful not to "judge a dream by its cover," and instead take time and care to unwrap it. A nightmare about someone we love dying very likely does *not* mean that they are actually about to die; it is much more likely to be symbolic of our own inner change, a change in our relationship with the person, or the act of letting go in some respect. The best way to find out is to work with the dream. As Kim's dream so beautifully shows, sometimes what first appears to be a worrisome nightmare can turn out to be a blessing and a release, and the beginning of a marvellous new way of being in the world.

practice 39

QUESTION YOUR BELIEFS,
ASSUMPTIONS, AND EXPECTATIONS

It can be fascinating to check in with ourselves about our basic stance on the nature of reality, consciousness, dreams, physics, and death. Try mulling over these questions for starters, and add more of your own, to come up with your current worldview. There's no need to judge your responses: everyone is different, so just go with whatever feels right for you. You may notice that your deepest beliefs were formed in childhood, or you might realise how much your worldview has changed over the course of your life. Skip the questions you feel are too much to focus on for now—there are some very deep ones. Many people barely consider these questions as they move through life, so well done if you actually sit down and give this practice some serious thought!

1. Do my waking thoughts, beliefs, and intentions have an impact on the physical universe? In what way? And how about my dream thoughts and the actions I take in my dreams—do these also impact the physical universe in some way?

2. Which beliefs do I hold about consciousness? What is it and where does it come from? How did human consciousness begin?

3. Is my brain the creator of consciousness, or does it mediate consciousness, a bit like a radio receiver that receives waves and decodes them into sounds?

4. Where does the "real me" reside (my "self")? In my physical body? Why? What about when I dream? Where am "I" then? Who is the dreamer of my dreams?

5. Does time move only in one direction: forward, in linear style? Or might it move seamlessly between past, present, and future?

6. How separate am I from other people? Are thought transference and telepathic communication possible in the waking state?

7. Are dreams "all in my head," or might there be a vaster dream matrix where it is possible to connect with other minds?

8. Do I believe that the laws of physics as we know them today are absolute?

9. What do I believe happens when we die? Does consciousness continue after death? If I view this as impossible, why is that? How do I know for sure?

10. How certain am I that my current worldview is correct? Would I feel threatened if something occurred that radically altered my worldview, or do I feel open to learning more as I go through life?

Out-of-Body Experiences (OBEs)

At ages seven and eight, I used to have recurring lucid nightmares where I'd be lying on a beautiful green and sunny hill, then suddenly thick, black, buzzing power lines would begin to crisscross the sky, darkening it to blackness and building into a massive electrical hum that shook the whole hill and terrified me. Even though I was aware in those nightmares, I was unable to control my fear and would wake myself up by screaming. It's possible that these nightmares were actually the onset of out-of-body experiences. Some OBEs begin with buzzing noises and strong vibrations, shaking, and the sense of being lifted up by a force greater than oneself. It can be a horrifying experience if we aren't ready for it. Some people think they are dying!

But we are not dying. We are fully alive and consciously aware of a natural transition out of the physical body and into what we might think of as an energy body. However, no "body" needs to be present at all; we are just all so attached to the body concept that we tend to experience ourselves as being in one in most states of consciousness. (We'll touch on bodiless OBEs at the end of this section.)

Maybe the concept of an out-of-body experience seems weird or disturbing if you believe that the centre of consciousness—the "self"—resides uniquely within the physical body. But think about it: we all "leave our body" every night when we transition into a dream body. How else do we fly over dream mountains, transform into a gazelle and run with the herd, or reach out and pick up a melon in a dream supermarket? In that sense, the OBE is no more of an esoteric experience than is ordinary sleep. It may occur rarely in most people, but it's a state of consciousness experienced by healthy people.[58] Here's my definition of the out-of-body experience and how it arises:

> The OBE is a state in which self-perception (perceived sensory input, self-location, and self-identification) seems external to and independent from the physical body; a state that may be entered spontaneously, involuntarily, and abruptly from diverse waking and sleeping states of consciousness. In terms of onset, the OBE differs from lucid dreams in that an OBE might arise from the waking state, trauma, meditation, fainting, or in the midst of great physical danger. But an OBE can also arise from sleep states such as hypnagogia, sleep paralysis, non-lucid dreaming, and lucid dreaming.
>
> The numerous entries into the OBE state seem non-exclusive in terms of reported onset phenomena: a lucid dreamer may experience either earthquake-like shaking at the onset of a lucid dream-induced OBE, or a gentle transition. A meditator may suddenly find herself

---

58. Levitan and LaBerge, "Other Worlds: Out-of-Body Experiences and Lucid Dreams."

floating above her body, or she may experience diverse kinaesthetic and auditory sensations (such as vibrations and buzzing) before the experience of being "out of body" seems complete.[59]

Unlike lucid dreams, OBEs can occur in a deeply relaxed waking state. British consciousness researcher Sue Blackmore explains that "many OBEs take place when the person is wide awake, and physiological studies using EEG, heart rate and other measures show that experimental OBEs occur in a relaxed waking state similar to drowsiness."[60] OBEs are not dreams, but for sure when an OBE begins from within the dream state, there can be plenty of overlap between these states. Neuroscientific studies show that the area of the brain supposedly activated during OBEs is the temporoparietal junction. Such studies indicate that OBEs can occur when sensory input and the body image are disrupted. Dr. Bigna Lenggenhager led an experiment in 2007 using virtual technology to induce "full body illusions" in the lab. Subjects were shown a film of themselves viewed from behind, then their backs were stroked to trigger a perceptual leap into the virtual body that they could see being stroked before them.[61]

Commonly reported sensations linked to out-of-body experiences are vibrations that move throughout the whole body, an invisible hand grasping you to help you out of your body, rushing or buzzing noises, sensations of shaking, and a whooshing "liftoff" feeling as you shoot out. People may see their prone body as they hover above it. Others report seeing a silver cord linking them to their physical body. However, often none of these sensations or visions occur; sometimes we just find ourselves floating in midair, with no discernible exit. Seeing your physical body does not mean you are dead, and not seeing a silver cord doesn't either! Just relax and enjoy exploring.

We can use the OBE state to overcome fears, just as we can in nightmare work. A number of the transformative nightmare practices in this book are helpful for any kind of frightening nocturnal experience, including scary OBE experiences. Practice 40: How to Release Fear During an OBE may

59. Johnson, "Surfing the Rainbow: Fearless and Creative Out-of-Body Experiences," 130–131.

60. Blackmore, *Consciousness: An Introduction*, 406.

61. Lenggenhager et al., "Video Ergo Sum: Manipulating Bodily Self-Consciousness."

come in handy if anything about OBEs frightens you, as will Practice 1: How to Release Fear and Become Calm. If you feel yourself shooting out of your physical body, relax and enjoy the ride! You're not going to die. William Buhlman, author of the fascinating book *Adventures Beyond the Body*, reports on a terrifying personal OBE in which he stands firm, confronts his fear, and experiences profound change. To induce this particular OBE, he continually repeated while falling asleep, "Now I'm out of body," and soon found himself floating just above his body. He then called out, "Clarity now!" to raise his awareness, and found himself staring down into a dark basement, where he saw…

> A huge hairy creature, a giant sloth, standing nine feet high; it has a bear's head and the face of a dog. My entire being is paralyzed with fear. I desperately want to run, but I hold my position… [It] climbs the stairs and wraps its huge hairy arms around me. All I can think is, *This thing can snap my neck in a heartbeat.*
>
> Suddenly the creature gives me a warm hug and licks my face like a dog. All my fear dissipates as I realize that this ugly creature is powerless to harm me. An intense feeling of empowerment and joy explodes through me; I feel completely free from my fear and limits. The creature looks directly into my eyes, smiles, and disappears. A surge of energy flows through me as I recognize a new form of freedom—an absolute freedom from fear." [62]

Following this transformative experience, William reports knowing for certain that he could achieve anything he desired. He understood that he could overcome his biggest enemy—his own fears. It seems clear that frightening OBEs can be approached in much the same way as any other high-awareness sleep-induced experience, from sleep paralysis to lucid nightmares. We find ourselves highly aware in a thought-responsive environment, able to respond consciously to whatever we encounter. In such a state, we can recall that it can be transformative and healing to face scary manifestations and discover what they want from us, and this gifts us with the courage to stand our ground or

---

62. Buhlman, *Adventures Beyond the Body*, 249–250.

react in helpful ways, rather than panicking, fleeing, or desperately trying to wake up.

When we release fear in any state of consciousness and instead adopt an attitude of wonder, we open the door to fabulous adventures, healing gifts, and states of unimaginable bliss. It's possible that I had my first OBEs when I was seven, but looking back through so many years I can't say for sure if they were lucid flying dreams or OBEs. I remember that magical feeling of flying up out of my bedroom into the cool night air, and gazing with wonder over the fields and hedges that were our back garden. (We lived on a 300-year-old converted farm among the rolling hills of Devon, England.) I also recall knowing with glee that I was doing "that special flying thing" again.

During these regular flying trips, which happened intensely for at least a year or so, I would also meet beings who hid in the hedgerow and never showed themselves. They would giggle cheekily and rustle the leaves around. What they did show me almost every time I went out to them was an ancient book filled with handwritten symbols and magic, something I thought of as a "spell book." They would turn the crackling pages and show me different things. I remember returning to that hedge next to the sandpit in daylight and searching in vain for those elusive beings and their book!

Years later, in my early twenties, I had hundreds of full-blown out-of-body experiences, sometimes starting from sleep paralysis, other times from lucid dreams, the void, and the waking state. Although at first I had plenty of scary OBEs where I felt out of control and uncertain of "the rules" of this state, when I worked with my fear, I quickly began to love them. I began to have what I've termed *bodiless lucid experiences*,[63] where I would become a speck of conscious awareness and fly, or expand into blissful oneness. I began to discover the Lucid Light, which will be explored more in the final chapter. Here's one of these beautiful experiences:

> I hover up, vibrating, and fly again. I'm in whitish space, endless neutral light. I try flying as fast as I can and it's so quick it's impossible to describe—I could go around the circumference of the world in a second at this speed. There's enough room in this white space for absolutely anything and I'm alight with exhilaration. It strikes me that

63. Johnson, "Surfing the Rainbow: Fearless and Creative Out-of-Body Experiences."

in experiences like this there can be no doubt that we are more than just a physical body. We are physics itself; gravitational pull and light particles and the energy-force that pulls everything together … There's something so harmonious and natural about flying so fast, as if I become the energy of the air itself. There's no resistance and with wonder I think to myself: "This is soul-flying." [64]

The following practice shows how to react in order to reduce fear during an OBE so that we can enjoy this potentially wonderful experience. [65]

practice 40

HOW TO RELEASE FEAR DURING AN OBE

1. **Relax.** Panicking is possibly the worst thing a person can do during an OBE. I cannot overstress the importance of relaxing and breathing calmly when the freight train version of an OBE entry runs you over. It's remarkable how simply accepting the experience can transform it fairly quickly into a calm, beautiful event. Practising yoga and meditation is an excellent way of learning to connect with the peaceful centre we all have somewhere inside us. Once the "Breathe–Grow calm–Relax" structure has been strengthened (and it takes only minutes of regular practice), it becomes second nature to turn to the breath in any state of consciousness as a way to calm emotions and release fear. Yes, in bodiless lucid experiences we have no sense of inhabiting a body, but even in this state, the decision to calm down and relax will trigger an automatic response. Combine it with an affirmation, such as "I am safe," and it will be even more effective.

2. **Visualise.** Another useful practice is that of visualisation. If we visualise ourselves moving easily away from our physical body towards a beautiful landscape or safe place, the thought-responsive environment generally tends to react by materialising that place. Feeling and projecting love is also a very good way of dissolving fear and fearful visions or sensations: when we explore lucid states with love in our heart, the

---

64. Ibid.

65. This practice first appeared in *Llewellyn's Complete Book of Lucid Dreaming*, 319.

lucid environment responds warmly. Summoning a feeling of love can be done by imagining warmth or colour emanating from the chest, breathing freely, and smiling.

3. **Be curious.** Adopting an attitude of curiosity when observing strange visions or scenes that arise during an OBE is an effective way of gaining perspective and clarity. If you're in search of creative inspiration for a painting or story, these visions are imbued with creative potential, so try to notice everything about them: watch them like a film. Remind yourself that after all this, you will find yourself safely in your bed. Don't forget your ability to fly in the OBE state; kick out a little or wriggle upwards like a mermaid. If you are truly desperate to escape the OBE experience and return to your body, try wiggling your toes, which brings your attention to your physical body, or hold your breath for as long as you can. This second technique can shock the body into returning to regular waking consciousness.

4. **Daydream.** If you have had a previous scary OBE, instead of wishing it will never happen to you again, it's far less psychologically stressful to think of something fun to try out in case it does happen again. Relax and have a little daydream about how your ideal OBE might go—would you fly over mountains, experiment with putting your hand through a wall, or enjoy the sensory explosion of doing floating somersaults? Once we open ourselves to the creative possibilities of OBEs, we soon find ourselves hankering after more experiences and working on inducing them. Personally, I've found that curiosity burns stronger than fear. If we get curious about OBEs, any fear rapidly diminishes. Reading widely on the subject and talking to experienced practitioners is also helpful, as the experience will seem less foreign.

5. **Balance the seesaw.** The golden rule of fearlessness in OBEs can be visualised as a seesaw, because it's all about balance and reciprocity. If you tip too far down into fear, the fear factor of the experience rises in response. If you are relaxed and calm while out of body and feel balanced within yourself, your OBE is far more likely to be a relaxed and calm one.

....

Now let's pay a brief visit to an experience that breaks through sleeping and waking realities and touches what lies beyond both: the near-death experience, or NDE.

Distressing Near-Death Experiences

Near-death experiences, or NDEs, occur when we almost die due to physical trauma or when we are actually pronounced clinically dead by doctors due to lack of a heartbeat, breathing, brain activity, and other vital signs. Studies have found that even in the latter cases, remarkably cogent experiences were reported once the patient was resuscitated. Dr. Penny Sartori remarks, "People were reporting clear, lucid, conscious experiences at a time when their brains had ceased to function or were not functioning optimally." [66]

You may have heard about typical NDE visions, such as a tunnel of light, a meeting with a deity, or an encounter with blissful, mystical light. Sometimes a life review is experienced, where people are shown their lives, their actions, and the effects these had on others. At times, a choice seems possible: to stay in this afterlife or return to the body. Other times, no choice is given: the experiencer is told to return or simply finds themselves being sucked back into their body. People often return from a positive NDE transformed. They find a deeper meaning in their lives, have more clarity about their life purpose, and feel more joyful and compassionate, understanding the interconnectedness of all lives and knowing that death is not the end of everything but merely a spiritual transition.

However, NDEs are not always glorious, soul-enhancing events. Since this is a nightmare book, I'll focus on distressing NDEs. Studies show that around 15 percent of NDEs are distressing.[67] These are rarely talked about, yet they can leave the experiencer with lasting fears about death and dying or a sense of their own failure as a human being. Some people who had negative NDEs where they were approached by demons return feeling they are unworthy people who will not make it to heaven. This can have the positive effect of transforming their waking behaviour as they strive to become more compassionate to others,

---

66. Sartori, *The Wisdom of Near-Death Experiences*, 177.
67. Atwater, *Beyond The Light: Near-Death Experiences.*

but these people could also benefit from knowing that distressing NDEs can be worked with and processed in a similar way to nightmares.

Let's look at an example of a negative NDE from Dr. Rajiv Parti, a former chief of anaesthesiology. He was in intensive care with sepsis following surgery when he had an NDE that changed his life. Dr. Penny Sartori recounts his experience in *The Wisdom of Near-Death Experiences*.

> He was taken to a place that he believed to be hell … He encountered grotesque entities and could smell burning meat. He witnessed the suffering of others and was himself subjected to tortures such as being stabbed with needles and made to lie on a bed of nails and blood oozed from wounds on his body. The experience of hell came with a revelation about his life which he described as being one of materialism and a selfish attitude of putting himself before others. He realized his life had been lived without being loving, kind and compassionate … He was deeply remorseful … As soon as he realized this … his father and grandfather appeared at his side and guided him towards a tunnel with a bright light. Dr. Parti then went on to experience a very deep NDE where he believed he went to what could be described as heaven.[68]

For those of you who have had a negative NDE, you might like to try working with it as if it were a nightmare. Practical dreamworking tools such as the ones given in this book could be very beneficial in helping you to make sense of your experience and resolve any trauma it may have caused. Practice 13: The Lucid Imaging Nightmare Solution (LINS) in particular can be easily modified to enable an NDE reentry in which the experiencer can ask questions, interact fearlessly with the imagery, and emerge with greater understanding, a sense of resolution, or deep healing. One book I know of on the subject of distressing NDEs is *Dancing Past the Dark* by Nancy Bush. More general books about NDEs are listed in the bibliography.

Reducing fear of death following a distressing NDE can be even more challenging than reducing fear of death in the average person. For this reason, it is good to work with the fear rather than turn our back on it. Many of

---

68. Sartori, *The Wisdom of Near-Death Experiences*, 22.

the practices in this book help us to work with fear in any area of our lives. When we transcend the most crippling fears we carry with us, we free ourselves to live larger, brighter, more compassionate and energised lives. We empower ourselves to make bold and graceful moves into the life we have always wanted to live, the life we can be proud of at all moments, including that most transformative of moments when we must leave our family, our job, our body, and our material wealth and possessions and journey onward with conscious awareness into whatever death may hold.

Fear of death is basically fear of separation, yet ironically our fear causes an even greater separation between ourselves and the heart of life. When we die, all we can take with us is our conscious awareness, so surely it makes sense to work on raising our level of consciousness, living compassionately, and helping others around us as we all navigate the ups and downs of this rich and precious life.

Here's a beautiful practice in which we can familiarise ourselves with liminal states and raise our consciousness.

practice 41
YOGA NIDRA: BALANCE BETWEEN THE WORLDS

Yoga nidra is the ancient tantric practice of conscious deep sleep. It is rooted in the yoga tradition and was first referenced in the Upanishads. A profound form of meditation, this alert, deeply relaxed state helps us to balance between the worlds of wake and sleep, just as one day we will balance between life and death. It's an excellent practice for maintaining lucid awareness in the face of shifting levels of consciousness so that we become more adept at exploring liminal states. It's also a very natural practice, and easier for most than sitting meditation: our body falls asleep every night, so we are deeply familiar with this process. In yoga nidra, the body sleeps (rests in deep relaxation) while the mind remains effortlessly aware.

Yoga nidra is more than just lying down and chilling out. It can help us heal on many levels. Physiologically, yoga nidra is known to cause blood pressure and cortisol levels to drop, while the heart rate slows. The health benefits it offers are many: when my private clients or workshop participants begin a daily yoga nidra practice, they often refer to it as life-changing—their anxiety levels drop, their depression is alleviated, their emotions feel more balanced, and those who suffer from intense anxiety dreams find that their dream life becomes calmer and their sleep more restful. People with insomnia find it a helpful and soothing practice to guide them back into sleep. Wannabe lucid dreamers find that with the right affirmations and guidance, yoga nidra can become a wonderful way of remaining consciously aware while falling asleep, so that they immediately enter a lucid dream. It is a fantastic way of surfing hypnagogic imagery and learning to navigate liminal spaces such as the lucid void and sleep paralysis with equanimity. It's a beautiful tool for exploring consciousness.

Yoga nidra can be practised at any time of the day or night; it's there for you whenever you need it. I have developed audio yoga nidra visualisations for various aspects of sleeping and dreaming, from releasing fear in liminal states to invoking lucid dreaming. Some people prefer to be guided by a voice, but you can also practise yoga nidra on your own.

1. Lie down comfortably on your back. If you're someone who falls asleep quickly, lie on a yoga mat rather than in bed. Close your eyes.

2. Relax with some regular, deep breaths. Feel your body grow heavy. If you like, you can do a body scan, bringing your attention to each of the different parts of your body and consciously relaxing them. With every exhalation, you release any tension and allow your thoughts to slow.

3. Notice your mind beginning to drift slightly. You may become aware of light forms advancing and receding, or geometric shapes. Strange, vivid imagery may appear, such as bizarre faces, intricate machinery, or random visions. Stay aware; observe any imagery as if it's a surrealist movie, without getting attached to it. You may experience sensations of floating or falling, or hear random noises or voices. These images and sensations are all a natural part of the hypnagogic state: relax and observe with detachment. Notice as your body awareness shifts: at some point, when you become deeply relaxed, you will be unable to feel it unless you try to.

4. The moment when you can't feel where your body begins and ends signals a golden threshold: you are floating on the very cusp of sleep, so

stay alert and don't allow yourself to be sucked in by beguiling dream-like imagery. Stay present to this threshold state; stay lucidly aware.

5. Stay present in this floating, bodiless state for as long as you like. While here, you might wish to ask for healing or knowledge, or ask to be shown your life purpose or the nature of the universe. You might conjure the face of a deceased loved one and speak words of love or forgiveness. You may wish to focus on a luminous dream you had, or do some deep nightmare work. You may prefer not to "do" anything in this golden state, but just float in liminality, enjoying the sensation of having no body. You may spontaneously experience the Lucid Light. You may decide to move consciously into the dream state—effectively remaining conscious throughout the process of falling asleep—and have a lucid dream.

6. When you are ready, come out of the experience by taking a few deep breaths and bringing your attention to your body. Wriggle your fingers and toes, turn your head from side to side, open your eyes, and smile.

In this chapter, we've looked at precognitive and telepathic nightmares, OBEs, and NDEs, and considered the big questions of consciousness, life, death, and the afterlife. We've considered nightmares that form a bridge between us and deceased loved ones, the different types and meanings of suicide dreams, and how death can be a metaphor for change. We've seen that some of the techniques in this book can be used to work with psi nightmares, out-of-body experiences, and even distressing NDEs.

In the final chapter, we'll look at spiritual nightmares, the wonders and terrors of the lucid void, and dying as a spiritual transition. We'll also encounter the golden oneness of the Lucid Light.

тнe Luminous sнadow: spiritual Niɡнtmares

The shadow side of ourselves is not only made up of qualities that we view as negative or harmful and that we repress or ignore, like jealousy, fearfulness, shame, or greed; it is also made up of "positive" qualities that we deny or suppress, such as our unexplored talents, our higher potential, and our spiritual connection. The shadow is all of the parts of us that we have not yet embraced and illuminated. It's shadowy because the light hasn't entered yet. Nightmares reach out forcefully to show us that we need to make changes in our lives and deepen our connection with our inner light.

This final chapter of the book explores how nightmares strengthen our connection with death, the deceased, and the divine, and illuminate our journey towards spiritual healing and enlightenment. We'll look at examples of how the luminous shadow makes itself known through nightmares and how to handle frightening experiences in "the void"—an endless dream space devoid of habitual dream imagery, where we feel ourselves to be floating, falling, spinning, or rushing through darkness or coloured light. We'll look at how the most terrifying nightmares can spontaneously shift into the numinous. We'll investigate nightmares that touch death and the divine. We'll look at nightmares that arise from a dark night of the soul, and explore the wonders of the Lucid Light—the blissful light that is the baseline state of consciousness, a source of infinite healing that we can encounter in any state, including nightmares!

Let's dive into the transformative process that spiritual nightmares can trigger by considering the powerful role of fire in dreams and nightmares.

The Transformative Element of Fire

Think about how almost every substance changes form in a fire: it melts, evaporates, burns to ashes, or explodes. Fire is a highly transformative and powerful element in any state of consciousness, so unsurprisingly it has a strong transformative energy in dreams. Fire destroys, and in doing so, it makes way for new creations. Fire emits energy in the form of heat and light. It purifies and clears. Flames can symbolise spiritual enlightenment and mysticism. Fire in the form of the burning sun represents the essence of life. Fire is a powerful archetype and can symbolise change of the highest order. It's no coincidence that there are plenty of fire nightmares in this chapter. Psycho-spiritual transformation often involves nightmares of fiery destruction, light, and illumination.

During an intense period of introspection and spiritual seeking, one of my ocean retreat attendees, Graziano from Italy, had the following dream:

> I am with a woman and there is a bullying person with us carrying a bag with him. I think there is money or something valuable inside. The man wants to know something from us, and he is aggressive. Then he becomes meek and I decide to react. He walks away to his motorbike and I see that he drops his bag in a trash can. I approach, spread gas on him and his motorbike, and set everything on fire. He doesn't even try to escape, and he doesn't argue or scream.

At first, Graziano felt this dream was about destroying a dark shadow aspect of himself: an old part of his personality represented by the motorbike man. But when we worked on it together, the dreamwork revealed deeper layers. During a dream reentry, he discovered that the motorbike man was seeking treasure in the form of self-knowledge, and that together, the man, the woman, and himself symbolised the three parts of the brain: reptilian, neocortex, and limbic. In the dreamwork, the three of them agreed to work together and combine their strengths to find the knowledge they were seeking.

The motorbike turned out to be powerfully symbolic: Graziano had always owned a motorbike, but for the previous two years, since the breakup of his relationship, his bike has sat unused in his garage. When he thought about the motorbike in the garage as symbolic of part of himself, he said, "It's like I don't want to move. A stationary bike is like a lack of energy; frozen energy. I want to shift my frozen energy." When he imagined himself riding the bike, he spoke of power and freedom. I asked him about the act of setting the motorbike and the man on fire, and we talked about the nature of fire. Graziano said, "Fire is a way to purify, to light something up, to illuminate. I have to illuminate the free, powerful part of myself."

It's very powerful symbolism in a dream to set something on fire. It shows a strong wish for change, a readiness for transformation. It was interesting that the motorbike guy seemed fine about being set on fire! This indicates that it is the right time to reignite that lost power and freedom, release the frozen part of the self, and move on. The psyche is ready; the dreamer has permission from all parts of himself to reclaim his power and freedom. This is a "luminous shadow" dream, one that illuminates the dreamer's higher potential and his readiness to reach for spiritual connection. It's also a transformation ritual, preparing the dreamer for psycho-spiritual change.

Even the most terrifying nightmares can become symbols of strength and succour. Let's look at how they can help us through the worst of times.

"Dark Night of the Soul" Nightmares

Nightmares can provide us with an awesome metaphor for upheaval and change during the darkest times in our lives, and can provide us with a sense of spiritual guidance. Delia shares her experience:

This "dark night of the soul" experience preceded a complete upending of my entire life—spousal abuse, divorce, family tensions, health issues, career change—but most of all, a complete revaluation and shedding of old views, values, and aspirations. The dream gave me a visual and metaphorical context that helped me grasp some kind of understanding during a time of much unknowing and upheaval. Its pervasive nature—timelessness and persistence in my awareness—helped me as a guiding presence rather than simply a symbol or message.

Delia shares her nightmare:

I am lying on my back on a bare stone altar or table, awaiting a terrible ceremony I am dreading with every fibre of my being. As much as I want to avoid it, I know it must happen, being important and inevitable. The ceremony involves a fancy, bejewelled sword being plunged into my chest, all the way through. As I wait indefinitely for the appointed time, panic leaves me breathless, sweating, with a racing heart. The altar stands in an empty room; the only presence seems to be the sword itself somehow. Although I don't see it, I know it's a magnificent, finely crafted one dedicated to this service. In my mind's eye, I can almost see the coloured jewels and glinting gold.

What significantly distresses me more than anything is knowing it will shatter my rib cage. I can almost tangibly preview the felt sense, the sound and texture of the cracking bones. I sense a vague parallel between the bare, exposed stone surface of the altar and my vulnerable, waiting rib cage so prone to breakage. The longer I wait, the more I seem to become familiar with the sword. In some ways, I begin to admire it. It seems rather magnificent and elicits the kind of awe and admiration one might develop for a beloved guru, wise mentor, or omniscient being.

Reflecting on her experience, Delia comments:

The dream foretold the impending psycho-spiritual processes unfolding ahead of me; in many ways, my ego structure was shattered as I lay defenceless against these processes. By being able to focus on a majestic presence behind the unbearable processes, I was able to better recognise and grasp the holy and life-giving forces behind that otherwise unbearable phase; somewhat like realising there's a caring, well-meaning doctor behind the dreaded jab of a needle.

Dr. Tadas Stumbrys from Lithuania shared this powerful dream with me for my Amazing Dreamers feature in the IASD magazine, *DreamTime*.[69]

---

69. Johnson, "Amazing Dreamer," *DreamTime*.

I dream there is a pandemic virus that is killing all the people on Earth. Everybody around is dying in the dream. At the end, it is just me and my grandma who are the only survivors, but she is lying in her bed very sick. I am pleading with her not to die.

I have a very strong feeling in the dream that if my grandma dies, the whole world will collapse and the whole of existence will halt, because there will only be a single point of awareness/perspective left (i.e., myself), and for the world to exist, at least two perspectives are needed. Like opposites: you need darkness for light to exist, or cold for heat to exist, as one cannot exist without the other.

Then my grandma dies in the dream.

To my biggest surprise, the world doesn't end. Immediately I have a realisation that it's me who is creating the world. With this sense of awe and numinosity, I become lucid and with my thoughts I start to creatively shape the dream environment which readily responds. I feel empowered and in a flow.

Tadas comments:

There was obviously some emotional processing, as my grandmother died a couple of years before the dream and she was my last family member. One of the key messages of this dream was how we create our dreaming and waking realities, often not explicitly recognising that. On a deeper level, it also connected with the notions of Atman and Brahman in Hindu philosophy, of an individual "soul" and the world "soul," and how both are essentially one and the same.

Nightmares can have a profoundly spiritual nature. They bring us insights about who we are and why we are here so that we can clarify our purpose and do the work we need to do during this lifetime. We do all co-create the world together. The knowledge that it is not only our inner world that we create but our outer, collective world, too, helps us to feel deeply connected to all others on the planet. We need each other, and we are not separate!

A pandemic forces us to realise how intimately connected we are as a species and confronts us with the mortality of ourselves and others. Death is a major spiritual transition, and awareness of its constant proximity can raise our consciousness, connecting us to the cosmic soul. When we act fearfully in the world, we generate panic, bad decisions, and feelings of separation and disconnection. But when we do dreamwork to transcend our worst fears, we become more balanced humans and can contribute more to the collective health and balance of humanity. It is wonderful to experience the support and joy of spiritual dreams during times of hardship and loss.

Let's move on to explore a different type of nocturnal experience. Have you ever had a nightmare where there is no imagery present? This may sound strange, because we are so familiar with nightmares as streams of vivid and distressing imagery, but in fact the scary experience of floating lost in pitch blackness is one that many people write to me about. "What is this frightening dream space?" they ask. "How do I escape from it?" Let's explore an imageless dream space that we can choose to fill with fear or wonder, a space where anything is possible. That's right—we're going to dive into the lucid void!

The Lucid Void: From Terror to Wonder

Have you ever found yourself falling unstoppably through infinite space at great velocity? Or floating in a universe composed entirely of dots of light? Have you ever felt lonely and bodiless in a vast black space? Or have you been sucked through a twisting wormhole of rainbow light? How about finding yourself in an entirely luminous space, or flying through endless white clouds at incredible speeds? If you've had any of these experiences, congratulations! You are officially a lucid void explorer and have encountered one of the most creative and meditative dream spaces out there, a space filled with infinite potential.

We are often effortlessly lucid in the void, and we may experience ourselves as not having a body, but existing as a dot of conscious awareness. The void may appear empty at first glance, but it is really more of a fullness. It may appear pitch black at first, but it is steeped in light. The void can be composed of light of any colour. It's a great place for initiating spiritual encounters with the Lucid Light, as described later in this chapter. I call the void "the gap between dreams," because although this is dream space, it lacks the vivid, realistic stream of imagery that manifests in most dreams.

In fact, from the creative blank screen of the void, we can have the fascinating and enriching experience of watching dreams and visions build up from scratch. We can also actively create sound, light, shapes, vibrations, and imagery. We can float meditatively and experience oneness. We can play around: we can spin, tumble, or plummet like a rock. We can shapeshift into a mermaid or a phoenix. We can seek profound healing by inviting healing light of any colour to pour into us. Of course, we can also choose to freak out, struggle to wake up, and generally have a terrible time in the void. It's really up to us.

There's no doubt that anybody's first encounter with the void can be terrifying. I've been there too! As you know, much depends on the mental attitude we take with us into these mysterious states. If we panic when we can't see anything we're used to seeing, like regular people, streets, or nature, then we may feel powerless and insignificant in the void. We may think we're about to die—or even that we have already died! Our own fear may well attract fearful visions and sensations. In the thought-responsive, creative space of the lucid void, once we allow our own worst fears to manifest, it becomes an awful lot harder to keep calm. As we've seen so often in this book, remaining calm is the key.

Plenty of people ask me how to cope with fear when they enter the void and how to avoid being sucked into the void ever again. Others ask me for a well-signposted map of how to reach the void, as they're so curious to experience it. In a comment on the lucid void page of my website, Jessica reports a typical first void encounter:

> I had a dream I was standing in a closet shuffling through the clothes hanging on the rack, then all of a sudden this unseen force pulled me into a black void. I was floating and feeling a bit scared, so I woke myself up.[70]

The sense of being pulled forcibly into another space happens often in dreams. This can be seen as an invitation for us to explore our dreams and consciousness more deeply. When I first started being ripped out of a dream and flung through space at a zillion miles an hour, I was surprised and confused

---

70. Johnson, Deep Lucid Dreaming, "The Lucid Void," https://deepluciddreaming.com/2015/05/the-lucid-void/.

about what was happening. But soon I was actively seeking these experiences, because when we relax into them and take a curious, open-minded approach, they become part of a fascinating personal journey and help us to understand life's mysteries and the deeper questions of the cosmos. When we embrace the void without fear, we are open to incredible spiritual experiences of love, oneness, and compassion. Also on the lucid void page of my site, Nyomi shares such an experience:

> I simply was in space. I wasn't scared; I was at total peace. Below me I could see a bubble. In that bubble I could see myself walking around, talking and interacting with family. I felt the most intense love that I've ever felt, but it was for myself. I thought, "You just don't know how beautiful and wonderful you are!" My consciousness felt so overwhelmed by this concept, because I knew once I was back in my body, I would have all life's truths and past experiences and future worries on my shoulders, but it was so peaceful. I woke up thinking, "That's the place before birth and after life: this eternal bliss and love in the void."[71]

In the void, Nyomi accessed the blissful state that we find when we enter the Lucid Light, the loving light that we emerge from at birth and reenter at death. The Lucid Light is always there because it's an intrinsic part of us, our baseline state of consciousness, and it's easily accessible in lucid dreams. The wonderful thing about this type of lucid experience is that we will always carry within us that inner knowledge of the oneness we share with every other living being, and the total bliss and peace we will likely return to when we die. The following practice gives tips on how to navigate the void so that we can transcend fear and make the most out of this deeply meditative experience.

practice 42

HOW TO NAVIGATE THE LUCID VOID

- Practise calming techniques during the day, or recall a moment in your life when you felt totally safe and loved. Allow this feeling of wellbeing to envelop you. In the void, bring this feeling of wellbeing into your

---

71. Johnson, Deep Lucid Dreaming, "The Lucid Void," https://deepluciddreaming.com/2015/05/the-lucid-void/.

heart. Stay calm and curious. Breathe calmly. (In the dream state, you have control over your breathing.) Say a mantra like, "I am safe, I am safe," to remind you that there is no need to freak out.

- Following a scary void experience, it can help to reduce fear if you practise entering the void in your imagination while awake and deeply relaxed. Try a dream reentry technique such as Practice 8: Reenter the Nightmare, where you close your eyes and mentally imagine yourself back in the scene. Lucidly aware in this waking dream reentry, you could either reexperience the void without fear and see what happens, or you could take on the role of a wise dream mentor and reassure your frightened void self that they are safe and free to relax and explore this marvellous world.

- If you are scared that you'll die during a weird sleep experience, please know that you won't die—you will wake safely from this strange experience! If people died each time they found themselves floating fearfully in the void, thousands of healthy people would be found dead in their beds each morning. You will survive this experience!

- Plan a few exciting experiments you can try the next time you enter the void. You could manifest an object—one woman said that she manifested an apple on her first attempt. Or you could intend for something glorious to appear—you could call out, "Void, show me something amazing!" and see what it comes up with. It can be such a magical experience.

- If you're falling through the void, smile to yourself as you recall the common expression "falling asleep." Feelings of falling are part of the natural sensory transition we experience as we shift from the waking state into the sleep state. There will be no hard landing, so release any fear and enjoy the ride!

- Experiment with your dream body, if you have one. You can shrink to the size of a pinhead, expand to infinity, grow new limbs, or do acrobatic feats such as backflips, impossible twists, and balletic leaps. Do anything that makes you giggle—laughter is the best antidote to fear.

- Create a fresh dream: set an intention to watch a dream build up step-by-step. This may start with spinning lights or sheets of luminescent colour. It may involve sound and motion, or you may simply see a highly realistic image of something very normal, like a shiny red car. Play with your intention while allowing spontaneous manifestations, and let the dream create itself around you. Then move into it, lucidly aware.

• It can be wonderfully relaxing to chant "Om" in the void. The voice is powerful; it sends out calming vibrations that emanate through dream space and can cause beautiful ripples of light to occur. You could build up an entire orchestra of sound, as I've done before. It's incredibly realistic and moving to create music in the void.

• If you're keen to have a spiritual experience in the void, then the next time you find yourself there, meditate. In any dream state, we are able to forget the body very easily. The light, flexible, and largely pain-free dream body is easily transcended. This makes it much easier to enter a state of deep and blissful meditation. The lucid void is a gift because we are often effortlessly aware—perfect for mind-expanding experiences.

These simple techniques and ideas were ones I stumbled across through trial and error when I had a long series of intense encounters in the lucid void about twenty-five years ago. Soon, I eagerly looked forward to my time in the void, because I understood that it's a space of infinite creative potential. If you're seeking a lucid void experience, the most common entry points are the pre-sleep imagery of hypnagogia; sleep paralysis; lucid dreams (just do a backflip with the intention of entering the void, or dive through a portal, or meditate); non-lucid dreams (in these, you often just get sucked into the void, willy-nilly); and out-of-body experiences. Once you're in the void, the dreamworld is your oyster.

....

Now that we've done more work on releasing fear, let's dive more deeply into the bliss of the Lucid Light.

What Is the Lucid Light?

The Lucid Light is pure conscious awareness: the underlying oneness that binds everything and everyone together.[72] Many people assume that the

---

72. A far more in-depth exploration of the Lucid Light can be found in *Llewellyn's Complete Book of Lucid Dreaming*.

waking state is our baseline state of consciousness, but my theory is that the Lucid Light is the state from which all forms and matter emerge; it is the original, alive, aware light from which all states of consciousness and all energy, matter, and physical forms emerge. As such, it is always present, and imageless dream spaces like the void and the "gap between dreams" are composed purely of the Lucid Light, which can be any colour, including black and white. We can have immersive Lucid Light experiences during meditation, in dreams where we experience luminescence, during out-of-body experiences, and in ultra-lucid waking-life moments, as well as during near-death experiences. This is the light we emerge from as conscious beings and the light we return to when we die. Experiences of the Lucid Light can be blissful, energising, and healing.

My advice to anyone interested in having a deeper and more spiritual life is to go towards the light in your dreams, in your meditations, in your heart. The luminosity is always present. When we go to the place of deepest fear, we will find light. And sometimes, the light finds us.

Let's explore some different encounters with the Lucid Light to see how it arises in dreams and nightmares. This first example is one of my own, when a waking nightmare provoked a wonderful Lucid Light–filled dream.

Encounters with the Lucid Light

When I was twenty-one, I lived alone in the South of France. Well, not completely alone: two lizards also lived in my apartment, and soon they had a baby. I loved that baby lizard—tiny, quick, delicate, its skin nearly translucent so you could see its heart beating. It had round black eyes and a flicky tail. I was so happy that my home was his home. One boiling day, I struggled back from town with four heavy shopping bags cutting into my wrists, unlocked the front door, burst into the apartment with all my bags, and kicked the door shut with my foot. My head whipped around as I remembered that I *never* shut that door without checking for the lizard … I saw him scamper up the inside of the doorjamb just as the door slammed shut.

For hours, I couldn't bring myself to open the door. I kidded myself that perhaps he'd survived. When I finally eased the door open, the baby lizard was flat as a pancake and very dead. Poor baby, poor parents! I was so sorry, and went to sleep feeling unhappy about it. Later that night, I became aware that my bedroom was illuminated by green light. I sat up, not sure if I was awake or lucid dreaming. The light seemed so real, and it was coming from the hallway, shining all around my doorframe. I rose from bed with such ease that I figured I must be dreaming. Still—there was something peculiar about this light. Slowly, I opened the door.

The entrance hall to my apartment was filled with a green luminosity, and as I looked up to the ceiling to discover its source, I saw the most enormous green lizard! She was much bigger than me, made from pure green light, and I knew this was the mother of all lizards. Immediately, and without words, I offered her a heartfelt apology for killing the baby lizard. She felt my regret and responded with such love and forgiveness, letting me know that everything was very much all right: this was a natural spiritual transition. I watched in awe as she collected the bright light of the baby lizard and brought it into her own light. Then she disappeared and the green light faded away.

I was left standing in the hallway, still with a strong sense of presence. The physical reality of my hallway was so real that it felt like I was sleepwalking. I returned to bed. This experience felt very spiritual and it helped me not to feel quite so awful about the baby lizard (but it was still tough to watch his little body shrivel and dry up over the next weeks—I couldn't bear to scrape him off the door!).

So many times in my life, when I've needed it, the Lucid Light has reached into my dreams and waking consciousness to gift me with loving energy, beautiful visions, and profound insights. I've experienced immersive Lucid Light from yoga nidra states of deep relaxation where I've been recharged from exhausted to energised simply by floating in the light. The Lucid Light can astonish us by appearing from unexpected sources, as in the following nightmares, two of which feature the majestic power of a dragon.

Luminous Dragon Nightmares of Fire and Light

Keith, an artist from the US, wrote to me sharing the following transformative spiritual dream. It started out as a nightmare, but when Keith faced the danger with courage, he was gifted with a vision of a luminous universe.

Inside a European castle, I see two duelling figures and a large wooden lever next to a steel portcullis. There is a fierce and fiery demon/dragon secured inside. I don't fully grasp the consequences of releasing such a figure. When I pull the lever, an overwhelming feeling of regret washes over me. I had no idea what I was unleashing. This demon is intelligent and all fire. Who could ever stop it? I descend the spiralling stairs with swift feet. In the car, I speed away down the road, trying to leave it all behind. And I may have gotten away, too, but I begin to hear the dragon. And the screams. A glimpse of the castle in smoky ruins flashes in the rearview mirror. I have to take responsibility for my actions. I released him. I have to go back.

I make a strong U-turn and head back. Somehow this dragon knows who I am and that I am in this car. It picks my car up in its talons and hoists me up, high in the air. I see its head. It is gesturing as if to lash out. In this moment of utter hopelessness, I feebly push my door open and vigorously flail it at my foe, as if this were some kind of weapon. What am I going to do? Bash him with the door? But Fire Dragon is actually pleased that I am fighting back. "Good!" he says, almost like a mentor.

I begin to realize that the fire is not harming me. Fire Dragon leans in close and begins to open his massive jaws. When I look into the dragon's open mouth, I see the most awe-inspiring sight, as if looking into the center of all creation. As I peer into this luminous universe of raw creative wonder, a burst of white flower blossoms emanates in a beautiful mandala that fills my gaze, and I wake up.

In Keith's dream, a shift from terror to courage results in the Lucid Light revealing itself in the form of a luminous archetypal image: the mandala—a sacred circle that represents unity in Jungian psychology and symbolises the universe in the Hindu and Buddhist religions. The dragon's mouth seems symbolic of a gateway opening into the deeper mysteries of life, a glorious glimpse of the infinite.

Maomi, an experienced lucid dreamer, wrote to me from Hawaii to share a lucid dream with a wholly unexpected ending:

Near the end of my lucid dream I saw a shadowy figure. I was afraid to look on the face. And because I have been in the practice of facing those fears in dreams, I chose to go up to the figure and look upon their face. The creature was human-like with dark, long, mangled hair. The posture was crouched, hunched up in a corner of the room where there was hardly any light to see. They had their face against the wall. It took everything I had to walk up to this being. As I approached, the figure turned around and faced me. The ragged exterior of the person didn't match what I saw.

When I looked at the face, it was pure, brilliant, bright light and its beauty was so humbling and overwhelming.

I woke up thinking, "What the F*** was that about!" I couldn't get the whole sequence out of my mind. Was that part of my psyche? Was that something outside of myself? Where do I go when I lucid dream? Lucid dreaming feels so powerful and between worlds, like a place yet not a place.

This is such a beautiful example of the luminous shadow. When we courageously face the darkness in whatever form it takes, we are sometimes gifted with the truth in the form of blazing light. When Maomi shared this powerful lucid dream, it made me think of a quote commonly attributed to the fourteenth-century Persian Sufi poet Hafez Shirazi: "I wish I could show you, when you are lonely or in darkness, the astonishing light of your own being!" We are all made of this brilliant light. It's a wonder to behold and sometimes shocking to us. From my own encounters with this light, my feeling is that this is the light of the soul, the essence of all that we are.

Vivid dreamer Jessica shares an amazing, luminous dragon dream that involves a kind of baptism by fire, death, and purification.

I'm at the ocean. The water is rising and dangerous, an uninviting dark teal colour. Next, there is a deafening crack—and I mean SO loud—CRACK—and instead of lightning, a big black fork comes down from the clouds and the sky. I feel fearful and doomed, as if the end of the earth is upon us.

Out of this black fork emerge flying black creatures with hooked wings. Almost like angel wings. It's as if they want to destroy the entire human race. They begin to breathe huge streams of fire, burning the city and town. I turn to run, but only a few steps later, a magnificent, terrifying dragon swoops out from the sky. I know this is it: I will not make it. I know it is too late. It is the end for me.

Dragon rains down fire.

His face and presence take up the whole scene—his eyes stand out, beady and intense, and he opens his mouth to release fire. The colour is a wonderful combination of yellows, golds, tinges of warm and red. I can see each individual scale on his face and the pointed horns on his snout. He wants to kill me.

The fire consumes me. I am dying.

The fear of feeling nothing is so great as I'm dying, but as the fire hits, I feel ALIVE with glowing white energy; it is blinding bright and reaches every part of my body, my mind, my existence. It is an amazing feeling. Like liberation. Purification. Cleansing. There is no fear or pain. Just being consumed by the fire and bright light, bringing with it an entirely different state of mind, a new realm.

Jessica says, "That was the beginning of a turbulent period that resulted in me finding my faith, so to speak." This kind of transformative spiritual nightmare can give us a profound understanding of how fear can be the greatest barrier to knowledge. Look at how we dress our fears: they emerge in nightmares as monstrous, predatory creatures whose apparent goal is to annihilate us. Of course we run away at first! Yet when we face the monster, we transcend our crippling fear and enable transformation, healing, and enlightenment.

practice 43

TURN MYTHOLOGICAL BEASTS INTO PROTECTIVE ALLIES

Sometimes the most terrifying nightmares involve monsters of mythological power and presence. In this book alone, there are nightmares that star serpents, dragons, a hideous goat, tigers, and mythological mixes of animals, such as the chimera in chapter 4. I especially love these nightmare combo-animals, because they are transformation in progress! They embody different powers. The fire-breathing chimera from Greek mythology has the head of a lion, the body of a goat, and a serpent's tail. It embodies the power and qual-ities of all of these animals, combined with the transformative power of fire. Wow! This nightmare beast could become a major ally if you take steps to merge its energy with your own and make it part of your inner power; your wilder, larger self.

- Whenever a mythological beast or any kind of powerful animal or monster shows up in your dreams, take time to consider its qualities. One man dreamed about a combo-animal that was half-crocodile, half-dolphin. If you have this kind of dream and feel the animal might repre-sent a part of you, ask yourself, which part of me is a bit like a crocodile? And a dolphin? Look for both positive and negative attributes. These can help you identify which qualities and characteristics about yourself you would like to change, and guide you to becoming your best self. If you feel the combo-animal represents a person in your life, ask your-self why it is showing up in this form in your dream. Is there something you can learn from this person?

- Investigate the way that this nightmare creature has been portrayed in myth, its role in history, and any other associations you want to explore in order to get a vaster picture of the energy it brings.

- Look for a personal association—does anyone in your life remind you of this beast? Wanwilai, a film producer from Thailand, dreamed of a wondrous white snake wearing a crown, with diamond eyes that spar-kled with da Vinci symbols. But then the snake spat poison onto the dreamer's chest. Soon afterwards in waking life, a dear friend of hers behaved in a poisonous fashion towards her, hurting her deeply. Wan-wilai dreamed again of the white snake. This time it turned black and lost its tail, indicating the ugly end of the friendship.

- Take action in your life in any way that feels right to honour your night-mare beast and bring its energy into your life. Draw it, write a poem about it, enact its movements in dance, or drum a story around it. I have dreamed many times of tigers. They often symbolise my creativ-ity. When I felt overwhelmed by other people's traumatic nightmare accounts at the start of writing this book and was unsure of how to organise my material, I dreamed a baby tiger let me pick him up and hold him. Our bodies buzzed together harmoniously. When I woke up, the block had shifted and I started to write at about a hundred miles per hour. Right now, a female tiger and her blue-eyed cub are eyeing me from across my desk in the form of tiny, lifelike models. They remind me to be brave as I work with all of these fiery nightmares and to let volcanic lava and creativity flow freely through the book.

- Meditate on your nightmare creature. Bring it into your mind's eye fearlessly, knowing that this wondrous beast has entered your dreams to help and heal you. If it has destructive energy, remember that sometimes old behavioural patterns and unhealthy attachments or thoughts need to be destroyed in order to clear the path to a new, healthier way of being in the world. If you feel repulsed by the beast, either allow it to transform into something else or focus on any positive qualities it has. Play with different scenarios as you engage imaginatively with the beast, and see what resonates and brings you insights into its place in your psyche and your life. Ask your beast to protect you and share its power with you.

- Call on the powerful energy of your nightmare creature in waking-life situations. If your boss is being critical and unfair, bring Lion energy into your heart and don't let yourself be bullied or subdued.

- Thank your beast from the heart for arriving on your path to help you towards wholeness and self-understanding. This could be the beginning of a beautiful friendship!

Luminous Lucid Dreams

Light and luminosity seem linked to higher states of consciousness in dreams. We've seen that spiritual nightmares may spontaneously morph into intense experiences of brilliant light, and super-aware dreams also tend towards luminosity. In lucid dreams over the past few decades, I have spontaneously found myself in a luminous white space where I have high-level, coherent, and illuminating conversations about the nature of consciousness, the journey of the soul through life and death, lucid dreaming, and the nature of being. Here, I have interactions with both living and deceased consciousness explorers and also meet guide-like super-conscious figures I've never seen before, who share knowledge with me, often in a stream of imagery. My lucidity in these dreams is effortless and unquestioned; it's as stable as in waking reality.

There are several interesting things to note about the people I meet in these luminous lucid dreams. First, they are usually around 20 percent bigger than regular humans. Second, they appear in vibrant physical health, radiating energy and well-being. Third (and please don't ask me why!), they are dressed entirely in white clothes. I refer to the space we meet in as a "white room" because there is sometimes minimalistic furniture in there, for example, a table and chairs (white, of course—seems it all has to match!). For someone like me who loves colour and has incredibly bright, colourful dreams, this is surprising and very different, yet these spaces feel luminous and alive. The walls are not like white-washed solid walls; this "room" seems to be a space made from white light. I think of it as a meeting place.

In one lucid dream, an old woman led me into a luminous white room with two massage-type beds in it. She lay down on one and crossed her arms over her chest and closed her eyes. I assumed the same position on the other bed and was instantly taken into the most profound state of meditation. I knew I was in the presence of a powerful meditator. I was then shown a stream of disturbing imagery that I felt tangibly in my body—one image was of a granite gravestone crushing me. I had no idea why I was being shown these multisensory images. However, despite the upsetting nature of the imagery, I felt safe, serene, and connected in this deep meditation, as if I were plugged in to a source of peace.

When the slideshow finally ended, the old woman left the room without speaking a word to me, even though I tried to ask her about what I'd seen. Shortly afterwards, in waking life, those scenes sadly came true in my life in the form of an unexpected situation of loss and grief. Amazingly, I was strong in this situation, able to connect to that sense of deep oneness and peace despite the circumstances, so that I was able to provide help and loving support for others who were affected by it too. It was as if the old woman had warned me of what was coming but had simultaneously reminded me of my inner resources so that I was able to tap into the peaceful centre we all have within us.

In another "white room" encounter, I found myself with the deceased sleep researcher and psychoanalyst Dr. Ernest Hartmann. We had met only once in waking life, at an IASD dream conference in 2005, when I was awarded an IASD student research award for my PhD work on lucid dreaming, and I'd found him to be a kind and thoughtful man. In this white space (where he was 20 percent bigger than his physical self was), we talked about the journey of the soul through life. I was saying how precious it was to be alive and experience this beautiful world in a human body, and I asked him what it was like after death. He conveyed to me that it was delightful. His eyes sparkled with health and joy. A dark-haired woman whom I didn't know entered the room, and we had a group hug that felt marvellous, as if I were being charged with energy. Midway through the hug, I noticed my feet were not touching the ground—Ernest and the woman were carrying me! I felt so incredibly loved and supported, and returned to waking reality feeling revitalised and with a strong feeling that this had been more than just a lucid dream—it felt like an actual encounter.

In dreams, it's good to watch for light and luminosity (also in the form of glowing colours, a shining moon, sparkling water, or vibrantly healthy dream people, plants, or animals). There may be healing there, or a gift of knowledge, or an immersive experience of the Lucid Light where you float in deep bliss and experience oneness. When you see the light in a dream or nightmare, move towards it.

Let's take a look now at how lucid dreaming and imaginal journeying can help us to prepare for the event that so many of us fear; the ultimate transition of death.

Preparation for the Ultimate Transition: Death

We can use lucid dreaming, out-of-body experiences, meditation, yoga nidra, and imaginal journeying, such as the drumming journey in practice 45 later in this chapter, as tools through which to explore death and prime ourselves for an experience of conscious dying. Some people might wonder why on earth anyone would want to be conscious of dying. Surely dying is an awful thing? Wouldn't we rather just slip into unconsciousness (and therefore death) and *not* know about it? Well, that's one way of doing things. Choosing to sleepwalk aimlessly through life and trip reluctantly into Death's arms at the end of it does seem to be a fairly popular approach in some cultures. But for those who wish to wake up in their lives and ignite their own vast human potential, consciousness in all things seems a far more exciting choice.

Are you afraid of dying? Where does this fear of death come from? It's good to make time in your life to question your beliefs about life and death. Practice 39: Question Your Beliefs, Assumptions, and Expectations in the previous chapter may help you to pinpoint the origins of your fear. It's helpful to consider the nature of the universe and wonder what happens after death. It's something we can all benefit from. We'll all definitely die one day—what's the point of fearing this natural transition? Fear can be pretty pointless, except when it kick-starts our survival instinct to help us escape from an imminent physical threat, such as a charging rhinoceros, or to keep us at a sensible distance from sheer drops. Fear in the dreamworld usually serves no real purpose, and excessive fear in waking life prevents us from living our fullest life. Releasing fear doesn't mean we become reckless about our personal safety; it means we live a lucid, joyful, responsible, and caring life. Whenever you encounter fear, examine it, go into it, … and release it.

Lucid dreaming can prepare us for death, because when we are consciously aware in a dream, we can transcend not only the physical body but also the dream body. Freed from the body concept, we can explore pure conscious awareness. We can exist as a floating point of consciousness in a lucid dream, or move beyond even that into nondual awareness where there is no longer a sense of the ego-self, or indeed any "self" at all. Such awesome and transformative experiences free us from fear. There is so much fear about dying, but advanced lucid dreamers know that there is no need to be frightened of this natural transition from one state of consciousness to another. Fear is an incredibly potent force in life. It restricts us, it reduces us, and it creates massive intellectual and emotional blocks that cause us to live a small life. When we work to transcend fear, we free up masses of energy with which we can live more consciously and help others on their own journey through life.

Spiritual lucid dreams and out-of-body experiences can help us to prepare consciously for death. We can practise dying in a lucid dream in wonderfully imaginative ways, such as by allowing ourselves to get eaten by a dinosaur or flying into the sun. We can ask to experience death and dying—but only do this if you're sure you really want to know! I would not recommend this for people with anxiety, depression, or mental health issues, or those who feel psychologically unstable. Some people report highly realistic experiences of drowning or being killed in some other way after formulating this kind of request in a dream. I have never had that; for me, this type of request usually results in the complete dissolution of all forms, including the dream body (or energy body), and the ego-self, and an experience of blissful white light. Whether unpleasant or pleasant, such lucid dream experiences can aid in the psychological and emotional understanding that we, too, will surely die one day! This awareness of death intensifies our life, sharpening our sense of purpose, bringing us closer to our heart's desire, and encouraging us to live consciously, with joy and compassion.

My experiences within the Lucid Light have helped me to transcend my fear of death. I'm very familiar with being consciously aware in bodiless, seemingly infinite dream spaces and raising my level of consciousness in these states via meditation (which is easy, as there are none of the usual physical distractions when we meditate in a lucid dream!). While I'm in no hurry to die, because I love life and feel that I'm doing the work I was meant to do, I am intrigued by what death will be like. I'm so curious about this big spiritual transition and I'm determined to remain consciously aware throughout and beyond death. It'll be a fascinating lucid adventure.

Deep meditation, yoga nidra, lucid dreaming, out-of-body experiences, and imaginal journeying effectively train us to raise our level of conscious awareness in life and prepare in reassuring and healing ways for the ultimate transition of death. In these states, we can travel towards our own death to take a clear-eyed look at our fears and register our own mortality. Such exercises often naturally result in greater clarity about our life path and a more compassionate engagement with the people in our lives. One thing I have done for decades, when facing important life decisions, is to engage in an imaginal journey where I travel forward in time to the age of eighty-five and imagine myself looking back at my life. Taking on this perspective not only makes any problems look less significant, but also reminds me of my life's trajectory and how I want to live.

The next practice helps us to cross thresholds with ease and connect with our inner light. It can also be a beautiful way of falling asleep!

practice 44

MEET YOUR INNER LIGHT

This is a guided visualisation that you can change and personalise in any way that feels right and use to connect to your deeper self when you are about to fall asleep at night.

Imagine you are standing on a sunny, flower-covered mountain. Everything in this place is at the height of its beauty, and you feel happy. Ahead of you is a beautiful waterfall. It sparkles with light and vitality. You approach it and stand very close to it, enjoying the feel of the spray on your skin. Then you walk effortlessly through the water-fall, as if it were a curtain made of light.

As you cross this natural threshold, you feel an increased sense of wellbeing and aliveness. Beyond the waterfall is a spacious chamber with an aura of tranquillity. This sacred space is warmly lit with can-dles that cast an orange glow. Being here makes you feel like you have finally come home. You feel safe and happy because this sacred place belongs to you.

Up ahead of you, in a stone circle lit with candles, you see your inner light, your soul, your deeper, wiser self. Everybody's soul looks different, but you recognise yours instantly. It may appear as a wise-eyed person or animal, a pool of crystal-clear water, a swirling sphere of coloured light, an ancient book, a radiant, compassionate presence, or anything else. Go up to your soul and greet it in any way that feels right. You may wish to ask a question about your life path, or listen to any message it has for you. You may choose to sit and absorb its loving energy. Take as much time as you need.

When you feel it is time to leave, thank your soul or inner light, and take three deep breaths to return to your body and your reality. You might want to write about your encounter or draw it. Bring your inner light with you into your dreams and make it part of how you see and experience yourself: *I am the man whose soul is a lithe jaguar.* Or, *I am the woman whose soul is a healing hand.*

When we maintain a connection with our inner light, we become more able to respond to life's fears and challenges from the soul level rather than the ego level. We also become closer to death in the most positive of ways, because we develop an idea of ourselves as more than just a body and a brain. When we grow our soul connection, we become more lucid in life and in dreams. As a result, spiritual dreams may become more frequent. The most luminous and lucid of spiritual dreams can teach us to die.

One remarkable woman, Aiha Zemp, was an accomplished meditator and lucid dreamer. She was born without forearms and legs, suffered from an incurable disease, and was in pain, so she chose to die in her native Switzerland when she was fifty-eight. In the year of her death, she reported over thirty spiritual lucid dreams in which she would float in light and experience oneness. She told her Zen meditation teacher, Dr. Peter Widmer, "These dreams teach me to die."[73] One week before her chosen time, she had the following lucid dream.

> I'm lying dead in this room with the view of the Rhine. Just after I die, you five carers go out onto the balcony and are holding sparklers … You light the sparklers. Part of me leaves my body and this part is completely porous, it looks like a breath, slightly bluish, like evaporating steam rising from a humidifier, except in a different form, a sort of body form but not really; and it's much bigger than you all are on the balcony. I float through the window without opening it and begin to pluck the stars from the sparklers out of the air as if I had hands, and start to play and dance with them. It's wonderful. Then I go away, up into the air, and dissolve. I wake up feeling happy.[74]

One week later, at the time of her death, Aiha's carers honoured her lucid dream in the most beautiful and touching way. Peter told me, "We did exactly what the dream described. We went out onto the balcony and lit the waiting sparklers."

73. Johnson, *Llewellyn's Complete Book of Lucid Dreaming*, 369.
74. Ibid.

Lucid dreaming can provide us with a safe space within which we can transcend the boundaries of the physical body and our innate body concept to experience incredible freedom and boundless awareness within Lucid Light states. It is hard to put into words the depth and beauty of such experiences. These states prepare us for the final act of releasing our physical body with joy rather than fear.

The following practice can be used as a basis for a myriad of wonderful imaginal journeys to take you wherever you want to go, whether you want to explore death, experience the Lucid Light, encounter spiritual allies, or befriend power animals to protect you both in and out of your dreams.

practice 45

DRUMMING JOURNEY:
CREATE YOUR OWN SPIRITUAL DREAM

Many different cultural traditions use rhythmic drumming to enter trance states. When we listen to rhythmic beats, we can follow the sound of the drum into the imaginal world and go on a dreamlike journey where we encounter power animals and immensely beautiful nature, or experience oneness by merging with the Lucid Light. It can be wonderfully vivid.

At a Gateways of the Mind conference in London at which I was invited to speak, there was a great lineup of events, one of which was a shamanic drumming journey led by Martin Duffy. My experience as I sat with so many others was as vivid as a super-lucid dream. During my journey that day, I met a powerful Bengal tiger on a beach. We stomped our feet to the beat in synchrony, then to my amazement he raised his paw, and with his curved claws he ripped me open from throat to navel! Looking down at my body in surprise, I saw the opened flesh, within which were six shining pearls of light, suspended in a vertical line, like a row of shirt buttons. I knew they were precious and beloved things I had lost and still grieved over, so I sent them healing energy and closed my chest back together. Then I was lifted by kind, invisible beings and set down by the shore. I stood naked and gazed out to sea, feeling whole, my heart and body ringing with the beat of the drums.

After the drum sounded the recall, it was weird to return to the auditorium and open my eyes to find hundreds of sleepy-eyed people blinking all around me! (I was relieved to note that I was still wearing all my clothes.) The point being that it is easier to lose yourself in an inner vision or journey when you have rhythmic accompaniment.

- Find a drumming recording that is 5–10 minutes long, preferably with nobody speaking or giving directives on it, but just the rhythmic sound of drums. If you search on YouTube using words like "meditative/shamanic/relaxing drumming journey," you should find something suitable. Of course, you can choose any music for your imaginal journey, from classical to chill-out ambient music or nature sounds such as ocean waves, whatever you prefer. If you do decide to go with drumming, I'd quickly skip through the recording first to check that there is some sort of "recall" signal included at the end, where the drumbeat changes slightly to let you know it's time to return. Returning is important!

- Make sure you won't be disturbed by anyone or by your phone. Dim the lighting to your liking. Then lie down comfortably (unless you're someone who falls asleep very quickly, in which case, lie on a yoga mat or sit up).

- If your thoughts are all over the place, take a minute or so to calm down through deep breathing. Use this moment to set an intention for your drumming journey. This might be general, such as "I want to have a beautiful, spiritual experience," or it might be more specific, such as "I'd like to meet a power animal who will protect me," "I'd like help with my anxiety/my relationship," "I'd like to heal my body," or "I'd like to face my fear of death." Intention is important, so take the time you need for this. You might wish to choose a luminous, spiritual aspect of a dream or nightmare to explore and deepen while journeying. This can be incredibly rewarding.

- When you feel ready, start the drumming recording and close your eyes, allowing yourself to fly free of your body and follow the beat. You may see a scene appear before you, or find yourself diving into the depths of the ocean or walking barefoot into a cave or forest. Allow the visuals to appear, and when you feel ready, remember your intention for this journey. Allow the drumming and your own imagination and dreamlike state to carry you into the imaginal world. You may receive words of wisdom or gifts. You may feel love and experience healing, or be bathed in light. You may feel an energetic shift during your journey, or waves of emotion, or a strong heart connection with one of the animals or guides you encounter. Surprising things may happen. Remember, you can guide this waking dream. You are safe and can halt the experience anytime you wish, by taking a deep breath and opening your eyes.

- When the drum sounds the recall, take leave of the animal guides, people, or spiritual spaces you have visited. Thank them and return by flying effortlessly back to your body, feeling the weight of it on the ground and taking a few deep and grounding breaths before opening your eyes. You may want to meditate to complete your journey, or write down your waking dream. You may wish to take action to honour any imagery, power animals, or wisdom you received on your journey.

In this chapter, we have explored the spiritual nature of nightmares and the movement towards transcendence that some of them naturally bring. We've looked at how nightmares can show us which parts of ourselves are ripe for transformation, and we've seen how even terrifying dreams can bring us solace during the darkest moments of our lives. We've looked at death as the ultimate transition and seen how lucid dreaming and imaginal journeying can help us to prepare for conscious dying. We've explored the Lucid Light and seen how to create a spiritual dream to carry us through the tough patches in life, fortified and supported by power animals, guides, and beautiful experiences of wisdom and transcendence.

conclusion

When we transcend excessive fear and bring conscious awareness to our nightmares through waking dreamwork, and when we truly desire to learn and heal, we enable powerful transformation that can influence all areas of our life.

I have met plenty of people who self-medicate to suppress their nightmares. One young woman smokes pot and drinks wine every night to avoid the sleep paralysis incidents that plague her. She wants to stop this unhealthy habit but is too fearful of what the night may bring. People who work in the healthcare industry tell me patients ask them if there is a pill to stop their nightmares. There are so many desperate people out there looking for nightmare solutions. Usually they have no idea that working actively with nightmares for insight and healing can reduce nightmare frequency and enable wonderful and life-affirming transformation. A seventy-one-year-old woman, Margaret, kindly shared her eureka moment of how to handle her chronic nightmares:

> For most of my adult life, I had nightmares starting at around twenty-five. My old nightmares usually involved someone chasing me and trying to kill me either with guns or knives, or a version of the out-of-control dream where I am in a car and going down a hill and the brakes fail. I have worked and worked to solve this situation. Finally, I have been nightmare-free for about nine months. How?

1. Sleep with a total darkening sleep mask
2. Sleep with silicone (swimmer's) earplugs
3. Take 1.25 mg of Time Release Melatonin when I go to sleep

You may wonder why I'm only sharing Margaret's nightmare solution at the very end of the book. Surely I could have spared myself a lot of work and saved you a lot of time by simply handing you this solution right at the start?

Hopefully you'll have read deeply enough in this book to spot the flaw of this "solution." It may provide a temporary nightmare band-aid and feel like a big relief, and I understand the need for relief, the need to be able to sleep without fear. But I invite you to consider what happens when we close our eyes so tightly that we can no longer see ourselves? What happens when we block up our ears so we can't hear our inner voice? What happens when we pop pills so that we bypass or forget the powerful stories, warnings, and blessings our strongest dreams bring us?

I know that ostriches don't actually bury their heads in the sand (although I do wonder how that myth got to be so well known!), but in any case, it never struck me as a wise response. When we know how to work with nightmares, we open the door to immense possibilities of healing, creativity, and clarity on everything from our intimate relationships to our life's purpose. We don't need to run from our "bad" dreams, hide, bury our head in the sand, and hope for the storm to pass. Ostriches can't fly, but in dreams and imagination, we can. We can fly right into our stormiest dreams, engaging with love and compassion and awe in the face of such wild creativity and intense emotion, until we reach the calm eye of the storm. This is the place where we take stock, gather wisdom, and arm ourselves with the tools we need to fly back into life on powerful wings.

In every area of our lives, we get to choose how conscious we are. Some people sit on the lid of a seething emotional cauldron their entire lives, ignoring their dreams, nightmares, and deepest desires. This is their choice (although it may not feel like a choice to them). Others go to the opposite extreme, dissecting every morsel of their existence, analysing every damn thing until they drive themselves and the people around them crazy! We don't need to get obsessive about dreams and nightmares. It's entirely possible to give them more space in our hearts and welcome their guidance to whatever extent feels beneficial. The vital thing to remember is that we have a choice. We get to choose how we live this precious life of ours. On a global level, the more people there are in the world who work on healing their old wounds and conflicts, the happier and more harmonious the world will become.

In the course of reading this book, you've likely discovered more about the kind of sleeper and dreamer you are, the type of nightmares and scary sleep experiences you are prone to, why they occur, and how to work with them. If you're serious about improving your dream life, you will have created a tailor-made, flexible Nightmare Solution Programme to reflect your unique needs and your preferred steps towards peaceful, healing sleep and wondrous dreams. You'll find your dream life will begin to shift into new dimensions, so it's wise to revisit the Nightmare Quiz now and then to check your current nightmare status and gather new practices and tips to help you as your journey into healthful sleep continues. Any practice in this book can be tweaked to personalise it so that it fully reflects your individual needs to maximise its effectiveness.

In *The Art of Transforming Nightmares*, we've explored how to transform a wide range of upsetting and disturbing sleep experiences, from recurring nightmares to those caused by trauma, and from frightening experiences of floating in nothingness in the lucid void to scary sleep paralysis visions. For all of these experiences and more, I have shared my best practical techniques to help you handle them and access their creative, healing, and spiritual gifts. We've discovered that nightmares act as red flags, shouting out, "Healing is needed!" We've looked at the thought-responsive nature of nightmares, and there is a strong focus throughout the book on releasing fear to enable us to dissolve inner blocks and benefit from the dazzling creativity and transformative power of dreams. We've encountered the four major steps in dreamwork: remembering our dreams, uncovering the message of the dream or nightmare, releasing fear and other unhelpful emotions, and taking positive action in our lives.

We've looked at how to unlock the symbolism of nightmare images, and we've familiarised ourselves with their incredibly alive energy, their metaphoric aptness, and their visceral emotions. We've looked at the storytelling power of nightmares, and how empowering it can be to change that story through waking dreamwork. We have explored the nature of lucid dreaming and seen how it can help us work with a nightmare while it's actually happening. I've shared my original waking lucidity practices, such as Lucid Writing and the Lucid Imaging Nightmare Solution, which enable transformation by combining nightmare imagery with lucid awareness. Lucid dreaming may be the world's most innovative and much-needed approach to insomnia. I hope those who try my Insomnia Freedom Technique will let me know how it plays out for them.

Creativity, healing, and transformation play a huge role in *The Art of Transforming Nightmares*, with practices on bringing healing imagery into the body, reentering nightmares safely to rehearse happier outcomes, and gathering courage in the scariest of dream environments. We've discovered how to do shadow work with nightmares and the value of employing different imaginative responses. Mythological nightmares, childhood nightmares, and lucid nightmares have been explored, along with how to enlist dream mentors and power animals for protection. We've stepped closer to our nightmare animals and flown with fire-breathing dream dragons, and we've heard dream warnings delivered by deceased loved ones. We've touched on suicide nightmares and learned how to navigate the lucid void and explore the beautiful nature of the Lucid Light. It's been quite an adventure.

The various states of consciousness we've explored, from trance states to sleep paralysis, can be viewed as portals to profound levels of creativity, healing, and self-understanding. Nightmare work can help us expand our natural compassion and deepen our knowledge of the luminous nature of consciousness and our journey through life as spiritual beings.

I hope you've enjoyed the fiery energy of transformation present in many of the nightmares throughout this book. Writing this book was quite a ride! I sent out a call for nightmares … and they began to pour in. It felt as if I activated a volcano churning with nightmares, ran from the scalding stream, and was then buried in it. But when I stood up in the lava stream and channelled the flow of liquid fire into my book, things got really crazy: the writing began to move very fast, and astonishing synchronicities occurred as warm-hearted people sent me new nightmares that fitted exactly with what I was writing at the very moment I got their message. It was a transformative process, with volcanic energy. This book is pure alchemy, with the raw material of people's worst nightmares turning into the gold of wisdom and healing. It isn't me who is the alchemist here; it's the brave people who worked on their nightmares and generously shared their process with me. They are the beating heart of this book. I am grateful to all those who kindly shared with me the best and worst of their nightmares to help others see the scope and potential of so-called "bad" dreams.

I'm also grateful to my magnificent dream tigers who showed me the way through the writing. At one point, I walked into an entire cave full of tigers who prowled around me, and one breathed warm, gentle breath onto the back of my neck! It's thrilling when they come that close. Aren't dreams wonderful? I hope that, having read this book, you know nightmares to be amazing gifts of the soul that we can work with for healing transformation.

Now that you've nearly reached the end of this book, the next steps are to keep engaging proactively and consciously with your dreams and nightmares, night after night! Dreams are honest mirrors, and your dream life reflects the inner work you do. Once you start putting the principles of this book into action, by doing dreamwork to transform your fears and heal your wounds, and by allowing your dreaming mind to become your new best friend, you will notice changes for sure. You may find that animal allies show up in a constant stream to lend you strength and support. While I grappled with the volcanic energy of this book through the dark winter months, some of the animals who came to me in my dreams were a tame silver wolf with amber eyes; a white owl as tall as my shoulder; a baby tiger; seven large and mysterious mythological birds with curved beaks; a blue-eyed husky as large as a bear; a whole cave of prowling adult tigers; and a wild, lithe leopard with a lush pelt who morphed into a little boy.

There was a lot of shapeshifting in my dreams and in my dreamwork as I worked with all of the transformative nightmare energies in this book. I experienced drumming journeys where I spontaneously morphed into a mermaid, a tiger, and a golden eagle. Despite all of the nightmare material I was engrossed in each day, I had no nightmares myself while working on this book. Perhaps I was so flooded by other people's nightmares that my dreams compensated by sending me a menagerie of power animals instead.

As you befriend your dreams and nightmares and give them an honoured role in your life, you might notice an increase in experiences of light and happiness in any (or every!) state of consciousness, as well as an abundance of spiritual dreams, or dreams where knowledge is shared with you. For example, in one memorable dream, I was alone in a white room with a woman who was singing an achingly sad song that I resonated with on a deep emotional level. She walked right up to me and I gazed into her beautiful amber eyes … and suddenly, her two eyes merged into one massive third eye! I was awed and highly conscious as her third eye beamed knowledge into me. At the end, there was a burst of light that went right into my heart. I woke slowly with this light tangibly present in my heart and the knowledge that we are all made of light.

When working with nightmares in imaginative and fearless ways becomes natural to you, you may discover that as soon as a dream threatens to become a nightmare, your lucidity levels automatically rise. You might notice that you have the awareness to react in healing, accepting, or empowering ways within that would-be nightmare, and this can lead to enlightening moments. For example, in the following dream, you'll see that at the tipping point when the dream could have become a screaming nightmare, instead of being consumed by fear, I became lucid. This lucidity jolt in the face of unease or anxiety has long been a typical reaction for me.

> I'm in a luminous cave with a crystal-clear lake, when suddenly I see a massive green snake coiled on some rocks to my left. It's watching me from very conscious black eyes.
>
> "Hmm," I think. "That's a big snake!"
>
> I realise I need to get my little daughter safely out of the cave. But as we're leaving the cave, I'm aware that the snake is gliding towards me! My unease rises.
>
> The moment the snake touches my back, three things happen. First, I become lucid, so I relax, ready to embrace the experience. Second, I realise the snake hasn't come to hurt me. It doesn't want to bite me; it wants to share its power and knowledge with me. And the third thing is that when it touches me, there's this incredible buzzing feeling that begins at the base of my spine and travels all the way up my spine, right up to the crown of my head, so the whole of my spine is buzzing with this energy. Then everything dissolves into blissful light.
>
> I wake up and my spine is still buzzing with serpent energy.

This lucid kundalini snake dream caused transformative energy to rise up through my entire spinal cord, dissolving any blocks and releasing new energy. I was navigating a challenging situation at the time of the dream, and when I woke up, I acted with purpose and clarity to resolve that situation and manifest something new. Things ended up resolving so much better than I could have imagined: I ended up signing two book deals with Llewellyn Worldwide within the space of two weeks! One was *The Art of Lucid Dreaming*, and—you guessed it—the other is its dark and luminous twin: *The Art of Transforming Nightmares.*

Would-be nightmares spontaneously change in marvellous ways when we have a habit of working closely and intuitively with our dreams. The more we listen to our dreams and nightmares, the more clarity we get on our life's purpose and how to manifest our best gifts to help others and create the life we'd love to live.

Sleep is a threshold we cross alone each night. I hope very much that this book helps you cross that threshold fearlessly, in the knowledge that you can remain calm and act with power in any sleep state and that you fully deserve a happy, enriching night of dreams.

I'll say it one final time, though: nightmares are gifts.

Yes, we all know that the wrapping paper can be pretty nasty, but when we gather our courage and unwrap a nightmare, we reveal its creative, healing, and transformative gold. Nightmare work is an alchemical art, and when we become adept at transforming nightmares into the gold of the soul, we free ourselves to step with wonder into a bolder, brighter life.

I wish you courage on your journey!

unique Nightmare solution programme template

Here's where you combine the best practices for different sleeper/dreamer types from the fifteen Nightmare Solution Programmes in chapter 5 to reflect your individual needs. Creating your own Nightmare Solution Programme personalises your practice and fast-tracks you to a happier, more peaceful dream life. Programme examples are given in appendix II.

Template

Sleeper/Dreamer Combination of Types:

After taking the Nightmare Quiz in chapter 5, sum up the categories you most identify with in one phrase; for example, "Sleep paralysis explorer, nightmare sufferer, imaginative thinker."

_____

_____

_____

Core Techniques:

The fifteen Nightmare Solution Programmes in chapter 5 recommend core practices for each sleeper/dreamer type. Navigate to the types that correspond with you, and choose a total of three practices that most appeal to you. Note the best time of day or night to practise them.

Practice X: _____

Timing: _____

Practice X: _____

Timing: _____

Practice X: _____

Timing: _____

Pre-sleep Routine and Techniques to Use during the Night:

Create an inspiring routine; for example, pre-sleep ritual + meditation + call on power animal for protection.

_____

_____

_____

Nightmare Journal:

Do you plan to journal your dreams each day? Will you write the dreams down or sketch them? Will you underline moments where you reacted with fear, and reenter these nightmares to relive a fearless outcome? How many dreams will you choose per week to vividly reimagine and practise nightmare solutions in? Set a couple of realistic goals for yourself.

Goal 1: _____

Goal 2: _____

Duration:

Decide on a minimum length of time to follow this Nightmare Solution Programme … and stick to it if you can!

_____

_____

_____

Examples of unique Nightmare solution programmes

I've picked three common sleeper/dreamer combinations and created Unique Nightmare Solution Programmes for each, so you can see how it works.

Unique Nightmare Solution Programme 1

Sleeper/Dreamer Combination of Types:

Nightmare sufferer, insomniac, anxious dreamer.

Core Techniques:

Practice 13: The Lucid Imaging Nightmare Solution (LINS)
Timing: Directly upon awakening from a nightmare, or as a dream reentry technique during the day.

Practice 38: The Insomnia Freedom Technique
Timing: During periods of sleeplessness in the night.

Practice 23: The Egg of Light and Other Nightmare Protections
Timing: During the day and right before bed.

Pre-sleep Routine and Techniques to Use during the Night:
Practice 5: Create a Soothing Bedtime Ritual, combined with Practice 41: Yoga Nidra: Balance Between the Worlds.

Nightmare Journal:
Goal 1: Write down every dream or nightmare you remember. Jot down associations and underline core emotions.
Goal 2: Choose one nightmare per week and use Practice 12: Ten Key Questions for Unwrapping a Nightmare.
Duration: Two weeks, maintaining a steady habit of dream journaling and perfecting a calming pre-sleep routine.

Unique Nightmare Solution Programme 2

Sleeper/Dreamer Combination of Types:
Traumatised dreamer, visual and imaginative thinker, lucid dreamer.

Core Techniques:
Practice 30: Imagery Rehearsal Therapy: Rewrite a Nightmare for Healing Resolution
Timing: Daytime, and rehearse the new, healing ending before bedtime.

Practice 28: Bring Soul Dreams and Healing Imagery into the Body
Timing: Several times a day.

Practice 25: Nightmare Work to Protect Your Inner Child
Timing: Any time of day, with a supportive friend available if need be.

Pre-sleep Routine and Techniques to Use during the Night:
Meditate to music and begin a calm bedtime routine such as the one in Practice 5: Create a Soothing Bedtime Ritual.

Nightmare Journal:
Goal 1: Write down all dreams every morning and during the night if you wake up with one fresh in your mind, then work with them using the techniques in chapter 2.

Goal 2: Choose a nightmare and imagine becoming lucid in it and responding with awareness, as in Practice 14: Creative Nightmare Responses.
   Prime yourself to become lucid the next time you experience fear or
   anxiety in a dream.
Duration: Two weeks, then integrate some different practices depending on
   your progress.

Unique Nightmare Solution Programme 3

Sleeper/Dreamer Combination of Types:
Sleep paralysis explorer, spiritual dreamer, child prodigy dreamer.

Core Techniques:
Practice 37: Change Your Sleep Paralysis Story
Timing: Take twenty minutes one day to answer these questions thoroughly
   and change the story.

Practice 33: How to Release Fear in Sleep Paralysis
Timing: Visualise this practice during the day, then put it into action the
   next time you have a sleep paralysis episode.

Practice 16: Become the Monster—Try this if you have spiritual nightmares
   involving frightening figures, or if you have met such figures during sleep
   paralysis.
Timing: Daytime.

Pre-sleep Routine and Techniques to Use during the Night:
Before sleeping, integrate Practice 5: Create a Soothing Bedtime Ritual and
Practice 6: Pre-Bed Meditation to Calm the Mind. During the night, if you
wake up scared or uneasy, try Practice 36: Invoke Protective Powers: Ball of
Light or Practice 1: How to Release Fear and Become Calm.

Nightmare Journal:
Goal 1: Write in your nightmare journal each morning or if you wake up in
   the night. Jot down a title for the dream, and any associations you have
   with it.

Goal 2: Pick one nightmare a week to work on using transformative techniques such as Practice 13: The Lucid Imaging Nightmare Solution (LINS), or try Practice 45: Drumming Journey: Create Your Own Spiritual Dream.

Duration: Two weeks, maintaining a steady habit of journaling and a relaxing pre-sleep ritual.

Bibliography

Atwater, P. M. H. *Beyond The Light: Near-Death Experiences: The Full Story.* London: Thorsons, 1994.

Banerji, Bhaskar. "Using Dreams to Elicit Inner Healing Resources: An Exploratory Study." PhD diss., Saybrook University, US, 2017.

Barasch, Marc. *Healing Dreams: Exploring the Dreams That Can Transform Your Life.* New York: Riverhead Books, 2000.

Barrett, Deirdre. *The Committee of Sleep: How Artists, Scientists, and Athletes Use Dreams for Creative Problem-Solving—And How You Can Too.* New York: Crown Publishers, 2001.

———. *Pandemic Dreams.* Oneiroi Press, 2020.

Beck, Aaron T., and Clyde H. Ward. "Dreams of Depressed Patients: Characteristic Themes in Manifest Content." *Archives of General Psychiatry* 5, no. 5 (1961): 462–467.

Belicki, D., and K. Belicki. "Nightmares in a University Population." *Sleep Research* 11 (1982): 116.

Bernert, Rebecca A., Carolyn L. Turvey, Yeates Conwell, and Thomas E. Joiner Jr. "Association of Poor Subjective Sleep Quality with Risk for Death by Suicide during a 10-Year Period: A Longitudinal, Population-Based Study of Late Life." *JAMA Psychiatry* 71, no. 10 (Oct. 2014): 1129–1137.

Bjorklund, Anna-Karin. *Dream Guidance: Interpret Your Dreams and Create the Life You Desire!* Newport Beach, CA: Crystal Souls, 2012.

Blackmore, Susan. *Consciousness: An Introduction.* London: Hodder Education, 2010.

Buhlman, William. *Adventures Beyond the Body.* New York: HarperOne, 1996.

Bulkeley, Kelly. "Nightmares as a Gift: The Surprising Value of Frightening Dreams in Childhood." In *Sleep Monsters and Superheroes: Empowering Children through Creative Dreamplay*, edited by Clare Johnson and Jean Campbell. Santa Barbara, CA: Praeger, 2016.

Bulkeley, Kelly, and Alan Siegel. *Dreamcatching: Every Parent's Guide to Exploring and Understanding Children's Dreams and Nightmares.* New York: Three Rivers Press, 1998.

Burch, Wanda Easter. *She Who Dreams: A Journey into Healing through Dreamwork.* Novato, CA: New World Library, 2003.

Burk, Larry. "Warning Dreams Preceding the Diagnosis of Breast Cancer: A Survey of the Most Important Characteristics." *Explore: The Journal of Science and Healing* 11, no. 3 (2015): 193–198.

Bush, Nancy. *Dancing Past the Dark: Distressing Near-Death Experiences.* Nancy Evans Bush, 2012.

Carr, Michelle, and Tore Nielsen. "A Novel Differential Susceptibility Framework for the Study of Nightmares: Evidence for Trait Sensory Processing Sensitivity." *Clinical Psychology Review* 58 (2017): 86–96.

Cartwright, Rosalind, and Lynne Lamberg. *Crisis Dreaming.* London: The Aquarian Press, 1993.

Clark, Laurel. *Intuitive Dreaming.* Windyville, MO: SOM Publishing, 2012.

Coalson, Bob. "Nightmare Help: Treatment of Trauma Survivors with PTSD," *Psychotherapy* 32, no. 3 (1995): 381–388.

Cortelli, Pietro, Giovanna Calandra-Buonaura, and Antonio Culebras. "Autonomic Dysfunction in Sleep Disorders." *Medlink Neurology*, July 21, 2003. www.medlink.com/article/autonomic_dysfunction_in_sleep_disorders.

Davis, Joanne L. *Treating Post-Trauma Nightmares: A Cognitive Behavioral Approach.* New York: Springer Publishing, 2008.

De Foe, Alexander, ed. *Consciousness Beyond the Body: Evidence and Reflections.* Melbourne, Australia: Melbourne Centre for Exceptional Human Potential, 2016.

Delaney, Gayle. *Sexual Dreams: Why We Have Them and What They Mean.* London: Piatkus, 1994.

Ellis, Leslie. *A Clinician's Guide to Dream Therapy: Implementing Simple and Effective Dreamwork.* New York: Routledge, 2020.

Epel, Naomi. *Writers Dreaming.* New York: Vintage Books, 1994.

Erlacher, Daniel, Tadas Stumbrys, and Michael Schredl. "Frequency of Lucid Dreams and Lucid Dream Practice in German Athletes." *Imagination, Cognition and Personality* 31, no. 3 (Jan. 2011): 237–246.

Fenwick, Peter, and Elizabeth Fenwick. *The Art of Dying.* London: Continuum, 2008.

Frank N. C., A. Spirito, L. Stark, and J. Owens-Stively. "The Use of Scheduled Awakenings to Eliminate Childhood Sleepwalking." *Journal of Pediatric Psychology* 22, no. 3 (June 1997): 345–353.

Garfield, Patricia. *The Healing Power of Dreams.* New York: Simon & Schuster, 1991.

———. *Pathway to Ecstasy: The Way of the Dream Mandala.* New York: Prentice Hall Press, 1989.

Germain, Anne, et al. "Increased Mastery Elements Associated with Imagery Rehearsal Treatment for Nightmares in Sexual Assault Survivors with PTSD." *Dreaming* 14, no. 4 (Dec. 2004): 195–206.

Goodwin, Jenifer. "Sleeptime Head-Cooling Cap Eases Insomnia, Study Finds." HealthDay, June 14, 2011. https://health.usnews.com/health-news/family-health/sleep/articles/2011/06/14/sleeptime-head-cooling-cap-eases-insomnia-study-finds.

Gordon, David, and Dani Vedros. "The Power of Dreamwork with Traumatized Adolescents." In *Sleep Monsters and Superheroes: Empowering Children through Creative Dreamplay*, edited by Clare Johnson and Jean Campbell. Santa Barbara, CA: Praeger, 2016.

Gratton, Nicole, and Monique Seguin. *Dreams and Death: The Benefits of Dreams Before, During, and After Death.* Quebec: Flammarian, 2009.

Green, J. Timothy. "Lucid Dreaming in the Treatment of Veterans and Others with Post Traumatic Stress Disorder." June 11, 2007. http://jtgreenphd.blogspot.de/2007/06/lucid-dreaming-in-treatment-of-veterans_11.html.

Greenwald, R. "Eye Movement Desensitization and Reprocessing (EMDR): A New Kind of Dreamwork?" *Dreaming* 5, no. 1 (1995): 51–55.

Grey, Margot. *Return From Death: An Explanation of The Near-Death Experience*. London and New York: Arkana, 1987.

Guadagni, Veronica, Ford Burles, Michele Ferrara, and Guiseppe Iaria. "The Effects of Sleep Deprivation on Emotional Empathy." *Journal of Sleep Research* 23, no. 6 (Dec. 2014): 657–663.

Harb, Gerlinde C., Janeese A. Brownlow, and Richard J. Ross. "Posttraumatic Nightmares and Imagery Rehearsal: The Possible Role of Lucid Dreaming." *Dreaming* 26, no. 3 (2016): 238–249.

Hartmann, Ernest. *Dreams and Nightmares: The New Theory on the Origin and Meaning of Dreams*. New York: Plenum Trade, 1998.

Hayley, Arnie C., et al. "The Relationships Between Insomnia, Sleep Apnoea, and Depression: Findings from the American National Health and Nutrition Examination Survey, 2005–2008." *The Australian and New Zealand Journal of Psychiatry* 49, no. 2 (Feb. 2015): 156–170.

Hearne, Keith. "Lucid Dreams: An Electro-Physiological and Psychological Study." PhD diss., University of Liverpool, England, 1978.

Hoffman, Jan. "A New Vision for Dreams of the Dying." *The New York Times*, Feb. 2, 2016. https://www.nytimes.com/2016/02/02/health/dreams-dying -deathbed-interpretation-delirium.html.

Holecek, Andrew. *Dream Yoga: Illuminating Your Life Through Lucid Dreaming and the Tibetan Yogas of Sleep*. Boulder, CO: Sounds True, 2016.

Hoss, Robert J. "Trauma and PTSD Nightmare Content." In *Parasomnia Dreaming: Exploring Other Forms of Sleep Consciousness*, edited by James F. Pagel. New York: Nova Science Publishers 2020.

Hoss, Robert J., and Robert P. Gongloff, eds. *Dreams That Change Our Lives: A Publication of the International Association for the Study of Dreams*. Asheville, NC: Chiron Publications, 2017.

Hurd, Ryan. *Sleep Paralysis: A Guide to Hypnagogic Visions and Visitors of the Night*. Los Altos, CA: Hyena Press, 2010.

Hurd, Ryan, and Kelly Bulkeley, ed. *Lucid Dreaming: New Perspectives on Consciousness in Sleep*. Santa Barbara, CA: Praeger, 2014.

Jalal al-Din Rumi, Maulana. *The Essential Rumi*. New York: HarperOne, 2004.

Jay, Clare [Clare R. Johnson]. *Breathing in Colour*. London: Little, Brown, 2009.

———. *Dreamrunner*. London: Little, Brown, 2010.

Johnson, Clare. R. *The Art of Lucid Dreaming: Over 60 Powerful Practices to Help You Wake Up in Your Dreams*. Woodbury, MN: Llewellyn, 2020.

———. "Amazing Dreamer." *DreamTime*, Spring 2020. Magazine of the International Association for the Study of Dreams.

———. "Celebrating 40 Years of Lucid Dream Exploration: A Dynamic Exploration of Lucid Dream Science, Therapy, Healing, Creativity, and the Dream Body." Event with Keith Hearne hosted by the Dream Research Institute, London, March 2015. www.youtube.com/watch?v=y6wX8Syuf Mw&t=17s.

———. "Creative Lucid Dreaming: Waking Up in Dreams, in Life, and in Death." Paper presented at the Gateways of the Mind Conference, London, Nov. 9–10, 2013.

———. "Dream Magicians: Empower Children through Lucid Dreaming." In *Sleep Monsters and Superheroes: Empowering Children through Creative Dreamplay*, edited by Clare Johnson and Jean Campbell. Santa Barbara, CA: Praeger, 2016.

———. *Dream Therapy: Dream Your Way to Health and Happiness*. London: Orion Spring, 2017.

———. *Llewellyn's Complete Book of Lucid Dreaming: A Comprehensive Guide to Promote Creativity, Overcome Sleep Disturbances & Enhance Health and Wellness*. Woodbury, MN: Llewellyn, 2017.

———. "Lucid Dreaming and the Creative Writing Process." Paper presented at the Dream Writing Conference, University of Kent, Oct. 15–16, 2005.

——— "Lucid Dreaming, Synaesthesia, and Sleep Disorders: Dreaming into Fiction." Paper presented at the 26th conference for the International Association for the Study of Dreams, Chicago, IL, June 26–30, 2009.

Johnson, Clare. R. "Magic, Meditation, and the Void: Creative Dimensions of Lucid Dreaming." In *Lucid Dreaming: New Perspectives on Consciousness in Sleep*, edited by Ryan Hurd and Kelly Bulkeley. Santa Barbara, CA: Praeger, 2014.

———. *Mindful Dreaming: Harness the Power of Lucid Dreaming for Happiness, Health, and Positive Change*. San Francisco, CA: Conari Press, 2018.

———. "The Role of Lucid Dreaming in the Process of Creative Writing." PhD diss., University of Leeds, UK, 2007.

———. "Surfing the Rainbow: Fearless and Creative Out-of-Body Experiences." In *Consciousness Beyond the Body: Evidence and Reflections*, edited by Dr. Alexander De Foe. Melbourne: Melbourne Centre for Exceptional Human Potential, 2016. http://deepluciddreaming.com/wp-content/uploads/2016/02/Consciousness-Beyond-the-Body.pdf.

Johnson, Clare R., and Jean M. Campbell, eds. *Sleep Monsters and Superheroes: Empowering Children through Creative Dreamplay*. Santa Barbara, CA: Praeger, 2016.

Jung, Carl G. The Archetypes and the Collective Unconscious. Vol. 9, part 1, of *The Basic Writings of C. G. Jung*. Translated by R. F. C. Hull. 1959; repr., London: Routledge, 1991.

———. "Marriage as a Psychological Relationship." In *The Collected Works of C. G. Jung, Vol. 17: The Development of Personality*. 1954; repr, London and Henley: Routledge & Kegan Paul, 1981.

———. *Memories, Dreams, Reflections*. Edited by Aniela Jaffé. New York: Random House, 1961.

———. *Psychology and Alchemy*. Vol. 8 of *The Collected Works of C. G. Jung*. 1960; repr., Princeton, NJ: Princeton Bollingen, 1990.

———. *The Structure and Dynamics of the Psyche*. Vol. 8 of *The Collected Works of C. G. Jung*. Edited and translated by Gerhard Adler and R. F. C. Hull. 2nd ed. 1960; repr., Princeton, NJ: Princeton University Press, 1969.

Kaempffert, Waldemar, ed. *A Popular History of American Inventions*. New York: C. Scribner's Sons, 1924.

Klein, Stefan. *The Science of Happiness: How Our Brains Make Us Happy—And What We Can Do to Get Happier*. Cambridge, MA: DaCapo Press, 2006.

Kohen, Daniel P., et al. "The Use of Relaxation–Mental Imagery (Self-Hypnosis) in the Management of 505 Pediatric Behavioral Encounters." *Journal of Developmental & Behavioral Pediatrics* 5, no. 1 (Feb. 1984): 21–25.

Krakow, Barry. *Sound Sleep, Sound Mind: 7 Keys to Sleeping through the Night.* Hoboken, NJ: Wiley, 2007.

———. *Turning Nightmares into Dreams.* Albuquerque, NM: Maimonides Sleep Arts & Sciences, 2002.

Krakow, Barry, R. Kellner, D. Pathak, and L. Lambert. "Imagery Rehearsal Treatment for Chronic Nightmares." *Behaviour Research and Therapy* 33, no. 7 (1995): 837–843.

Lask, Bryan. "Novel and Non-Toxic Treatment for Night Terrors." *British Medical Journal* 297 (1988): 592.

Lenggenhager, Bigna, T. Tadi, T. Metzinger, and O. Blanke. "Video Ergo Sum: Manipulating Bodily Self-Consciousness." *Science* 317, no. 5841 (Aug. 24, 2007): 1096–1099.

Levitan, Lynne, and Stephen LaBerge. "Other Worlds: Out-Of-Body Experiences and Lucid Dreams." *Nightlight* 3, nos. 2–3 (1991).

Litman, R. E., "The Dream in the Suicidal Situation." In *The Dream in Clinical Practice,* edited by J. Natterson. New York: Aronson, 1980.

Lyons, Tallulah, and Wendy Pannier. "The Healing Power of Dreams and Nightmares: The IASD Dream Work with Cancer Patients Project." http://www.healingpowerofdreams.com/Pannier_Lyons[1].pdf.

Mallon, Brenda. *Dream Time with Children: Learning to Dream, Dreaming to Learn.* London: Jessica Kingsley Publishers, 2002.

———. *Dreams, Counselling and Healing.* Dublin: Newleaf, 2000.

Mascaro, Kimberly R. *Extraordinary Dreams: Visions, Announcements and Premonitions Across Time and Place.* Jefferson, NC: McFarland, 2018.

Mellick, Jill. *The Natural Artistry of Dreams.* Berkeley, CA: Conari Press, 1996.

Michaels, Stase. *Nightmares: The Dark Side of Dreams and Dreaming.* New York: Sterling Ethos, 2018.

———. "Pulsing Ball of Fear." https://www.interpretadream.com/.

Morgan, Angel K. *Dreamer's Powerful Tiger: A New Lucid Dreaming Classic for Children and Parents of the 21st Century.* Ashland, OR: Dreambridge, 2018.

Morley, Charlie. *Dreaming Through Darkness: Shine Light into the Shadow to Live the Life of Your Dreams*. London: Hay House UK, 2017.

Moss, Robert. *Dreaming the Soul Back Home: Shamanic Dreaming for Healing and Becoming Whole*. Novato, CA: New World Library, 2012.

———. "Liminal Complaints: Demons, Night Hags and Sleep Paralysis." Beliefnet. Accessed Aug. 14, 2020. https://www.beliefnet.com/columnists /dreamgates/2011/01/im-reading-a-lucid-and.html.

Nadorff, Michael R. "Bad Dreams and Nightmares: Causes, Correlates, and Interventions." Presentation given at the 37th annual conference of the International Association for the Study of Dreams, June 14, 2020.

Naiman, Rubin R. *Healing Night: The Science and Spirit of Sleeping, Dreaming, and Awakening*. Minneapolis, MN: Syren Book Co., 2006.

Neidhardt, E. J., B. Krakow, R. Kellner, and D. Pathak. "The Beneficial Effects of One Treatment Session and Recording of Nightmares on Chronic Nightmare Sufferers." *Sleep* 15, no. 5 (Oct. 1992): 470–473.

Newmark, Amy, and Kelly Sullivan Walden. *Chicken Soup for the Soul: Dreams and Premonitions: 101 Amazing Stories of Miracles, Divine Intervention, and Insight*. Cos Cob, CT: Chicken Soup for the Soul Publishing, 2015.

Nielsen, Tore. "The Stress Acceleration Hypothesis of Nightmares." *Frontiers in Neurology* 8 (2017): 201.

Nielsen, Tore, and Michelle Carr. "Nightmares and Nightmare Function." In *Principles and Practice of Sleep Medicine*, edited by M. Kryger, B. Roth, and W. Dement, 546–554. New York: Elsevier, 2016.

Nielsen, Tore, et al. "Early Childhood Adversity Associations with Nightmare Severity and Sleep Spindles." *Sleep Medicine* 56 (March 2019).

Ohayon, M. M., P. L. Morselli, and C. Guilleminault. "Prevalence of Nightmares and Their Relationship to Psychopathology and Daytime Functioning in Insomnia Subjects." *Sleep* 20, no. 5 (May 1997): 340–348.

Parnia, Sam, et al. "AWARE—AWAreness during REsuscitation—A Prospective Study." *Resuscitation*, 85, no. 12 (2014): 1799–1805.

Paul, Marla. "How Traumatic Memories Hide in the Brain, and How to Retrieve Them." Northwestern Medicine. Aug. 17, 2015. https://news

.feinberg.northwestern.edu/2015/08/how-traumatic-memories-hide-in
-the-brain/.

Pennebaker, James W. *Opening Up: The Healing Power of Expressing Emotions.*
New York: Guildford Press, 1997.

Perls, Frederick S. *Gestalt Therapy Verbatim.* 1969; repr., Gouldsboro, ME:
The Gestalt Journal Press, 1992.

Peters, Roderick. *Living with Dreams.* London: Rider, 1990.

Radin, Dean. *Entangled Minds: Extrasensory Experiences in a Quantum Reality.*
New York: Paraview Pocket Books, 2006.

Sartori, Penny. *The Wisdom of Near-Death Experiences: How Understanding
NDEs Can Help Us Live More Fully.* London: Watkins, 2014.

Sartori, Penny, and Kelly Walsh. *The Transformative Power of Near-Death
Experiences.* London: Watkins, 2017.

Schenck, Carlos H. *Paradox Lost: Midnight in the Battleground of Sleep and
Dreams.* Minneapolis, MN: Extreme-Nights, 2005.

———. *Sleep: A Groundbreaking Guide to the Mysteries, the Problems, and
the Solutions.* New York: Avery, 2007.

Schiller, Linda Yael. *Modern Dreamwork: New Tools for Decoding Your Soul's
Wisdom.* Woodbury, MN: Llewellyn, 2019.

Schredl, Michael, et al. "The Use of Dreams in Psychotherapy: A Survey of
Psychotherapists in Private Practice." *The Journal of Psychotherapy Practice
and Research* 9, no. 2 (Feb. 2000): 81–87.

Sevilla, Jorge Conesa. *Wrestling With Ghosts: A Personal and Scientific
Account of Sleep Paralysis.* Bloomington, IN: Xlibris Corporation, 2004.

Sharpless, Brian A., and Jacques P. Barber. "Lifetime Prevalence Rates of
Sleep Paralysis: A Systematic Review." *Sleep Medicine Reviews* 15, no. 5
(Oct. 2011): 311–315.

Sharpless, Brian A., and Monika Klikova. "Clinical Features of Isolated Sleep
Paralysis." *Sleep Medicine* 58 (June 2019): 102–106. https://doi.org/10.1016
/j.sleep.2019.03.007.

Sheldrake, Rupert. *The Sense of Being Stared At: And Other Aspects of the
Extended Mind.* London: Arrow Books, 2003.

Spoormaker, Victor, and Jan van den Bout. "Lucid Dreaming Treatment for Nightmares: A Pilot Study." *Psychotherapy and Psychosomatics* 75, no. 6, 2006: 389–394.

Spoormaker, Victor I., Jan van den Bout, and Eli J. G. Meijer. "Lucid Dreaming Treatment for Nightmares: A Series of Cases." *Dreaming* 13, no. 3 (2003): 181–186.

Stevenson, Robert Louis. "A Chapter on Dreams." In *Across the Plains: With Other Memories and Essays.* London: Chatto & Windus, 1892.

Stickgold, R. "EMDR: A Putative Neurobiological Mechanism of Action." *Journal of Clinical Psychology* 58, no. 1 (2002): 61–75.

Stumbrys, Tadas, and Michael Daniels. "An Exploratory Study of Creative Problem Solving in Lucid Dreams: Preliminary Findings and Methodological Considerations." *International Journal of Dream Research* 3, no. 2 (Nov, 2010): 121–129. doi: http://dx.doi.org/10.11588/ijodr.2010.2.6167.

Sunderland, Margot. *Using Story Telling as a Therapeutic Tool with Children.* London: Speechmark Publishing, 2000.

Taylor, Martha. "The Influence of Community on Children's Dreams." In *Sleep Monsters and Superheroes: Empowering Children through Creative Dreamplay*, edited by Clare Johnson and Jean Campbell. Santa Barbara, CA: Praeger, 2016.

Ullman, Montague. *Appreciating Dreams: A Group Approach.* New York: Sage Publications, 1996.

Ullman, Montague, and Stanley Krippner, with Alan Vaughan. *Dream Telepathy: Experiments in Nocturnal ESP.* Baltimore, MD: Penguin, 1974.

Van der Kolk, Bessel. *The Body Keeps the Score: Mind, Brain, and Body in the Transformation of Trauma.* London: Penguin, 2014.

Voss, Ursula, Romain Holzmann, Allan Hobson, Walter Paulus, Judith Koppehele-Gossel, Ansgar Klimke, and Michael A. Nitsche. "Induction of Self Awareness in Dreams through Frontal Low Current Stimulation of Gamma Activity." *Nature Neuroscience* 17, no. 6 (2014): 810–812.

Ware, Bronnie. "Regrets of the Dying." Accessed Aug. 14, 2020. https://bronnieware.com/blog/regrets-of-the-dying/.

Wiseman, Ann Sayre. *The Nightmare Solution: Simple, Creative Methods for Working Out Your Dream Problems*. Brattleboro, VT: Echo Point Books & Media, 2013.

Zadra, Antonio, and Robert Pihl. "Lucid Dreaming as a Treatment for Recurrent Nightmares." *Psychotherapy and Psychosomatics* 66, no. 1, 1997: 50–55.

Resources

If you are looking for community support in the area of dreams and nightmares, the IASD, described below, is a wonderful organisation. If you need individual support, research your area to find a therapist who has experience working with dreams and nightmares, and see a sleep medicine doctor if you suffer from sleep disturbances. All over the world there are psychotherapists, crisis hotlines, and mental healthcare services to be found. I have included in this resources section a range of books that expand on many of the topics explored in *The Art of Transforming Nightmares*.

The International Association for the Study of Dreams (IASD)

For readers who would like community support with their dreams and nightmares or who want to deepen their exploration of dreamwork, I highly recommend becoming a member of IASD. This vibrant and friendly organisation brings dreamers together from all walks of life, creates fabulous dream conferences (easy-to-access online ones and others in global locations), and provides a wealth of expert dream advice, insight, and information through its member-exclusive *DreamTime* magazine and its academic journal, *Dreaming*. IASD is community-based, supportive, and fascinated by all aspects of dreaming. For me, it's like a second family. Find out more at www.asdreams.org.

Deep Lucid Dreaming

If you want to go deeper into lucid dreaming and healing through dreams, on my website you can explore everything from lucid dream healing and the sparkling black void to sleep paralysis and nightmare solutions. You can pick up a free e-book on how to get and stay lucid, as well as one on how to heal nightmares. You can watch lucid dreaming videos, and contact me for advice. (Please understand that I get a lot of messages, but I do my best to reply as fast as I can.) I look forward to connecting with you. Visit www.DeepLucid Dreaming.com.

If you like the idea of exploring the healing, creative, wild, and spiritual aspects of dreams, nightmares, and lucidity in a small, relaxed group by the ocean, you may wish to join me on one of my lucid dreaming retreats. We share clifftop meditations at sunset, morning dream groups, and workshops on everything from healing dreams to conscious death and playful creativity. I offer my best practices to help you become more lucid in dreams and in life, and we share illuminating lucid discussions over dinner in local restaurants. I also lead online Transformative Lucidity workshops, Yoga Nidra for Lucid Dreaming courses, and Lucid Immersion weekend intensives.

I offer private, one-to-one mentoring sessions where I create personalised nightmare solutions and lucidity programmes for people and advise them on aspects of sleep, from transforming upsetting dreams and sleep paralysis to encouraging healthy sleep and higher lucidity. I have created video courses on lucid dreaming, nightmare solutions, and yoga nidra for lucid dreaming and blissful sleep, with more to come. For more information, write to me at deeplucid dreaming@gmail.com or see my website.

My YouTube channel, "Deep Lucid Dreaming Dr Clare Johnson," has plenty of short videos where I talk about different aspects of lucid dreaming: https://www.youtube.com/channel/UC3P-H6MiXL4oRQjocOrcxlw. You can also contact me on Twitter @LucidClare or visit my Facebook pages: https://www.facebook.com/DeepLucidDreaming/ and https://www.facebook.com/LucidClare. I'm on Instagram as clare_johnson_lucid_dreaming.

I wish you an illuminating path into your dreams, and a happier, healthier dream life!

Book Resources

The world is full of riches and there are many wonderful books out there on the topics covered in *The Art of Transforming Nightmares*. I'm giving you a couple of suggestions per category, just to start you off. Please see the bibliography for many more great titles.

Children's Nightmares—Guides for Parents

Bulkeley, Kelly, and Alan Siegel. *Dreamcatching: Every Parent's Guide to Exploring and Understanding Children's Dreams and Nightmares*. New York: Three Rivers Press, 1998.

Johnson, Clare R., and Jean M. Campbell, eds. *Sleep Monsters and Superheroes: Empowering Children through Creative Dreamplay*. Santa Barbara, CA: Praeger, 2016.

Mallon, Brenda. *Dream Time with Children: Learning to Dream, Dreaming to Learn*. London: Jessica Kingsley Publishers, 2002.

Sunderland, Margot. *Using Story Telling as a Therapeutic Tool with Children*. London: Speechmark Publishing, 2000.

Wiseman, Ann Sayre. *The Nightmare Solution: Simple, Creative Methods for Working Out Your Dream Problems*. Brattleboro, VT: Echo Point Books & Media, 2013.

Dream Creativity

Barrett, Deirdre. *The Committee of Sleep: How Artists, Scientists, and Athletes Use Dreams for Creative Problem-Solving—And How You Can Too*. New York: Crown Publishers, 2001.

Mellick, Jill. *The Natural Artistry of Dreams*. Berkeley, CA: Conari Press, 1996.

Dream Novels

Jay, Clare [Clare R. Johnson]. *Breathing in Colour*. London: Little, Brown, 2009.

———. *Dreamrunner*. London: Little, Brown, 2010.

Healing Through Dreams

Barasch, Marc. *Healing Dreams: Exploring the Dreams That Can Transform Your Life.* New York: Riverhead Books, 2000.

Johnson, Clare. *Dream Therapy: Dream Your Way to Health and Happiness.* London: Orion Spring, 2017. (US title is *Mindful Dreaming: Harness the Power of Lucid Dreaming for Happiness, Health, and Positive Change.* San Francisco, CA: Conari Press, 2018.)

Healthy Sleep

Krakow, Barry. *Sound Sleep, Sound Mind: 7 Keys to Sleeping through the Night.* Hoboken, NJ: Wiley, 2007.

Naiman, Rubin R. *Healing Night: The Science and Spirit of Sleeping, Dreaming, and Awakening.* Minneapolis, MN: Syren Book Co., 2006.

Lucid Dreaming and Nightmare Solutions

Johnson, Clare R. *The Art of Lucid Dreaming: Over 60 Powerful Practices to Help You Wake Up in Your Dreams.* Woodbury, MN: Llewellyn, 2020.

———. *Llewellyn's Complete Book of Lucid Dreaming: A Comprehensive Guide to Promote Creativity, Overcome Sleep Disturbances & Enhance Health and Wellness.* Woodbury, MN: Llewellyn, 2017.

Near-Death Experiences

Fenwick, Peter, and Elizabeth Fenwick. *The Art of Dying.* London: Continuum, 2008.

Sartori, Penny. *The Wisdom of Near-Death Experiences: How Understanding NDEs Can Help Us Live More Fully.* London: Watkins, 2014.

Sartori, Penny, and Kelly Walsh. *The Transformative Power of Near-Death Experiences.* London: Watkins, 2017.

Out-of-Body Experiences

Buhlman, William. *Adventures Beyond the Body.* New York: HarperOne, 1996.

Johnson, Clare R. "Surfing the Rainbow: Fearless and Creative Out-of-Body Experiences." In *Consciousness Beyond the Body: Evidence and Reflections,* edited by Dr. Alexander De Foe. Melbourne: Melbourne Centre for Exceptional Human Potential, 2016. http://deepluciddreaming.com/wp-content/uploads/2016/02/Consciousness-Beyond-the-Body.pdf.

Post-Traumatic Nightmares

Davis, Joanne L. *Treating Post-Trauma Nightmares: A Cognitive Behavioral Approach.* New York: Springer Publishing, 2008.

Krakow, Barry. *Turning Nightmares into Dreams.* Albuquerque, NM: Maimonides Sleep Arts & Sciences, 2002.

Sexual Dreams

Delaney, Gayle. *Sexual Dreams: Why We Have Them and What They Mean.* London: Piatkus, 1994

Garfield, Patricia. *Pathway to Ecstasy: The Way of the Dream Mandala.* New York: Prentice Hall Press, 1989.

Sleep Disturbances

Schenck, Carlos H. *Paradox Lost: Midnight in the Battleground of Sleep and Dreams.* Minneapolis, MN: Extreme-Nights, LLC, 2005.

———. *Sleep: A Groundbreaking Guide to the Mysteries, the Problems, and the Solutions.* New York: Avery, 2007.

Sleep Paralysis

Hurd, Ryan. *Sleep Paralysis: A Guide to Hypnagogic Visions and Visitors of the Night.* Los Altos, CA: Hyena Press, 2010.

Sevilla, Jorge Conesa. *Wrestling With Ghosts: A Personal and Scientific Account of Sleep Paralysis.* Bloomington, IN: Xlibris Corporation, 2004.

Spiritual Dreaming

Holecek, Andrew. *Dream Yoga: Illuminating Your Life Through Lucid Dreaming and the Tibetan Yogas of Sleep.* Boulder, CO: Sounds True, 2016.

Moss, Robert. *Dreaming the Soul Back Home: Shamanic Dreaming for Healing and Becoming Whole.* Novato, CA: New World Library, 2012.

Telepathy and Psi Dreams

Mascaro, Kimberly R. *Extraordinary Dreams: Visions, Announcements and Premonitions Across Time and Place.* Jefferson, NC: McFarland, 2018.

Sheldrake, Rupert. *The Sense of Being Stared At: And Other Aspects of the Extended Mind.* London: Arrow Books, 2003.

Ullman, Montague, and Stanley Krippner, with Alan Vaughan. *Dream Telepathy: Experiments in Nocturnal ESP.* Baltimore, MD: Penguin, 1974.

Trauma and Dreams

Cartwright, Rosalind, and Lynne Lamberg. *Crisis Dreaming.* London: The Aquarian Press, 1993.

Mallon, Brenda. *Dreams, Counselling and Healing.* Dublin: Newleaf, 2000.

index

H

hag, 179, 204

healing gifts, 2, 7, 20, 157, 228

health, 43, 48, 49, 51, 58, 59, 65, 84, 128, 129, 132, 143, 151, 152, 160, 170, 198, 211, 213, 217, 218, 233, 239, 242, 254, 255, 257, 279–282, 292

health-challenged sleeper, 132, 143, 149

Hoss, Bob, 165, 213, 280

Howe, Elia, 111

hypnagogia, 31, 125, 185, 225, 246

hypnopompia, 31, 126, 182, 185

hypnotherapist, 105

I

imagery, 9, 14, 15, 17, 19, 22–25, 30–32, 39, 42–45, 47, 53, 55, 59, 64, 68–73, 84, 88, 89, 98, 101, 102, 111–115, 118, 125–127, 134, 135, 138–140, 143, 148, 154, 157, 160–165, 167, 170–175, 179, 182–186, 188–191, 195, 200, 203, 232, 234, 235, 237, 242, 243, 246, 254, 262, 266, 274, 279, 280, 283

imagery rehearsal therapy (IRT), 70, 134, 135, 138, 143, 171, 173, 174, 274

imaginal journey, 140, 257, 261

imaginative thinker, 132, 140, 149, 271, 274

incubate a dream, 33

incubus, 179

initiation, 64, 97, 201

inner child, 8, 93, 101, 115, 117–119, 135, 142, 163, 274

insomnia, 7, 9, 35, 124, 127, 137, 152, 182, 196, 198–201, 234, 266, 273, 279, 280, 284

Insomnia Freedom Technique, 9, 137, 199, 200, 266, 273

insomniac, 34, 132, 137, 148, 149, 198, 273

integration, 51, 66, 166

intentions, 16, 151, 224

To Write to the Author

If you wish to contact the author or would like more information about this book, please write to the author in care of Llewellyn Worldwide Ltd. and we will forward your request. Both the author and the publisher appreciate hearing from you and learning of your enjoyment of this book and how it has helped you. Llewellyn Worldwide Ltd. cannot guarantee that every letter written to the author can be answered, but all will be forwarded. Please write to:

Clare R. Johnson
℅ Llewellyn Worldwide
2143 Wooddale Drive
Woodbury, MN 55125-2989

Please enclose a self-addressed stamped envelope for reply,
or $1.00 to cover costs. If outside the U.S.A., enclose
an international postal reply coupon.

Many of Llewellyn's authors have websites with additional
information and resources. For more information,
please visit our website at http://www.llewellyn.com.

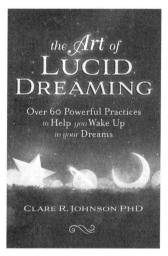

The Art of Lucid Dreaming is a quick and easy guide to help you get lucid fast. Dr. Clare Johnson, world-leading expert on lucid dreaming, provides an excellent introduction and practical tips so you can learn to "wake up" in your dreams. When you are awake and lucid in a dream, you can choose to ask your subconscious mind for guidance, perform healing magic, predict the future, seek creative solutions to problems, or explore the dream realm more deeply and more profoundly than ever before.

With more than sixty practices and fifteen tailor-made programs to help you get started, this hands-on book features a unique Lucidity Quiz that encourages you to discover your personal sleeper-dreamer type so you achieve lucidity as quickly as possible. Focusing on how to get lucid, stay lucid, and guide your dreams, this book shows how to transform your nightly slumber into an exciting spiritual adventure that fills your life with meaning.

978-0-7387-6265-4　•　$17.99

A lucid dream is a dream in which you become aware that you're dreaming. It's a powerful opportunity to solve problems, create new possibilities, take charge of your own healing, and explore the depths of reality. This book provides a range of practical techniques and activities to help you bring the creativity and superconscious awareness of lucid dreaming into your life.

Join international expert Clare R. Johnson as she shares the most up-to-date lucid dreaming techniques on how to get and stay lucid, guide dreams, resolve nightmares, deepen creativity, and integrate dream wisdom into everyday life. Drawing on cutting-edge science and psychology, this book is packed with inspiring stories of life-changing lucid dreams and fascinating insights into topics such as the ethics of dream sex, how to interact with lucid dream figures, and the nature of consciousness.

Whether you're a person who barely remembers your dreams or a lifelong lucid dreamer, this in-depth guide is the perfect next step as you cultivate the power of lucid dreaming.

978-0-7387-5144-3　•　$34.99